PILLARS OF FAITH

PILLARS OF FAITH

BIBLICAL CERTAINTY IN AN UNCERTAIN WORLD

HERMAN O. WILSON &
MORRIS M. WOMACK EDITORS

INTRODUCTION BY
WILLIAM S. BANOWSKY

BAKER BOOK HOUSE
Grand Rapids, Michigan

ISBN: 0-8010-9538-7 (paper) 0-8010-9540-9 (cloth)
Copyright, 1973 by Baker Book House Company
PRINTED IN THE UNITED STATES OF AMERICA

FOREWORD

"What's it all about, Alfie? Is it just for the moment that we live?" These lines, from the recently popular song and movie, raise the question which millions of people are asking today. And, perhaps, young people especially are asking it. Suicide is the second highest cause of death among American college students. Ethical confusion, which leads to disillusionment and despair, is characteristic of our time.

The despair arises from a sense of betrayal. There was a time when the world was simple, when questions had answers, when we were confident of solving all human problems. Earlier in this century we were certain that men could live together peacefully as brothers, that general prosperity for all mankind was possible. We placed our faith in rationalism and empiricism, and looked toward secular higher education to transplant us into Utopia.

Then came the wars, the bombs, the violent upheavals in our cities, the agony on our campuses. And with the collapse of confidence in rationalism, many turned to mysticism. In the past decade, our confidence shifted away from the cognitive, or knowing process, to the affective, or feeling process. And, as a consequence, we have seen the tremendous revival of hedonism. I recently saw a bumper sticker which put the matter tersely: "If it feels good, do it!"

It is because of this ethical confusion of our time that Herman O. Wilson and Morris M. Womack have produced this timely book. Dr. Wilson is a Professor of English and Dr. Womack a Professor of Speech on our faculty at Pepperdine University. By reason of training and talent, they are uniquely qualified to collaborate on this important study. They have assembled, for the writing of this volume, some of the most qualified Christian spokesmen of our time. They address, forthrightly, many of the hard, agonizing questions. This is a needed book, which speaks to the ultimate issues, and I predict for it a wide reading.

William S. Banowsky
President

Pepperdine University
Los Angeles

5

CONTRIBUTORS

John Scott is a professor at Harding College, School of Bible and Theology, Memphis, Tennessee.

Joseph F. Jones serves in the dual capacity of professor at Oakland Community College, Pontiac, Michigan, and minister at Troy Church of Christ, Troy, Michigan.

H. Douglas Dean is professor of biology at Pepperdine University, Malibu, California.

Arlie H. Hoover is associate professor of history, Pepperdine University, Malibu, California.

The late *J. W. Roberts* for many years served on the faculty of Abilene Christian College, Abilene, Texas.

Jack P. Lewis is professor of Bible at Harding College Graduate School of Religion, Memphis, Tennessee.

Frank Pack is currently serving as chairman of religion at Pepperdine University, Malibu, California, and as dean of the Graduate School.

Rex F. Johnston is president of Columbia Christian College, Portland, Oregon.

James D. Bales is professor of Bible at Harding College, Searcy, Arkansas.

Donald R. Sime is dean of the School of Business at Pepperdine University, Malibu, California.

J. P. Sanders is executive vice president of Columbia Christian College, Portland, Oregon.

Herman O. Wilson is professor of English at Pepperdine University, Malibu, California.

Morris M. Womack is professor of speech at Pepperdine University, Malibu, California.

6

CONTENTS

PART FOUR

Can the Bible Influence Man's Conduct?

PREFACE
The Predicament of Modern Man

No thoughtful person can fail to see the moral crisis of our time. Modern man, for all his science and technological achievements, is restless, troubled, uncertain of himself and his values, and vast numbers feel that life has neither purpose nor meaning. The old concepts and standards which for generations gave life direction and a degree of unity have been largely ignored or rejected, and in this vacuum life is characterized by frustration, futility, rebellion, and moral chaos. The search for meaning and happiness goes on, but as a rule the masses have sought for answers from science, medicine, and, in recent years, psychiatry. All sorts of fads and panaceas have been tried and discarded as man has sought some basis for unity in life and for direction. In the latter half of the twentieth century we find conflict, confusion, disillusionment, despair, and violence.

Matthew Arnold's lines, written in 1855, well depict our present era:

Wandering between two worlds, one dead,
The other powerless to be born . . . .
——Stanzas from the Grande Chartreuse
11.85-86

The world now "dead" is the age of faith which, in his view, was doomed by the advent of modern science, particularly the sciences of geology and anthropology. Many other Victorians agreed that the old views of man and the universe, and therefore man's view of God and the creation, were untenable; and yet no new force or unifying influence had arisen to bring unity, peace of mind, and an acceptable faith.

The symptoms of the crisis in our age may be summarized as follows: a widespread disregard for all forms of law and authority, leading to lawlessness; a craving for novelty, experimentation, and sensual pleasure; increasing crime, dope-addiction, and rebellion of many of the younger generation; a loosening of the moral codes and

9

a disposition to base all moral decisions on a personal rather than an inflexible ethic; a desire for "freedom" which has degenerated into license, that is, freedom to decide which laws, moral or political, one will obey.

Our personal and national problems are essentially moral problems. The restlessness, disillusionment, carnality, and violence which characterize so much of life today can be traced to a want of purpose and direction, or to the loss of any meaningful standards. In times past men agreed upon certain fundamental principles (e.g., the sanctity of one's word or oath) as binding in all situations. Today, relativism and "situation ethics" have undermined such ancient sanctions. Thus adultery can be "justified" if the consenting parties "love" each other. Many of the grave moral and social evils of our age finally resolve themselves to wrong relationships—exploitation of others; taking what one wants, regardless of the rights and wrongs involved; defying any authorities or laws of which one disapproves.

When Elton Trueblood was asked about the "ruling tenets of our time," he said that "the first of these is the extraordinary belief that all our problems are new." This view he characterized as "the disease of contemporaneity."[1] When he advised a group of pastors to study such works as Augustine's *Confessions,* the *Imitation of Christ,* and Pascal's *Pensees,* they felt that these classics had no value for men today because they regarded these books as out-dated and no longer relevant. But Trueblood sees human nature and therefore man's problems as unchanging. Our vaunted wisdom he finds "an intolerable conceit."[2]

Another of the ruling ideas of our time, he said, is the belief that the essence of life is to be found in things and the "infinity of sex." Contemporary men have assumed that fulness of life can be found in the abundance of things one can buy. Thus life is interpreted in physical terms rather than spiritual, and sexual indulgence has quite commonly become a substitute for love and self-fulfilment. When one lives primarily for pleasure, his life is wholly centered in self, and after a time pleasure fails and life then becomes empty, void, and intolerable.

If life is to have meaning and true value it must be based on something higher than self, possessions, or pleasure. The wisdom of other ages points to right relationships as the true foundation for a satisfying life. This concept involves not only one's relationships to the earth and its laws, but also one's relationship to neighbor, friend, stranger, and, on a higher plane, to moral and spiritual law and to God. If the relationships are warped or twisted by evil, frustration and failure are inevitable. And in all relationships with persons or God, one quality is basic. That is faith or trust.

Faith must be established before any human ties can have permanence or value. In business as well as social relations there must be trust or confidence. A good neighbor is one who is ready to show a trusting and benevolent spirit. The cynic characteristically trusts nobody.

When one is ill he wants a doctor whom he can trust. Our friends are persons who have been dependable in many situations and have proved their trustworthiness. Stable communities are those in which people have lived in close association long enough to know and trust one another. By contrast, those communities in which the population undergoes almost constant change have no loyalties, no binding ties, no real regard for what happens to those outside their immediate circle. The lack of community spirit can often be traced to the fact that there are few if any shared commitments; each man goes his own way, oblivious of his neighbor, and though they live on the same block they have no common interests or concerns. Whatever relationships are formed are temporary and shallow, for significant human relations take time to mature and depend on mutual faith.

Morality, or just and wholesome human relations, must be founded on fixed principles which give truth, fairness, justice, and compassion a very high value. These principles in turn must be based upon a code that elevates human values above money, property, or personal advantage. Such a code was the Mosaic commandment which bade all Jews "to love thy neighbor as thyself." This broad principle would prevent such wrongs as lying, cheating, stealing, adultery, and all kinds of violence and oppression, while at the same time obligating the faithful Jew to show kindness, mercy, and a readiness to help anyone in distress. This injunction applied not only to their neighbors but also to "sojourners" or strangers in their land.

Such a principle of benevolence (which strikes at the root of self-love and greed) must be based on conviction and a higher-than-human law. This leads one logically to the teaching of God's Word, where morality is given the sanction of divine authority, with its system of rewards and punishments. Morality, therefore, finds no fixed and unchanging foundation except in faith in the Creator, and His revealed will. Any other system must perforce be human and consequently temporary and imperfect. Man's law, which is constantly undergoing change and adding new offenses and new penalties, illustrates very well man's failure to respect his neighbor and to "do right." By contrast, the moral imperatives of the Ten Commandments and the Sermon on the Mount have never changed, or needed change, and yet they still stand as the highest expression of man's responsibility to his fellow creatures. To live by these principles is to live "above the law," for human law is written to control the lawless and evil men.

It can readily be seen that faith in God and a sense of accountability to Him have a powerful and direct bearing on human conduct. Lacking this faith, man follows his own course, which ends in lawlessness, self-interest, exploitation and distrust of others, and violations of the rights of the weak and defenseless.

Faith is fundamental to a right view of life. If man were only an animal, albeit a highly developed and intelligent animal, his antisocial acts could be explained even if not approved. But man does not and cannot live by instinct alone, as animals do. Animals act from certain urges or needs but they do not act from the motives associated with human conduct, such as pride or self-esteem, compassion, vengeance, obedience to a principle. Obviously some animals display traits which are interpreted in human terms as love, loyalty, gratitude, prudence, and so on; but these are qualities arising either from instinctual behavior or from conditioning. Another way to express this idea is to say that animals always behave as their species or kind has behaved for countless generations or as they have been *trained* to behave.

Man, on the other hand, lives by codes which have been handed down by his ancestors, and he passes judgment on himself or others according to the way an action satisfies or repudiates the generally accepted code. His "conscience" or inner voice (Anglo-Saxon *inwit*) approves or disapproves his conduct. When he has done wrong—gone against his code—he feels guilty, unworthy, unacceptable to those whose sense of guilt is a uniquely human trait. So far as we know, animals never kill for vengeance nor do they feel any sense of wrong for an action. But in human behavior the motive for any action is of tremendous significance. Law takes into account the difference between accidental and intentional killing, and it makes allowance for acts of passion (killing in the heat of anger) as compared to lying in wait to slay a man.

In the New Testament, man's behavior is traced to its springs in the "heart," i.e., the mind and will of the individual. Whereas the Old Testament punished the *act* of murder, Christ condemned the hatred which is the *cause* of murder (cf. Matt. 5:21-22). In like manner Christ examined a man's motives in almsgiving: if one gave to receive the plaudits of men, then he had received his reward; if, on the other hand, one gave without fanfare to a destitute family or to a worthy cause, he would have God's approval. Though the end result, so far as man can see, might be identical in the two acts of giving (the hungry are fed or the good cause is furthered), God looks at the motive and calls one self-interest, the other unselfish.

What is the relation, then, of man's conduct to faith? If one believes that God approves or disapproves certain actions and this faith is vital and strong, then one will strive hard to avoid what is forbidden (lying, adultery, for example) and we say that his conduct is motivated by faith. If one does not believe that he is accountable to God for his actions, if he rejects the Bible as having any authority over his life, then he must formulate his own code of conduct—and this is precisely what most persons, even in the "Christian" world, are doing. As we have noted already, man must accept God's teaching and His moral laws—or fashion his own. It is the widespread rejection of God's authority, or moral laws, that has brought about the chaos, confusion, and endless problems of this era.

Because man is by nature a responsible creature, able to choose a course of action deliberately and with some idea of its consequences, he feels the need of trustworthy information, and for his moral conduct the need of clearly defined rights and wrongs. Lacking such a guide, he is like a ship at sea without chart or compass. This is, broadly speaking, the situation of modern man.

Christian believers accept the word of the ancient prophet Jeremiah: "It is not in man that walketh to direct his own steps" (Jer. 10:23). This is why God directed His people in ancient times through patriarchs, prophets, and priests. This explains the reason for a covenant or agreement between God and His people, and why—at a later time—He sent His own Son to reveal His will and to offer a new way of life, based on faith, to all who would accept it.

Faith affects far more than man's morality; it determines his view of himself and other men and it gives his life meaning and purpose. Without faith in God's revelation, man has no knowledge of his origin, his reason for existence, or his final destiny. It is this lack of a clear purpose or *raison d'etre* that makes so many lives pointless and, in the view of many existentialists, "absurd." Conscious of the importance of his inner life, man seeks for an explanation of the laws of his own being and for some clue as to the purpose of living. In one of his philosophic poems Browning puts the following words into the mouth of the matchless musician, Abt Vogler:

> Therefore to whom turn I but to Thee, the ineffable Name?
>   Builder and maker, Thou, of houses not made with hands!
> What, have fear of change from Thee who art ever the same?
>   Doubt that Thy power can fill the heart that Thy power expands?
> There shall never be one lost good! What was, shall live as before;
>   The evil is null, is naught, is silence implying sound;

What was good shall be good, with, for evil, so much good more;
On earth the broken arcs; in the heaven, a perfect round.
                              ——"Abt Vogler" St. 9

Our Lord recognized the duality of man's nature and the need for understanding and sustaining the spiritual life when He declared, "Man shall not live by bread alone but by every word that proceedeth out of the mouth of God" (Matt. 4:4). Material things can never satisfy the hunger of the heart. Physical pleasures may for a time satisfy the physical man, but the claims of the spiritual are just as insistent as physical wants. When these are not satisfied, man becomes troubled, restless, searching for meaning and nonmaterial values. This yearning, the Christian believes, can be satisfied only by an enlightened faith. In the words of Scripture, "By faith we understand . . . " (Heb. 11:3).

The purpose of this book is to provide for the thoughtful person "a reason for the hope that is in him." In the following chapters a number of educators have explored the foundations of the Christian faith and have endeavored to show the reasonableness and the harmony of faith based upon God's Word. Each man was chosen to write on a subject for which he is especially trained—whether the ancient Hebrew texts, history, archaeology, or psychology. It is the conviction of the several writers that man is, rightly considered, a unified and integrated personality and that, in a corresponding sense, the universe also is a harmonious whole. Through the various "laws" of nature we believe that man can work his way back to the source of all light, power, and truth—the Maker of the universe. This series of essays is dedicated to this search for a fuller understanding of God's Word and its meaning for our lives.

                                                  The Editors

1. *Christianity Today*, (Jan. 6, 1967) Vol. XI, 7.
2. *Ibid.*, p. 4.

PART ONE

DOES THE BIBLE HAVE A MESSAGE FOR MODERN MAN?

INTRODUCTION

A frustrated twentieth century is crying out for answers—answers to problems of war, crime, immorality, and alienation. Many solutions have been sought for these problems—mainly through legislation and social programs—but none has satisfactorily solved the problem.

The editors and the several writers of this volume are committed to the concept that Christ is the answer to man's needs. The Bible remains the Book of books because it discloses man's relation to the Creator and shows the way of redemption through Christ.

Part I is devoted to the supreme worth of the Bible in man's search for answers. Modern scholarship has been both critical and complimentary in its analysis of the worth of the Bible. Often it has weakened man's faith in the credibility of the Word.

The editors have directed themselves in Part I to two vital themes: the unity and relevance of the Bible. They have supplemented their thoughts with the judgments of other Christian thinkers.

1

THE BIBLE SPEAKS TO MEN TODAY

Herman O. Wilson

In recent years the Western world has witnessed a wide-ranging and continuing attack on almost every idea, institution, or tradition associated with the past. History has shown again and again that each succeeding generation rejects many of the ways and standards of the older generation. This tendency has affected not only government and legislation, but also dress, speech, manners, and values.

Yet the revolution in thought and behavior in the past twenty years has been more sweeping, more violent and destructive than any in modern history. Disenchantment with the past has turned into open aggression and attacks on the foundations of society: the government, educational institutions, churches, and whatever constitutes "the establishment." Visible evidence of the change can be seen in the attitudes, the dress, the language, and the behavior of great masses of society. Institutions which have long been regarded as sacred, or at least honorable and permanent—such as marriage and the home, our judicial system, and traditional respect for law and the rights of others—have been challenged, denounced, and treated with contempt. These bastions of the common life, which preserved and transmitted most of the ideals and values of the past, have in recent days been assailed as outmoded, obstructionist, and unworkable.

To take a notable example, marriage, which in all societies has been considered the foundation of human life and culture and the protector and teacher of the children, has been derided as unrealistic, contrary to nature, and not suited to man's craving for freedom and change. Critics from many levels of society have charged that marriage is failing, that in the twentieth century social and economic changes have made it obsolete, and that eventually it will cease to exist as an institution.

In this climate of revolt and social upheaval, the Bible has also been widely attacked as belonging to another time and suited to a less complex and sophisticated society. Its critics see it as hopelessly out of date, too strict in its morality, too negative in its view of man's "sinful" nature, and—worst of all—"irrelevant." This over-worked word has been used to discredit anything which does not fit into the current craze for what is new, exciting, and pragmatic.

This questioning and rejection of nearly all that has been valued in the past and the exaggerated regard for what is recent, "scientific," or modish is one of the marks of our troubled age. Modern man's unreasoning devotion to what is new and up-to-date has been called by Elton Trueblood "the disease of contemporaneity." In an inter-view conducted by Carl F. H. Henry, editor of *Christianity Today,* on "Ideas that Shape the American Mind," Dr. Trueblood was asked to comment on "the reigning tenets of our time." His first response was as follows:

> The first of these is the extraordinary belief that all our problems are new. I would call this, really, the disease of contemporaneity. Shall I give you an example? Last winter I was speaking to a group of pastors in a certain state, and I advised these men to study Augustine's *Confessions* and the *Imitation of Christ* and Pascal's *Pensees,* and John Woolman's *Journal.* Right away one of the leading clergymen said, "Oh, those were all very well for another day. But so much has happened now that their appeal is utterly undermined. We are in a new world, and these books have nothing to say to our situation at this moment."[1]

Dr. Henry then asked about the implications of such a view upon our Judeo-Christian heritage, and received the following reply:

> It means that we cut ourselves off from the wisdom of the ages, including that of the Bible. It means that, if taken seriously, we are really an orphan generation that takes itself far too seriously, that is much too impressed with changes that may be only superficial. And, of course, if this is true of our generation, as your question indicates, there is no reason why it will not be true of another generation. Therefore, whatever we gain would natu-rally be rejected by our descendants. No civilization is possible this way. Contemporaneity when it is a disease is a very damaging disease, because it destroys the continuity of culture.[2]

Dr. Trueblood also stated that he considers modern man's "con-ceit" to be one of the serious problems of this age. He supports this observation by saying that many students today ask what Moses, Abraham, or Socrates can say to us today, who have learned or seen so much more than they. To this query Dr. Trueblood replied that those who say this "have not really considered carefully enough the nature of the human problem," that is, that the problems of hate, lust, unconcern for others, are not "modern" but age-old problems. And then he adds, quite pertinently, "and the notion that we are living in such a fresh time that wisdom has 'come with us' whereas nobody ever had it before—this I find to be an intolerable conceit."[3]

The tragedy of this kind of conceit is that it alienates this generation from the great minds and inspiring literature of past ages. As Mary Ellen Chase has pointed out in her popular *The Bible and the Common Reader,* the Bible is not merely a book, it is a remarkable library containing some of the finest narrative, character sketches, and poetry to be found in the whole range of literature. She quotes John Livingston Lowes, who called it "the noblest monument of English prose," and she shows through a number of statements from great British writers and poets the abiding influence that the Bible had in forming their ideas, values, and style. Eminent writers from Bacon and Shakespeare down to Lincoln and Churchill praised the Book of books for the beauty of its language and its influence on the molding of men's lives. Miss Chase remarks:

> The Bible belongs among the noblest and most indispensable of our humanistic and literary traditions. No liberal education is truly liberal without it.[4]

Interestingly enough, she points out that parts of the Bible antedate Homer, and most of it was written long before the time of Virgil. One reason why this book has held a high place in the lives of all classes of readers, rich and poor, learned or unlearned, down through the ages, is that it is a veritable storehouse of wisdom, human goodness, and folly; songs of joy, hope, sorrow, and penitence; stories of brave men and women—Abraham, Joseph, Deborah, Daniel, Elijah, Ruth, and scores of others; besides the stirring messages of the prophets who preached obedience and righteousness; and philosophers who, in such books as Job, Proverbs, and Ecclesiastes, wrestled with the most searching questions of life, and offered some of the profoundest answers yet given to men. In the Bible, as she shows by many fascinating studies, we encounter men and women like ourselves who sought to know the meaning of life, to understand their own minds and hearts, and who struggled with the same temptations and snares which trouble us today. Thus, to treat this great book as if it were just a dry and tiresome record of the wars and hardships of a small, obscure nation that existed centuries ago having no relevance to our times or our problems is indeed tragic.

One of man's needs, as Dr. Trueblood wisely observed, is a sense of continuity, an appreciation of what was thought and done by our predecessors. Unless such knowledge is studied and valued, man must try to learn for himself what is good, valid, and true, and is doomed to repeat the mistakes of the past. One of our principal needs, therefore, is something tested and trusted as a reliable guide—something to hold to in times of stress. In this connection, Calvin D. Linton, writing on "Delusion and Reality," says of man's present-day confusion:

> Totally lacking is any kind of national—much less of planetary—creed, set of beliefs, patterns and values, established goals. And none will ever be found, until we discover again a fixed center, a motionless center, to give meaning to our motion. Without a sense of direction, motion becomes meaningless, a mere waste of energy, leading to exhaustion and death. . . .[5]

What so many writers in this generation, both skeptics and believers, have singled out as a part of our human malaise, is the lack of any definite goal or purpose among the great masses of mankind. The result has been unprecedented motion or movement, but much of it frenetic and meaningless. Until men find a purpose for living, life becomes a race against time, to "live it up," to consume it in self-gratification, some fleeting pleasure; or else, in despair and disillusionment, to try to escape the demands of life by turning to alcohol, drugs, promiscuity, or some other delusion.

Two passages in the New Testament set forth man's need in every age for divine guidance and the way the Scriptures can meet his needs:

> For whatsoever things were written aforetime were written for our learning, that through patience and through comfort of the scriptures we might have hope.—Romans 15:4

> Grace to you and peace be multiplied in the knowledge of God and of Jesus our Lord; seeing that his divine power hath granted unto us all things that pertain unto life and godliness.—II Peter 1:2-3

These two statements agree that the Scriptures serve two important ends: to *inform* ("for our learning") and to *encourage* (that "we might have hope") and they deal with all things that belong "to life and godliness." The subject matter of the Holy Scriptures is life (both here and hereafter) and its theme (running through both Old and New Testaments) is righteousness or godliness. No other book even approaches the Bible in giving mankind such a clear and complete guide for living and such noble standards for living it well. Since man's nature and the nature of truth do not change, the moral teachings of Moses, Isaiah, Job, Christ, and the apostles are as vital and relevant today as when they were first announced. "The grass withereth and the flower falleth, but the word of the Lord abideth for ever" (I Peter 1:24-25).

The purpose of this study is to show that the Bible, far from being dated and irrelevant, is filled with truths, insights, and moral science which is as relevant to man's needs today as the latest findings in medicine, psychology, and the social sciences. This ancient book is the foundation on which Western culture was erected, and its great truths about God, man's nature and origin, sin and its effects, and the meaning of the good life are as vital today as they were in the past—and are needed even more now than ever. This essay will touch on such topics as self-understanding, race relations, sex and marriage, moral standards, concern for the poor and dependent, and a purpose for living.

Man's Nature

One reason why the Bible holds so much interest for man is that it gives him more information about his origin, his nature, his purpose and potential than any other book ever written. The record of the creation given in Genesis seems intended to show that man is not only God's creature, but is indeed the master-work of creation, and all other things were made for his use and enjoyment. The Scripture gives man great dignity and worth by declaring that man was made in God's image; "in the image of God created he him, male and female created he them" (Gen. 1:27). Only the most naive would give this statement a literal meaning; the very fact that God created both a male and a female rules out the idea of a physical likeness. Instead, the passage, like poetry, connotes much more than the bare words state: man is like God in three very important respects—in the ability to *think* and thus create, to *feel* and thus respond to other creatures and to God, to *will* and thus to act responsibly, that is, to choose deliberately among many possible ways to act. These are Godlike qualities.

Because man is first of all a rational creature, he is able, to a degree at least, to comprehend God's work, His laws, His will for man. The gift of intelligence makes possible communication between God and His creature man; we are able, as Kepler said, "to think God's thoughts after him." This light of intelligence lifts man above the animal level; it makes of him a dreamer, a builder, a seeker of laws and principles. Because of this capacity to think and thus to give order to life, man has learned to manipulate the forces of nature and to conquer the seas, the skies, and outer space.

In the second place, man has the capacity for a wide range of emotions. Like God he loves, he hates, he feels compassion or

revulsion, he yearns, fears, despairs. The Old Testament reveals God
as loving, hating, repenting, punishing, despising, forgiving, or de-
stroying. Man, since he is like God in nature, responds to love, reacts
to hatred and wrongdoing, rejoices in what is pleasing, and—over a
period of years—expresses every kind of emotional response. This
idea is beautifully expressed in the Old Testament:

> And he [God] humbled thee and suffered thee to hunger. . . that
> he might make thee know that man doth not live by bread alone,
> but by everything that proceedeth out of the mouth of Jehovah
> doth man live.—Deuteronomy 8:3

Man yearns for many things which cannot be satisfied with material
gifts; he wants words or ideals to live by, praise from those whom he
tries to please, and a life that is higher and better than what he has
known here.

In the Bible man learned that his "heart" or mind can be clean
and holy or wicked and defiled. This idea is epitomized in Ecclesiastes: "God made man upright; but they sought out many inven-
tions" (7:29). One of the prophets declares: "The heart is deceitful
above all things, and is exceedingly corrupt: who can know it?"
(Jer. 17:9). Modern history affords ample evidence of this ancient
truth. Christ also reveals that "out of the heart come forth evil
thoughts, murders, adulteries, fornications, thefts. . ." and many
other evils, since the heart is the source of man's inner life. Likewise,
out of the heart man may praise God, bless his fellowman, cheer the
discouraged and fallen, and inspire others to noble living.

Since man is a self-conscious being (looking back upon his own
thoughts and actions with approval or sorrow and shame), he is
capable of judging his behavior according to his own or external
standards. In the Bible this inner voice or judge is called the "conscience," and the New Testament makes clear that the conscience
can be hardened or seared by repeated sins (II Cor. 1:12; I Tim.
1:5; 4:2). Even the sinful and unbelieving man has a conscience
which serves to tell him when he goes against the truth of his own
nature.

Thirdly, man shares with God the capacity to will. Even the small
child has ways of making its will known, and it can be very emphat-
ic! The power of will is fraught with immense possibilities for good
or evil. God's will is expressed time and again in His dealings with
Abraham, Moses, and other patriarchs. These men, in turn, expressed
their own will by obeying or disobeying God, and by their course of
action. Joshua, for example, displayed his leadership by calling on
the wavering Israelites to choose whether they would serve Jehovah
or "the gods which your fathers served. . . the gods of the Amorites,"

and then by declaring his own stand: "but as for me and my house, we will serve Jehovah" (Josh. 24:15). The will is that which harnesses one's energies and directs these toward a chosen goal; it can be used to control one's weaknesses or appetites, or to carry out great plans for man's benefit (as Joseph did in Egypt), or to direct the conquest of a country (as Joshua did in Canaan).

The nature of man is further revealed in his origin, for he was made of the "dust of the earth;" and afterward, God "breathed into his nostrils the breath of life, and man became a living soul" (Gen. 2:7). The dual nature of man is thus clearly indicated (in physical respects he is like the animals and shares the same appetites but in the spiritual he resembles God and cannot be satisfied with eating, drinking, and "replenishing the earth").

> ... Gentiles that have not the law do by nature the things of the law. . . . [They] are a law unto themselves; in that they show the law written in their hearts, their *conscience* bearing witness therewith, and their thoughts one with another *accusing* or else *excusing* them. . . . —Romans 2:14-15

A clear conscience gives one a sense of well-being and satisfaction, but a troubled conscience arouses fear, unrest, and a sense of truth violated. "There is no peace, saith my God, to the wicked" (Isa. 48:22). And again, "The wicked flee when no man pursueth, but the righteous are bold as a lion" (Prov. 28:1). King David's deeply troubled conscience, as revealed in Psalm 51, shows the sorrow of a good man who went against the knowledge of the truth and suffered for it.

Marriage

Closely related to man's self-knowledge is his need of companionship. At the creation, God saw that it was not good for man to be alone and thus provided for him a help "meet" (that is, one answering to man's needs) to share his life. Because she was created with a mind, emotions, and spirit like those of man, she completed God's creative act and complemented man's physical and social life. The account of woman's creation adds a significant statement regarding marriage:

> Therefore shall a man leave his father and mother, and shall cleave unto his wife: and they shall be one flesh. And they were both naked, the man and his wife, and were not ashamed.— Genesis 2:24-25

This account shows that men and women were meant for one another (marriage is natural), each must be willing to leave father and mother to make a new home, and in their relationship to each other there was no shame or self-consciousness.

The Old Testament makes clear that sex is a gift of God: "male and female created he them. And God blessed them and said unto them, Be fruitful and multiply and replenish the earth, and subdue it. . ." (Gen. 1:27-28). God then looked upon His earth and the newly created creatures "and saw everything that he had made, and behold it was very good" (Gen.1:31). At the beginning marriage was monogamous, and the teaching of Christ shows that one man-one wife was God's intention for man (Matt. 19:4-8). Bigamy and polygamy are found in corrupt times, yet monogamy seems to have been the rule among the ancient Jewish people.

Sex had meaning only in marriage, and adultery was forbidden because it violated the rights of others (Exod. 20:14; Gen. 20:6; Lev. 18:20). Various kinds of sexual aberrations are explicit condemned: homosexuality and sodomy (Gen. 19; Lev. 18:22; Deut. 22:5); incest (Deut. 27:20); bestiality (Exod. 22:18); nudity (Gen. 9:21-23). It is worth noting that in Israel (surrounded by pagan nations with fertility cults) God was never worshiped by sexual rites.

In certain periods the Jewish nation was corrupted by the practices of heathen people, and their respect for the laws of marriage suffered. Ezra the prophet cried out against foreign marriages and their consequences (9:1—10:44); and Solomon sinned in taking many wives and in corrupting his faith (I Kings 11:1-8).

In the days of Christ polygamy was uncommon among the Jews but easy divorce (perhaps influenced by Roman laxity) brought about what some have called "consecutive polygamy." When certain Pharisees asked whether it was "lawful for a man to put away his wife for every cause," Jesus quoted the statement about God creating them for each other (Gen. 1:27) and added, "So they are no more two, but one flesh. What therefore God hath joined together, let not man put asunder." To a second question, "Why then did Moses command to give a bill of divorcement, and to put her away?" Christ answered, "Moses for your hardness of heart suffered you to put away your wives; but from the beginning it hath not been so" (Matt. 19:1-8). The Lord showed that Moses did not "command" but "suffered" or permitted divorce, but he asserted positively that this practice was not God's will ("in the beginning it hath not been so"). In other words, divorce was simply an accommodation because of man's weakness and was permitted lest worse evils occur.

The teaching of Christ on the subject of marriage is plain, positive, and definite. One man and one wife joined for life was the ideal, and this high standard, if generally accepted, would cause couples to be far more cautious about marrying and would also encourage them to strive to make the marriage succeed. Among Christians marriage is "a holy estate, blessed of God" and "not to be entered into lightly, but reverently, seriously," and "for better or worse, for richer or poorer" as long as the two shall live. That the New Testament approves marriage is shown in many passages (I Cor. 7:1-2; 8-39; 9:5; Eph. 5:22-23; I Thess. 4:3-8). The Hebrew letter declares, "Let marriage be had in honor among all, let the bed be undefiled: for fornicators and adulterers God will judge" (13:4). Although Paul the apostle did not marry, he declared that he had a right to, and in one epistle (I Tim. 4:3) he specifically says that in later times false teachers will forbid marriage. One of the qualifications given for an elder or bishop was that he be "the husband of one wife" or as some other versions translate it "must have only one wife" (Williams) or "he must be married to one wife only" (Phillips), a provision apparently meant to prohibit polygamy as well as to qualify the man as a godly and effective "ruler of his own house" (I Tim. 3:2, 5).

One other illustration of the sanctity of marriage is found in Paul's use of the marriage relationship to show Christ's love and sacrifice for the church, his bride:

> Husbands, love your wives, even as Christ also loved the church, and gave himself up for it . . . that he might present the church to himself a glorious church, not having spot or wrinkle or any such thing, but that it should be holy and without blemish.—Ephesians 5:25, 27 (cf. II Cor. 11:2)

What does the New Testament say about sex outside of marriage? Here again the teaching is plain and the ideal is quite high. Fornication, adultery, and all immorality is associated with the unregenerate or godless: for example, Christians are admonished to have nothing to do with fornicators, idolators, and other evil persons, but the context makes plain that the prohibition refers to those "in the world," that is, those who have no regard for the Christian's standards (I Cor. 5:9-12). A little farther on the apostle lists many of the common sins of the heathen (adultery, fornication, sensuality, unnatural sexual vice) and then adds:

> And these are just the characters some of you used to be. But now you have washed yourselves clean, you have been consecrated, you are now in right standing with God. . . .—I Corinthians 6:11 (Williams)

These deeds of darkness belonged to their past—not to their new vocation. Then, the New Testament gives us one of its truly grand insights: that both body and soul belong to the Lord, that the human body is the Holy Spirit's temple, and the person who has been "bought" by Christ's sacrifice belongs wholly to the Lord.

> But the body is not for fornication but for the Lord; and the Lord for the body. . . . Know ye not that your bodies are members of Christ? Shall I then take away the members of Christ and make them members of a harlot? God forbid. Or know ye not that he that is joined to a harlot is one body? . . . Flee fornication. Every sin that a man doeth is without the body, but he that committeth fornication sinneth against his own body.

Then follows the great principle regarding the relation of body and Spirit and of the Christian to Christ:

> Or know ye not that your body is a temple of the Holy Spirit which is in you, which ye have from God? And ye are not your own; for ye were bought with a price: glorify God therefore in your body.—I Corinthians 6:13-20

Relations with Others

Does the Bible offer any teaching on race relations? Of course it does, but not in a direct manner. It first lays down a number of principles about mankind in general, asserting that man is God's creation, that all men are descended from one, and that God is the father of all. The first proposition has been set out earlier; the second is declared in these words: "he [God] made of one every nation of men to dwell on all the face of the earth. . . ." (Acts 17:26). Paul is here addressing the Athenians, and after showing that God is not limited, does not dwell in "temples made with hands," he declares that all men, whatever their race or nation, are descended from one common progenitor. Man being made in God's likeness argues that God cannot be "like unto gold, silver, or stone," but on a higher level resembles His own intelligent creature, man. In this sense all men are related to God as the Father and to one another as brothers. One of the clearest statements of this important truth is found in the Old Testament: "Have we not all one father? hath not God created us? why do we deal treacherously every man against his brother, profaning the covenant of our fathers?" (Mal. 2:10). For any man to acknowledge God as Father is to admit that all other men are his brothers.

One wholesome and abiding principle regarding man's relations with his fellows is found running through the entire Bible: it is that of concern or love.

> Thou shalt not take vengeance, nor bear any grudge against the

children of thy people; but thou shalt love thy neighbor as thyself: I am Jehovah.—Leviticus 19:18

Again, the Mosaic law speaks directly to the point:

And if a stranger sojourn with thee in your land, ye shall do him no wrong. The stranger that sojourneth among you shall be unto you as the home born among you, and thou shalt love him as thyself; for ye were sojourners in the land of Egypt: I am Jehovah your God.—Leviticus 19:33-34

In the New Testament, Christ broadened the bounds of compassion to include all men, not merely those of one's clan or class:

For if ye love them that love you, what reward have ye? do not even the publicans the same? And if ye salute your brethren only, what do ye more than others? do not even the Gentiles the same?—Matthew 5:46-47

Here the "brethren" are Jews, or in many instances fellow Pharisees or Sadducees, and the Gentiles are "those lesser breeds without the law." Christ therefore raised His standard far above the appeal of class, race, or culture; even the despised Gentiles, He shows, love their own kind. His righteousness demands respect and concern for *every* man, regardless of his country or condition. Though Judaism was the religion of Israel, Christ came to save all men, and the scope of His teaching is worldwide in its appeal and demands.

Christ addressed the apostles just before leaving to them the task of evangelizing the world (cf. Matt. 28:19-20; Luke 24:46-49). It is especially interesting that in repeating His instructions (as found in Acts) the Savior specified that the witnessing in His name should begin in Jerusalem and then spread through Judea (the area around Jerusalem), "to Samaria, and unto the uttermost part of the earth" (Acts 1:8). Why, especially, did He single out Samaria? Was it not because the Jews held themselves to be superior to the Samaritans, whom they despised? Many times in the New Testament records we are shown the contempt which Jews had for their part-Jewish neighbors. The account of our Lord's conversation with the Samaritan woman at Jacob's well adds this explanatory note at the point where Jesus asked the woman for a drink of water: "For Jews have no dealings with Samaritans" (John 4:9). Later, when Jesus was upbraiding the Jews for their unbelief and saying that they were not truly Abraham's children, they began to hurl insults at Christ, and the worst charge they could make was "thou art a Samaritan" (John 8:48).

Perhaps it was because of the Jews' inordinant pride that Christ in two of His parables gave honor to the racially mixed but more loving

Samaritans—in the story of the Good Samaritan (one of the best loved of all the parables) and in the story of the one leper, a Samaritan, who returned to thank Him for being healed (Luke 17:16). No doubt the Savior wanted to show that those who were considered outside the pale were as acceptable to Him as any orthodox Jew, and often were more responsive.

After Pentecost a great change came over some of the followers of Christ, and we find that after the scattering of the Jerusalem church, the disciples "went about preaching the word. And Philip went down to the city of Samaria, and proclaimed unto them the Christ" (Acts 8:4-5). The result of this effort is summed up in one sentence: "And there was great joy in that city." When the apostles learned of the conversions in Samaria, they sent Peter and John to preach there and to confer the Holy Spirit on the new converts. After fulfilling this mission, the two "returned to Jerusalem, and preached the gospel to many villages of the Samaritans" (Acts 8:25). Here is the record of one of the first missions ever carried out by Christians, and that in the face of ancient prejudices.

Later, the Jerusalem church, and especially one of its "pillars," was to receive another lesson in the problem of overcoming racial prejudice. The detailed account of the conversion of Cornelius, an Italian soldier stationed at Caesarea, seems clearly intended to show the fear devout Christians had about entering a Gentile home, even on an evangelistic mission. It required a vision and a direct message from God ("What God hath cleansed, make not thou common") to convince Peter that he should go and preach to this Gentile. Even so, Peter felt compelled to take with him "certain of the brethren" who later were to serve as character witnesses for the reluctant Peter.

When the apostle finally entered the house of the honorable and god-fearing centurion, Peter began by saying, "Of a truth I perceive that God is no respecter of persons. . ." (Acts 10:34). Here was a new truth which finally had taken hold of this great leader, though he was slow of heart to believe. Back at home, reporting to his own brethren, he gives them step by step the object lesson which he had lately been taught, concluding:

> If then God gave unto them the like gift as he did also unto us, when we believed on the Lord Jesus Christ, who was I, that I could withstand God?—Acts 11:17

The record makes perfectly clear that not only Peter but the leaders of the church in Jerusalem had to overcome a strong feeling against the acceptance of men of another race. Unfortunately, many latter-day Christians have not yet learned to accept those of other races or cultures. The animosity of Jews against Gentiles continued to trouble the church long after the events just referred to. The letter to the Ephesians discusses the separation between the two groups, but shows that when men come into the fellowship of Christ these outer distinctions are forgotten:

> For he is our peace, who made both one, and brake down the middle wall of partition, having abolished in his flesh the enmity, even the law of commandments contained in ordinances; that he might create in himself of the two one new man, so making peace; and might reconcile them both in one body unto God through the cross, having slain the enmity thereby. . . .–Ephesians 2:14-16

As men move closer to Christ and His cross, they come closer to each other and finally lose their former identity in Him. The Jew had to give up his zeal for the law and the distinctions it conferred on him, and the Gentiles had to give up their gods, their worldly wisdom, their pagan rituals, and self-sufficiency. Each group had much to give up and much more to receive.

To many believers the crowning Scripture on the relations between different races and classes is found in Galatians 3:26-29:

> For ye are all sons of God, through faith in Christ Jesus. For as many of you as were baptized into Christ did put on Christ. There can be neither Jew nor Greek [race], there can be neither bond [slave] nor free [condition], there can be no male and female [sex]; for ye all are one man in Christ Jesus. And if ye are Christ's, then are ye Abraham's seed, heirs according to the promise.

The whole message of the New Testament on relations between men and races is this: "Treat other people exactly as you would like to be treated by them–this is the essence of all true religion" (Matt. 7:12, Phillips). Love means respect, consideration, acceptance; it is not (as often thought) a shallow, sentimental feeling. Love, as Paul says, comprehends all the other moral commands: "Owe no man anything save to love one another: for he that loveth his neighbor hath fulfilled the law" (Rom. 13:8, 10). It means doing good to another.

Christian Benevolence

What has just been said about the believer's relation to men of other classes and races can be applied to one's attitudes toward needy children, the sick, the aged, and all helpless persons. Many detailed provisions for the care of the sick, the infirm, and the poor are found in the Old Testament. God's leaders and prophets constantly reminded the Jewish people of God's care and compassion for them, and in turn the Jews were reminded to care for "the poor and the sojourner" in their midst.

Christ emphasized compassion by His teaching and His example. To the overscrupulous about the law, He said, "Go ye and learn what this meaneth, I desire mercy and not sacrifice. . ." (Matt. 9:13). "When he saw the multitudes, he was moved with compassion for them, because they were distressed and scattered, as sheep not having a shepherd" (Matt. 9:36). He healed their sick and afflicted, He fed the hungry on two notable occasions, He welcomed and showed kindness to strangers, and even on the cross He made provision for the care of His mother. In the picture of the final judgment (as given in Matthew 25), it is not doctrine but deeds of mercy shown to the hungry, the naked, the stranger, the sick and imprisoned by which men will be accepted or rejected. Compassion is one of the cardinal principles of Christianity.

Caring for helpless or poor persons is taught in the New Testament as an obligation. Christ strongly rebuked those Jews who used a technicality in the law to escape responsibility for caring for aged parents. By declaring their goods "Corban" (that is, promised or dedicated to God's service) they assumed no obligation to provide for needy parents. Jesus showed that the fifth commandment, "Honor thy father and thy mother," was abrogated by their selfishness and He said, "Ye have made void the word of God because of your tradition" (Matt. 15:1-9).

At a later period, after the church had spread over a good part of Asia Minor, the need for providing care for aged Christian widows brought this response from the apostle Paul: to Timothy he wrote saying that children or grandchildren should "requite their parents," for if "any provideth not for his own, and specially his own household, he hath denied the faith, and is worse than an unbeliever." Then he gave the qualifications of those widows to be cared for by the congregation:

> Let none be enrolled as a widow under threescore years old, having been the wife of one man, well reported of for good works; if she hath brought up children, if she hath used hospitality to strangers, if she hath washed the saints' feet, if she hath relieved the afflicted, if she hath diligently followed every good work.—I Timothy 5:9-10

How these women were cared for is not stated, but apparently the congregation organized this activity and provided lodging and food for qualified widows who had no family support.

One of the most commonly quoted passages on the care of dependents is this one: "Pure religion and undefiled before our God and Father is this, to visit the fatherless and widows in their affliction and to keep oneself unspotted from the world" (James 1:27). Williams puts this more plainly—"to look after orphans and widows in their trouble," and the New English Bible says "go to the help of orphans and widows in their distress." Again, no directions are given as to how this Christian benevolence is to be carried out. Various ways of caring for the needy ones have been used; and since no definite instructions have been offered, common sense would suggest that the church should concentrate on doing the work rather than quibbling about methods.

One could go on to name many topics discussed in the Scriptures which have reference to our daily living—divine and human authority, self-control, patience, trust, influence, and many more. Nearly every phase of life or culture, with the possible exception (noted by Matthew Arnold) of science and art is found in the Bible. But the grand theme of the Bible is *human conduct* which, Arnold says, concerns three-fourths of man's life. Even though it is necessary to remember that the Scriptures were written in ancient times and to people who knew slavery, who sometimes were conquered, exploited, and persecuted, their lives and problems were in no way radically different from the lives of the masses in the twentieth century. They suffered from wars, diseases, hunger, exploitation, and human greed, even as men do today. They knew the joys of home-life, of having children, of working to improve their lot in life, and they also knew the temptations of the flesh, of excessive greed, of pride, and the defeats and humiliations that are a part of human life. The Book of Ecclesiastes shows us the vanity of prosperity without piety; the moving drama of Job reveals the true dignity of a man of integrity who suffers without knowing why; and the Psalms are universally loved and read by rich and poor, young and old, the pious and the practical because they speak so clearly to the heart of man. In the Psalms we find words to express almost every mood, every longing, every noble aim of mankind. These are living oracles.

In the Holy Book we read of our origins, of the long struggle of mankind to understand and to discipline himself, and of the One who came to reveal the mind and heart of God and then, by His obedience, to become our example and our Savior.

In the pages of Holy Writ we find light for the mind, a true path for our feet, a guide to what is clean, noble, and uplifting, and stories of faithful men and women whose acts of trust, obedience, and heroism have inspired and strengthened generations of Bible readers.

Here is truth to make men free, counsel to make them wise, teachings to make them kind and compassionate, and promises to give men courage when life is difficult and the days are dark.

1. January 6, 1967, Vol. XI, p. 7.
2. *Ibid.*
3. *Ibid.*, p. 4.
4. New York: Macmillan, 1945, p. 9.
5. *Christianity Today* (Oct. 10, 1969), p. 4.

2

THE UNITY OF THE BIBLE

Morris M. Womack

The more man explores his world, the greater are the evidences of the ingenious and superhuman planning involved in its creation. Although the universe is filled with many diversities, an astounding unity permeates the whole of man's existence.

Aristotle taught that the whole of a thing is more fully understood when one understands the end, or the *telos*, of the thing. This principle may not necessarily be a universal truth, but its applicability to Biblical interpretation will be demonstrated in this chapter.

The relationship which exists between the Old and New Testaments is one of the oldest questions to command the attention of Christian thinkers. Viewpoints have varied from a total rejection of the Old Testament to placing the Old and New Testaments on an equal basis with each other. Some Christian teachers see the Old Testament as an antiquated, outdated, and irrelevant collection of Hebrew folklore, while others revere it as the inspired Word of God and the story of man's religious encounter with the Eternal.

Out of the many diversities existing among the several authors of this volume, one concept which they all hold as truth is the fact that the Old and New Testaments are both parts of a unified revelation from God to man. This volume will seek to demonstrate a number of areas wherein the unity of the Bible may be seen.

Background of the Problem

Augustine of Hippo, one of the greatest thinkers of the early church, made one of the clearest, most succinct declarations of the unity of the Bible. He believed that the Old Testament is the New Testament concealed, and the New Testament is the Old Testament revealed. Although his view has been the most widely accepted and is

35

the traditional interpretation of the relationship between the two Testaments, other more divergent attitudes have been prominent. A brief review of some of these differing views should assist the reader in developing a better understanding of the problem under consideration.

The Gnostic movement of the first two centuries of our era presents one of the earliest rejections of the Old Testament as a part of inspired writing. Gnosticism with its dualistic concepts laid a foundation for other attitudes which were contrary to the principles taught in the Old Testament. Many Gnostics rejected anything related to the materialistic needs of man; and the creative God of the Old Testament was distinguished from the redemptive God of the New Testament. The Gnostics saw a dichotomy between the two testaments which they could not reconcile.

Marcion (ca. A.D. 150) was the most notable person in the early days of Christianity to reject the Old Testament. He conceived the God of the Old Testament to be just but cruel; whereas, the God of the New Testament and the Father of Jesus Christ, he conceived to be loving and forgiving. He could not reconcile the personalities of the two Gods whom he saw in the Jewish and Christian Scriptures. In pointing out his rejection of the unity of the Bible, Marcion developed one of the earliest canons of Scripture known to Christian history. In this canon, he rejected anything which he regarded as remotely related to the Jewish religion and the Old Testament. Hence, several of the books of the New Testament, as we know it, were rejected by Marcion because they have an affinity to the Old Testament. This problem will be discussed later in this chapter.

After the Gnostic crisis, the rejection of the Old Testament was not a serious problem until modern times. Throughout the Middle Ages, the religious climate created by the dominance of the Catholic church was one of faith and dependence upon the church. Independent study of the Bible was discouraged and superstition was rampant in most of the western world as it groped with the religious needs of mankind. This period, often called the Dark Ages, produced very little significant literature, but rather was interested in passing on to ensuing generations such ideas as had been developed by previous ages.

While the age of the Renaissance opened the minds of men to become more cognizant of the world around them, the spirit of inquiry grew increasingly prevalent. Almost every idea which had commanded man's attention was questioned and scrutinized to determine its truthfulness and relevance to men. With regard to the subject at hand, the problem which the modern thinker faced is expressed by James D. Smart:

Of all the problems that arise in interpretation perhaps none is more basic than that of the unity of the Testaments. Can the Old Testament be given its rightful meaning in independence from the New? Can the New Testament be interpreted apart from the Old? Widely divergent answers are heard from competent scholars. Some insist that, since the whole of the Old Testament came into being long before there was any Christian gospel, the New Testament is irrelevant to the interpretation of the Old and that to draw it into consideration is merely to create confusion about what the text of the Old Testament was originally intended to say. At the opposite extreme are those, growing in number, who say that the movement of faith and thought and life that is evident in the Old Testament came to its climax in Jesus Christ, so that the whole story has to be read in the light of its climactic denouement in him.[1]

It would be difficult for one to state with accuracy when modern scholarship began to question the unity of the Bible. From the Renaissance onward skeptical modern thinkers have doubted the unity of the Scripture. (Surely it was preached by the prophets of doubt from the dawn of the new mind of the modern world.) However, during the last hundred years, the controversy has been more acute. Smart says:

> This problem of the unity of the Bible was thrust upon the European church with unusual force by political events in Germany in the 1930's. Both theology and church in Germany as in other lands had left this question in suspense for generations as though a decisive answer to it were not really necessary. But suddenly it became no longer a theoretical and academic consideration but an issue demanding a decision in the concrete life of the church. The proposal was made to remove the Old Testament from the Christian Scriptures. Christians in general and theologians in particular had to ask themselves what the consequences would be for the life of the church if the Old Testament were removed from any place of authority or influence within it.[2]

Consequently attacks continued to be made upon the unity of the two Testaments. Theological concepts were fragmented and many critics were convinced that not only were there divergent differences between the Old and New Testaments, but some weren't even convinced that there was a unity within each of the Testaments themselves. Smart further adds,

> The seriousness of the problem for the church in America, however, arises not from any external attack upon the Old Testament but from the church's inner uncertainty and embarrassment about what to do with the Old Testament.[3]

The consequences of denying the unity of the two Testaments have differed within the varying schools of theological thought. It is not within the purview of this study to trace in detail the historical development of this movement. It should be noted, however, that a number of prominent theologians have engaged themselves to show the dependence of the two Testaments upon one another.

One of the earlier attacks upon this false teaching in the present century was made by the renowned British scholar, H. H. Rowley. He wrote two books in which he defended a unified Bible.[4] One of the volumes is more extensive than the other, but both of them thrust upon the mind of Christian thought the importance of accepting the two Testaments as coming from a common author and as having the unified story of the salvation of mankind at its heart. Rowley declares that the Bible is a unified whole, but within that unity there are diversities:

> There is diversity in the Bible, and with all the emphasis on the unity of the Bible which will be found in the present work, the diversity in which that unity is found must not be forgotten. It is impossible to reduce all to a flat uniformity, and the effort to make Old Testament and New Testament say the same thing is dishonouring to both Testaments. . . . It is unnecessary to close our eyes to the diversity in order to insist on the unity, or to close our eyes to the unity in order to insist on the diversity.[5]

More recently another noted scholar has affirmed the unity of the Testaments. This writer was privileged to hear F. F. Bruce in the Payton Lectures for 1968 at Fuller Theological Seminary in Pasadena, California, on the theme of "The Relationship of the Old Testament to the New." These lectures were later included in a volume under the title of *New Testament Development of Old Testament Themes.* In this volume, Dr. Bruce states:

> As a New Testament student I gladly avail myself of the permission thus granted me to read the Old Testament in the light of the New. There is something more to be said: if we begin to atomize the Christian scriptures we cannot treat even the Old Testament by itself as a unity or the Old Testament theology as a single subject of study. The Old Testament is interpreted in the New, it is true, but the Old Testament is also interpreted in the Old. . . . Historic Christianity recognizes in the New Testament the goal or *telos* of the Old, and we do not need to go all the way with Aristotle to agree with him that anything is better understood in the light of its *telos*.[6]

This historical overview of the relation of the Old and New Testaments was not designed to be more than an overview. The reader will find a more detailed study of the problem in historical perspective by reading the material developed by Rowley, Smart, and Bruce,[7] although neither of these is, by any means, a comprehensive treatment of the historical problem.

In the balance of this chapter, the author will present three different, but we hope, interrelated viewpoints of the unity of the Bible. All of the writers of this volume are deeply committed to the belief that the Bible was given by the will of and through the inspiration of God. Having only one ultimate author, therefore, they further believe in the unity of the Bible. With this one principle in mind, those who planned the volume selected themes through which man has validated the truth and relevance of the Scriptures for these many centuries.

Unity in Diversity

It has already been noted that there are elements of diversity within the Old Testament and even between the Testaments themselves. Yet, it would be most incorrect to assume that because there are diversities, we must deny the authenticity or even the unity of the Bible. Rowley, on the other hand, says:

> The diversity of the Bible must be recognized fully and clearly, even though we see a more profound significant unity running through it all. Nor is it to be supposed that in arguing for the unity the writer is claiming an equal value for all the varieties in which that unity is to be found. There are differences of emphasis as between law and prophets, and it is permissible to value the one above the other, even though rich common elements are found beneath their antitheses.[8]

Who would deny that there is a great diversity between the deep spiritual experience which a reading of the Suffering Servant of Isaiah 53 creates in the reader and the response one gets from a reading of the historical war narratives of the Chronicles? Both of these are from the Old Testament, and no one can successfully deny that there is a great diversity between the contents of the two, but they complement each other as they contribute to the overall theme of the Bible. Or, how would one compare the concepts of justice in the Old Testament to the principle of love and mercy in the New? These are different concepts, but they are also parts of the unified story of God's entrance into time and circumstance.

The most dynamic factor to consider in comparing the unity of the Bible with its diversities is the completeness of the revelation. Or, to put it another way, the unity of the Bible can best be seen by looking beneath the variety of the message to see the overall theme of the Bible.

It has already been stated that the central theme of the Bible finds its highest expression in its declaration of the salvation of lost and sinful mankind. This theme has been revealed to man through the declaration of a number of divergent, yet closely unified, stories which persist throughout the Bible. Three such stories shall be suggested here to illustrate the unity which exists within the diversity of the Bible.

First, the Bible is the story of man's struggle with himself. Man's struggle began with his temptation and fall. He has since struggled with pain, sorrow, temptation, sin, and eventually death. The Book of Ecclesiastes is an excellent example of one man's struggle with life and with himself. In this treatise, Solomon was seeking to find what is good for man to do all the days of his life. In his encounter with life, Solomon concluded that life was nothing but vanity. But compare with Solomon's predicament of life the great feeling of victory and strength of conviction Joshua had when he presented his final address to the Hebrew nation (Joshua 24). So, even with the diversity which exists between two men like Solomon and Joshua, there is still a unity if one does not let himself become enveloped in the individual human differences of the inspired writers.

Second, the Bible is the story of man's struggle with his God. The diversity ranges from the story of a vagabond and fugitive Cain to the life of a faithful and worshiping Abraham. Each of these men was illustrating, through his mode of living, his own encounter and struggle with his God. Yet, between these two extremes, one may find a weeping Jeremiah, David the sweet singer of Israel, and Amos the prophet of reform. The diversity that exists in these individual people is far surpassed by the depth of unity that they represent. Each, in his own weakness or strength, is expressing his own personal story of his encounter with God.

Third, the Bible is the story of how God revealed Himself as the solution to the problems of life. Again, the diversity within the Bible is evident. In the words of the writer to the Hebrews, "In many and various ways God spoke of old to our fathers by the prophets; but in these last days he has spoken to us by a Son, whom he appointed the heir of all things, through whom also he created the world" (1:1-2). The inextricable union which is declared here between the revelation of the "fathers by the prophets" and "the Son" exists also when one considers other theological concepts which are declared by both the Old and the New Testaments. Paul is very explicit in his declaration of the unity between the Old and New Covenants, "for," he writes, "whatever was written in former days was written for our instruction, that by steadfastness and by the encouragement of the scriptures we might have hope" (Rom. 15:4). The whole theme of Bruce, in his treatment of the relationship between the two Testaments, was to "consider how the New Testament writers continue to use them [i.e., the chief themes of the Old Testament] to set forth the perfected revelation in Christ."[9] In fact, he declares that the New Testament not only "merely presupposes but positively and repeatedly emphasizes" between the Testaments "a continuity which is expressed preeminently in the history of salvation."[10]

There is a unity within the many diversities of the Old and New Testaments. In the next part of this treatise, we shall take note of some of the elements of diversity within the Bible and the nature of the diversities. But, regardless of how great they are, one overriding factor still exists: the Bible presents one predominant and persistent theme, namely, the salvation of mankind.

Diversity Out of Unity

The Epistle to the Hebrews opens with a declaration of the diversity present in God's revelation, for the writer states that God has spoken to man "in many and various ways" (1:1). Even a superficial reading of the Bible will show that God has spoken to man in dreams and visions, through inspired prophets and apostles, and even face-to-face, as He did to Moses on Mount Sinai. He appeared in thunderings and loud voices, and in the last days He has spoken to us directly through His own Son. The medium of revelation, therefore, presents more diversity than any man can claim for any other document that has thus far been written. But, the diversity does not stop here.

A tremendous difference between the various writers is paramount. They span a period of more than two thousand tumultuous years from the earliest writers until the end of the first century A.D. During these two or more millennia, the customs, circumstances, political and social conditions, and geographical locations varied drastically. The various writers included Amos, a shepherd from Tekoa; Moses, a tender of the flocks of Jethro; David and Solomon, the two most renowned kings of the united kingdom of Israel; Paul, a tentmaker; Matthew, a tax collector; and John, a fisherman. These are only a few of the diversities to be found among the writers of the Bible.

Charles Dickens refers to "the best of times" and "the worst of times" as he describes the conditions in *A Tale of Two Cities*. The Bible was literally written during the best of times as well as during the worst of times. Some of the writings were written during the times of stress and exile, while others, such as some of the psalms, must have been penned while the author was in a state of spiritual exhilaration. Wars, slavery, impending invasions, and persecution were some of the conditions experienced by the people when men directed by God's Spirit set down the immortal words of Scripture.

The diversity found in the Bible becomes even more individual than this. Even in the writings of the individual authors themselves, there is a great diversity. For example, Proverbs, Ecclesiastes, and the Song of Solomon represent some of the greatest elements of diversity to be found in the Bible. How can one compare the symbolic and allegorical teachings of the Song of Solomon with the sagest wisdom in the Proverbs, or the pessimistic interpretation of life which is presented in Ecclesiastes with Jesus' philosophy toward life or with Paul's statement, "I have learned, in whatsoever state I am, to be content" (Phil. 4:11)? Yet, there is no reason for us to accuse the Bible of irreconcilable diversity because of these variations in states or conditions of individual people. The diversities that exist are normal differences that in no way detract from the pervading unity of the Scriptures.

Another distinctive element of diversity that rises out of the unity of the Bible is seen in the many styles of language used. One great reason for these differences is the fact that at least two languages, possibly three, were utilized by the writers. Those acquainted with the structural and linguistic qualities of Hebrew and Greek, not to mention Aramaic, will recognize immediately the roots of diversity. This is compounded by the fact that several writers of the New Testament were Jewish, spoke and read Hebrew and Aramaic, yet penned their messages in Koine Greek. Often the thought tends to be Hebraic but the expression Greek. Then, again, the presence of individual vocabulary, and the emotional and personal differences of the various writers cannot be overlooked. Paul's writings, for example, show the impact of his Jewish training under Gamaliel, but one cannot escape the influence of the Hellenic culture of such a place as Tarsus. On the other hand, John writes in a simple, easy-to-read, devotional style which enhances the feeling that he was truly the beloved disciple. Whatever their variations are, they are still righteous men of God speaking the truth as God has given it to them. Or, as Peter stated it, "men moved by the Holy Spirit spoke from God" (II Peter 1:21).

Many other diversities arise out of God's unified message. Who can deny that there is diversity between the ethical and legal teachings of the Old and the New Testaments? Whereas one loved his neighbor and hated his enemy under the law of the Old Testament, Jesus demanded that His devoted followers should love their enemies and even to do good to them. Though this difference was present, Jesus could still say that the law of God can be summarized in two basic principles: implicit, total, and undivided love for God, and a self-denying, compassionate love for one's fellowman (cf. Matt. 22:34-40).

Thus, a definite diversity can be seen arising out of the Scriptures, yet that diversity does not express a necessary hostility, or even contradiction, between the various elements of inspiration. It does say that the Bible is not a mechanical or stereotyped message, nor does it even need to be. It is a living message about living issues to living people. As such, it will lend aid in the resolution of real problems in the lives of real people.

Unity Out of Diversity

Thus far in this chapter, it has been emphasized that there is a positive unity within the diversity of the Bible. This unity is centered around the Bible's dominating theme, the salvation of mankind. This unity is no accident, but rather emphasizes the all-seeing supervision of God. Within this unity, however, there is a variety of diverse elements. Yet, the diversity does not detract from the pleasantness of this unity.

In this concluding section, we contend that in spite of all the diversity which the Bible exhibits, still an abiding and living unity emerges. As a matter of fact, some of the very elements regarded as diverse in reality serve to demonstrate that unity pervades the whole of the Scriptures. Four Biblical themes will be used to illustrate that the unity of the Bible has great dynamism as the various themes move with eternal surety from the Old Testament shadows to their unity and culmination in Christ. The dynamism of the Scripture's unity is discussed in the following words by H. H. Rowley:

> It will be perceived already that the kind of unity which the writer sees in the Bible is a dynamic unity and not a static unity. He recognizes development, and in particular development from the Old Testament to the New. Yet, lest he be misunderstood, let it be said here, as he has often said elsewhere, that it is not to be supposed that development was brought about by the unfolding of the human spirit through the mere passage of time. There is no automatic spiritual growth of mankind, and the Bible nowhere tells the story of such a growth. It records how men of God, acting under a direction which they believed to be of God, mediated ideas and principles to men.[11]

Thus, a unity emerges out of the mystery of godliness which was kept hidden, but that is now made manifest to us. It presents itself in the following four dynamic themes which are woven through the Scriptures.

From the justice of God in the Old Testament comes the mercy of God in the New Testament. Marcion and the Gnostics in the first and second centuries after Christ saw these two concepts as so irreconcilable that they "created" another god to solve their apparent dilemma. But there need be no real divergence between the two concepts. The latter concept is merely a more complete development and revelation of the former. Had not the justice of God been demonstrated against the reality of sin, there would in truth be no need nor place for the entrance of mercy for its forgiveness. The one is the complement to the other, and together they show the infinite love of an eternal God. How could a Father as loving and forgiving as God neglect to be just in punishing sin and yet in His acts of mercy save His creature from its destructive powers?

The physical in the Old Testament is overshadowed by the spiritual in the New. The major emphasis within the Old Testament is upon physical deeds and manifestations of God. The Law itself was primarily physical in its dealing with and shaping of men's lives. Jesus emphasized the contrast in the Sermon on the Mount. An "eye for an eye" is replaced with "love your enemy," and the act of sin is regarded as the result of an impure heart's desire to do wrong. There is no real disunity between the two. Israel simply had to crawl before she could walk, and the immaturity of the physical manifestations is only made full when Christians can see the sublimity of an infinite God through spiritual truth and life.

Animal sacrifice of the Old Testament is replaced by the life of God's Son in the New. Truly "the blood of bulls and goats cannot take away sin" (Heb. 10:4), nor indeed did it ever. As the first covenant was only a part of the revelation of God which was completed through Christ, so the institution of animal sacrifice was only a temporary and partial remedy for sin. The scheme of man's redemption could not fully be revealed until God has given the ultimate of His love (Rom. 5:8), and this was not accomplished until He had made the gift of His only begotten Son (John 3:16). The enormity of man's sin must be matched with the generosity of God's gift.

Finally, it must be pointed out, the love of Law in the Old Testament is superseded by the law of love in the New. In the development of Jewish religion, especially in the postexilic era, there was an increasing emphasis on the love of law and legalism. The people of God in Jesus' day were intoxicated with their own traditional interpretations and legalistic forms. Seldom has a people ever relied so heavily on visible forms and the traditions of the past as they. As a response to their attempt to ensnare Jesus with their legalism by asking Him which was the greatest law, Jesus responded with, "You shall love the Lord your God with all your heart, and with all your soul, and with all your mind. . . . You shall love your neighbor as yourself" (Matt. 22:37, 39). Love of neighbor was replaced with an *agape,* a self-giving, self-denying love which has never had a superior, and it is doubtful that it has ever had an equal. The law of love will cause full surrender to the will of God and will bring sinful man to penitent knees for forgiveness.

Thus, there is no real diversity but only diverse ways through which the majestic and unified message of God has been revealed to man. I know of no more appropriate way to conclude this section than with the following final paragraph by the eminent scholar, H. H. Rowley:

> Here we must leave the large theme which has engaged our attention. Only a few of its aspects have been dealt with, and these have been but lightly touched. The threads of unity which run through both Testaments are many, and we have traced but a few of these, noting some of the correspondences between the Old and New Testaments which bind them securely together, and above all noting the fundamental conception of the nature of religion which belongs to the whole Bible. Everywhere it is man's response to the achieved work of God, his yielding to the constraint of grace, his fellowship with God and obedience to Him, his reflection of the Spirit of God in every aspect of his life, and the lifting of his life into the purpose of God. It does not despise symbols, though many of the symbols of the Old Testament are transcended in the New. It demands, however, that the symbols shall be invested with reality by being made the vehicles of the spirit. If Christ is the fulfilment of the hope of the Old Testament, He is also the satisfaction of the need of every man. It is in union with Him that man, who was made in the image of God, can reflect that image, for in union with Him he is lifted into the life of God, without Whose fellowship he cannot walk in God's way.[12]

1. *The Interpretation of Scripture* (Philadelphia: Westminster, 1961), p. 65.
2. *Ibid.,* p. 67.
3. *Ibid.,* p. 68.
4. *The Relevance of the Bible* (New York: Macmillan, 1944) and *The Unity of the Bible* (Philadelphia: Westminster, 1953).
5. *The Unity of the Bible,* pp. 2-3.
6. *New Testament Development of Old Testament Themes* (Grand Rapids, Eerdmans, 1968), p. 11.

7. Cf. the volumes already cited by these eminent scholars. Their purpose was not to develop a history of the unity problem, yet the facts they give are very significant.

8. *The Unity of the Bible*, pp. 3-4.

9. Bruce, *op. cit.*, p. 21.

10. *Ibid.*

11. *The Unity of the Bible*, pp. 7-8.

12. *Ibid.*, pp. 186-187.

PART TWO

IS THE BIBLE
SCIENTIFICALLY RELIABLE?

INTRODUCTION

Solomon, many years ago, declared that there is nothing new under the sun! This truth applies to the questionings of man about the reliability of the Scriptures. Almost from the beginning of the Christian era, there have been men who would argue against the Scriptures and their truthfulness. If it wasn't the resurrection they were questioning (cf. I Cor. 15) then it was the real nature of Christ or the authenticity of some book of the Bible.

In this section, four scholars are looking at different aspects of the reliability of the Scriptures. Dr. Scott, in chapter 3, will examine some of the archaeological arguments for the truthfulness of God. Many valuable findings have been made in recent years which will verify and vindicate the claims of the Bible for itself.

Chapter 4, written by Joseph F. Jones, looks at the relationship of historical studies to the whole theme of the reliability of the Bible. History tells many stories of the activities of mankind. But, in many ways, the past truly unfolds the answers to many of the problems which we face in religion today.

H. Douglas Dean has examined the problems of science as they relate to the Scriptures. There are many scholars today who will deny the relationship between the Scriptures and science. Dr. Dean points out that there is a rhyme between the two and that the Christian scholar does not have to decide between the two. He can accept both of them and, when properly understood, they harmonize.

In Chapter 6, Arlie L. Hoover examines the evidence for Christian miracles. After discussing the various objections made against Biblical miracles, he discusses the positive evidence for the miracles of Jesus Christ.

Whether it be the idea that God is dead or that the Bible is unreliable, a study of the past will tell us that there is nothing new. These "recent" ideas have been set forth in earlier times—in man's efforts to understand the Infinite.

3

THE EARTH CRIES OUT FOR GOD

John Scott

The Setting

Geographical Location: The Near East, The Oldest Civilization.[1]

There is no question but what the Biblical description of the Garden of Eden refers to an area which includes the Mesopotamian Valley.[2] The archaeologist and the ancient historian, without hesitation, support this contention in stating that the Mesopotamian Valley was the cradle of civilization. It is in doubt as to how wide an area the Garden of Eden covered, but most certainly the valleys of the Tigris and Euphrates rivers were included. There are a number of factors which contributed to making the area a suitable environment for developing man.[3]

1. It is known that the principal cereals grew wild here. This would encourage agriculture.

2. Geographical factors include sufficient natural resources to sustain the life and activities of early man. These resources would include water, clay for building materials and pottery, grass for grazing, etc.

3. Climatic factors were favorable—sufficient rainfall and a temperate climate which would keep early man from having too severe a struggle against the elements.

4. It was an area where the basic economic factor of marketing and trade could develop. This was simple and basic at first, to be sure, with simple barter of produce like wine, olive oil, wheat, and livestock among themselves. The location, however, was also ideal for the earliest trade routes, and as time went on the adjacent Palestinian area became the bridge between the other eastern areas and Egypt.

Of course, none of these factors is completely consistent. Nonetheless each played an important part, at one time or another, for the development of early man.

Sources and Means of Study of Prehistoric Civilization in the Area

A study of prehistoric Palestine is not in order here,[4] but for the benefit of those who are interested in what has been learned from excavations about life before the dawn of history, it is interesting to note that in the Mesozoic Age, Palestine was submerged by the sea which left marine sediments in the area. In later times the Pleistocene Age was characterized by four glacial periods. Palestine's fauna and climate have varied from tropical to arid, as shown by excavations which revealed pictures of ancient times in caves.

Actual skeletal material shows evidence of settlement in the Galilee area by a Neanderthal type.[5] Previously this type of man was thought to have been confined to Europe. However, in 1923, in a cave 130 feet above the Sea of Galilee, seven levels of human occupation were found. A human skull now known as the Galilee skull is the most famous of the area. In the years following, other caves have been explored and have yielded skeletal material and Stone Age tools. More recent prehistoric man in Palestine has been called "Natufian." The settlers were Caucasian of a Mediterranean type. Deductions made from the finds indicate that Natufian man engaged in agriculture but, seemingly used no pottery and no metals. Apparently he believed in life after death, and according to the dating of specialists, he began to live in the open some five thousand or six thousand years B.C. He made pins of bone and had other crude tools such as fish hooks, arrowheads, and the hoe.

It should be said here that the radioactive carbon method of dating now in wide use on such remains of civilization is controversial with regard to how precisely remains can be dated earlier than 4000 to 5000 B.C. For details of the problems concerning the method of dating, one should consult *The Creation Research Society Quarterly,* January 1966. The problem is that the dating is based on assuming the radio-carbon in the atmosphere today has not drastically changed since the time the sample picked up carbon from the air in its original setting. The further back one reaches into history, the more tenuous the date.

History of the Land

The Introduction of Writing

The crucial division between prehistory and history is the ability to leave written records. This line of demarcation is dated in this area at approximately 3000 B.C.[6]

The heading of "prehistory" includes a vast period of settlement of the Mesopotamian valley by nomads and ends with settlement in the first villages. Then there was an interlude as the villages were settled and the foundations for civilization and history were laid down. This period has been designated protohistory.[7]

Much can be known about the protohistoric period with regard to the basic races of people and their way of life by the remains that have been left. These remains include burials, jars, and implements of various sorts. During this dawn of history there were three basic ethnic divisions in Mesopotamia.[8] One was called the Irano-Semitic culture. Dating from perhaps 3750-3250 B.C., these early settlers were non-Semitic and non-Sumerian who lived in peasant villages. Another ethnic group were the Semites, who were the forerunners of the Assyrians, Babylonians, Hebrews, and others. A third group was the Sumerian. Perhaps they arrived by sea and settled in southern Mesopotamia about 3250 B.C. Although this is a much debated point, they appear to be intruders on the scene. Very little is known about their point of origin.

The available evidence seems to indicate that the oldest known villages of the world were in this area of the Near East, and as the urban centers emerge,[9] the necessity for keeping written records became compelling.[10] Without being able to record the language, ties with the past would be broken and the influences from the forefathers would be meager. Three primary motivating forces which prompted the invention of writing on Mesopotamian soil were religion, economy, and art. Seemingly, the Sumerians brought the idea of writing with them, but we can see the development of it before our eyes in the Tigris-Euphrates Valley. Crude drawings and systems of keeping numerical records developed into a pictographic script very early, and as time went on pictures became more schematized. The earliest written documents include lists of kings and battles, annals and chronicles compiled by scribes for palace records, hymns praising the gods or kings and events, laments over disaster and death, omens which were used for guidance in major decisions and, most important of all, writing was used for legal texts. The economy necessitated keeping records for grain, taxes and religious offerings. Signs and drawings were used to identify the persons involved in the economic and religious transactions. Of course, the precise year for the invention and development of writing cannot be given since it was a gradual process, but the period 3000-2500 B.C. gives us round numbers to work with.

The Beginning of History

   Writing affected the development of the peoples in many ways.
Some fundamental changes in the outlook of the people took place.
When an old temple was to be restored, the restorer was not only
concerned about his own times, but was greatly concerned to find
out as many details from its past as he could.

   The Sumerians are not only given the credit for the introduction
of writing, but apparently their concept of society and religion was
also a dominating influence on the peoples they found living in the
land. E. A. Speiser has emphasized that each major civilization must
come to terms with two fundamental issues: the relation of the
individual to society about him and the relation of society to the
cosmos.[11] With regard to the first of these, that is, the relationship
of the individual to society, the inhabitants of the Tigris-Euphrates
valley were remarkably constructive. They believed that the individual had certain rights, among these the right to own property, a view
which was not prevalent among the Egyptians.[12] These rights were
to be protected by the due process of law. Hence the Mesopotamian
concept of the state emphasized these individual rights, and it was
the responsibility of the rulers to protect them. With the introduction of writing, the laws could be clearly known and understood. It
would remain for a subsequent group of the Semitic family, the
Israelites, to contribute most to the second fundamental issue of
civilization, that of the relationship of society to the cosmos—that is,
to the Deity.

   With this brief résumé of the setting, we can see something of the
circumstances of the first empire. Sargon the Great of Akkad,[13] is
given the credit for being the first empire builder when he organized
what has come to be known as the old Assyrian Empire. The date of
2335 B.C. is surely not far wrong for this momentous event, and for
the next thousand years there would be a jockeying for power, first
between the Sumerians and the Semites, later among separate groups
of the Semites among themselves as, for example, between the
Assyrians and the Babylonians. The capital would be first in the
north, then in the south, and back in the north as the land rocked
beneath the marching feet of soldiers, and the balance of power
shifted from one nation to another. Thus, in the middle Euphrates
area the foundation is laid for the unfolding drama of man's relationship with his God; for it is here that the first eleven chapters of
Genesis set the stage in preparation for the appearance of the main
characters—the patriarchs.

The Reconstruction of Archaeology

Archaeology is a loaded word. To some it calls to mind the professor with a goatee, a bone in one hand and a pick in the other. Beyond such superficiality, many books and articles have been written which unfortunately leave an exaggerated impression that every turn of the spade in Bible lands brings additional "proof" of the inspiration of the Bible, for there have been times when the records in the dust have produced materials which at first appear to conflict with the Bible. Furthermore, difficulties and problems arise in translating and/or interpreting the material found in the process of excavation. In addition, synchronizing dates and rulers with the traditional chronological system of the Bible, as proposed by Ussher, proves to be a tedious problem.[14]

Archaeology literally means a discourse on old things. Certainly it has to do with the scientific study of antiquity and as such has come into its own, as one of the newer sciences. Indeed, it is both a science and an art. A few pages back attention was called to the fact that the remains of prehistoric civilizations include skeletal materials and many different kinds of artifacts, while the remains of historic civilizations include all of these, plus written records. It is the task of the archaeologist to discover and interpret these remains.

The site for excavation is selected with care and after certain arrangements are made with the government and an appropriate staff is selected, excavation proceeds meticulously.[15] Ancient cities were usually located on a high knoll or *tell* for purposes of a clear view over the surrounding countryside, whether looking for grazing sheep, travelers, or the approach of enemies. Usually the dwellings and buildings were made of sun-dried brick. Consequently, they deteriorated quickly when the inhabitants moved away or were killed. Later another band of settlers would level the mound and build on top of the previous settlement so that with the passing of several generations or hundreds of years, layers for different settlements, like a layer cake, accumulated and the mound became higher. Thus, in order to excavate, the archaeologist proceeds, usually layer by layer, from the surface down to virgin soil so that the farther down one digs the older the civilization uncovered; in each layer may be found the remains of the people who occupied the site at that time. By a careful study of the skeletal remains and artifacts, deductions may be drawn as to the race of people, where they came from, and how they lived. Naturally, in the case of finding written records, their accurate translation will reveal further details.

Obviously, there are many factors which must be taken into account when studying archaeology or comparing its finds with the Bible. It is true that many discoveries yield astonishing support of the Biblical record. Others, or at least the interpretation of others, have produced apparent conflicts with the presumed meaning of the Bible. Sometimes the traditional interpretation of a Biblical passage may prove to be in error as archaeology corrects the Biblical commentator. In other instances the archaeological record is corrected by the Bible.

For example: Isaiah 20:1 states that the Tartan (general) of Sargon captured the city of Ashdod. Some of the earlier higher critics regarded this as a corrupt text because Sargon wasn't known to them—so the critics "corrected" the Bible. Later Sargon's records came to light and he became quite well known for that time—so archaeology "corrected" the critics. Then the actual record of the battle with Ashdod came to light, but it stated that Sargon, not the Tartan, went to Ashdod—so there appeared to be a conflict between the clay tablets and the Bible. But as the study of many documents continued, it became apparent that it was the habit of kings, given to braggadocio, to take the credit for what their commanders did in their name—so, in conclusion, the scholars now agree that the Bible is undoubtedly correct in saying that it was the Tartan who did the dirty work while Sargon took the credit. Thus in the last analysis the Bible corrected archaeology.

In all fairness we must recognize that not every historical and archaeological difficulty is yet answered. We are still confronted by many problems and, as we press on, more of them are being resolved. We will consider some of these later in this chapter. As we compare the literature of the Bible with the literature of the land, we will see the contrasts in culture, dignity, and insight. As we study the people of the land, we will learn more about the life and times of the patriarchs. As we consider the remains of some sample cities, we will find records from the dust which corroborate the record of the prophets. And as we consider the law of the land, we will see how our own jurisprudence is based on the Law of Moses.

The Literature of the Land

Akkadian Religious Literature

As has already been stated, the first people on the face of the earth to reduce their language to writing were the people in the Mesopotamian Valley. Consequently, they were the first people to develop a literature. Myths and legends that had been handed down for many generations by word of mouth could now be put in a permanent form by using the recently developed "script." The Sumerian language, which was a monosyllabic, has been linked to many other languages, but the closest affinity is mongoloid, with which there is a possible connection. Originally, about two thousand signs were developed for words but later this was reduced to one thousand and eventually ended with a working list of about six hundred. The earliest writing on clay tablets is clearly traceable to a picture. Since the language of the native Akkadians was necessary to the emigrating Sumerians, grammars of the two languages were made about 2000 B.C. As a result of this, we have a great deal of literature—actually thousands of tablets—in both the Sumerian and Akkadian languages. Every type of literature is represented—myths, epics, legal texts, historical documents, incantations and rituals, hymns, prayers, wisdom literature, as well as other types.

It will be interesting to compare the Akkadian (Babylonian) account of the creation with Genesis. The most significant expression of the religious beliefs of Mesopotamia is contained in a work consisting of seven tablets called *Enuma Elish,* "when on high," which are the opening words of the text.[16] The epic deals with the struggle to bring order out of chaos in the creative period. The actual tablets came first from three main sources—Nineveh, Ashur, and Kish. The exact date of the composition of this epic is still in doubt. However, none of the other existing texts is dated earlier than the first millennium B.C.

The text presupposes in the beginning of time the existence of the creative force of the primordial waters, called "Apsu," and Tiamat, a goddess who seems to share in the creation of other gods and goddesses. These two forces beget Marduk, a grotesque god, along with other monsters which are a part of the pantheon. The condition of the heavens is now described in these words:

> Tiamat is jealous and disturbed and proposes: "Let us make monsters; Let us do battle against gods; They thronged and marched at the side of Tiamat. Enraged they plot without cease night and day. They are set for combat, growling, raging. They form a council to prepare for the fight. Mother Hubur, she who fashions all things, added matchless weapons, bore monster-serpents. . . . Roaring dragons she has clothed with terror. . . . She set up the viper, the Dragon, and the Sphinx. . . ."

Apparently the monsters that have been created get out of hand and a revolution threatens. Marduk agrees to defend the other gods from the onslaught of Tiamat and the monsters. When this agreement is made the gods have a celebration described as follows:

> They kissed one another in the assembly. They held converse as they sat down to the banquet. They ate festive bread, partook of

the wine; They wetted their drinking-tubes with sweet intoxi-
cant. As they drank the strong drink, their bodies swelled; They
became very lanquid as their spirits rose.

Finally the stage is set for the heavenly forces to struggle in
combat. We are told:

> They swayed in single combat, locked in battle. The lord (Mar-
> duk) spread out his net to enfold her. The Evil Wind, which
> followed behind, he let loose in her face. When Tiamat opened
> her mouth to consume him, he drove in the Evil Wind that she
> close not her lips. As the fierce winds charged her belly, her body
> was distended and her mouth was wide open. He released the
> arrow, it tore her belly; It cut through her insides, splitting the
> heart. Having thus subdued her, he extinguished her life. He cast
> down her carcass to stand upon it. . . .

After the chaotic Tiamat is killed, Marduk is now ready to engage
in creation. From this comes the heaven, the earth, and man:

> He split her like a shellfish into two parts: Half of her he set up
> and ceiled it as sky; He constructed stations for the great gods
> . . . Blood will I mass and cause bones to be. I will establish a
> savage, "man" shall be his name. Verily, savage-man I will create.
> He will be charged with the service of the gods; That they might
> be at ease!

Now read the Biblical account of creation from Genesis 1:6-8, for
the formation of the heavens, and 1:26-28 for the creation of man.
Keep in mind that in the fertile crescent some thousand years B.C.,
both of these accounts were in vogue. The Babylonian text was
prevalent in Mesopotamia and other areas while the Biblical account
was peculiar to Israel. The simplicity and the dignity of the Biblical
account, as well as the accurate order of the creative events, prompts
one to see in the Genesis record an aura of authenticity not found in
any other tradition.

Other examples could be given, such as the Akkadian record of
the Flood. When it is compared with the Biblical account one is
further impressed with the dignity of the Bible.

It is obvious that the Akkadian religious literature exemplifies the
building of hundreds of years of tradition, and is filled with exaggera-
tions and fantasy characteristic of a people who read into the
circumstances and religions of their gods all the foibles, problems,
and other features of their earthly society. These observations
prompt one to conclude that the literature of the land was the
literature of the people, whereas the literature of the Bible is the
literature of God's spokesmen, the prophets. This illustrates a princi-

ple mentioned earlier in this chapter, that the Mesopotamians had difficulty in resolving the issue of the relationship of society to the universe, even though they were able to work out a satisfactory relationship of the individual to society. It was with Israel in Palestine that the crucial problem of the relationship of society to the universe, that is, man's relationship with his God, was solved for all generations.

The Law of the Land

Mesopotamian Law[17]

Attention has already been called to the fact that the people of Mesopotamia believed that they had certain rights such as the right to own property and the right of protection by law, certain inheritance rights, and other privileges which were considered to be given them from their gods. Consequently, when they learned to write, their laws very early were put in concrete form so that they could be known and recognized by the whole society. The early kings of Mesopotamia were considered more as "counselors" than despotic rulers.

One of the earliest law codes in the area is known as the code of Lipit-Ishtar.[18] There were some thirty-eight laws on seven clay tablets, in fragments, dating from sometime in the first half of the second millennium B.C. The king, whose name the code bears, must have reigned somewhere around 1975 B.C. In the prologue to the code various achievements of King Lipit-Ishtar are cited, as well as how his gods reestablished equitable family practices through him. The laws have to do with hiring of boats, real estate transactions, treatment of slaves, defaulting on taxes, inheritance, marriage, and renting oxen.

Another body of laws which also had a part in laying the foundation for later codes is known as "the laws of Eshnunna."[19] The kingdom of Eshnunna was in the Diyala region, east of Baghdad; it flourished between the downfall of the third dynasty of Ur (ca. 2000 B.C.) and the creation of Hammurabi's empire. These laws may be earlier than those of Lipit-Ishtar, and are similar in subject matter. A sample taken at random states: "If a man buys a slave, a slave-girl, or an ox, or any other valuable goods, but cannot (legally) establish the seller, he is a thief." Another early code was known as the laws of Er-Nammu. All of these codes had a prologue followed by the body of laws, and concluded with an epilogue.

Chaos ensued after the decline of the old Assyrian Empire late in the first half of the second millennium B.C., that is, around 1700. During this time of confusion—a dark age also in Indo-Europe—the old Babylonia Empire, with Hammurabi as king, gradually developed. He established his throne in a more southerly direction from Akkad. His area of jurisdiction included the area referred to in Genesis 11:28 as "Ur of the Chaldees." An approximate date for the beginning of this period is 1850.

The system of laws for which Hammurabi takes credit for codifying bears his name.[20] Actually, he was the sixth of eleven kings of the Amorite dynasty in the old Babylonian Empire. He ruled for forty-three years, 1728 to 1686 B.C.[21] His law was "published" at the beginning of his reign. The laws were inscribed on a stele at the top of which the king is pictured as receiving his commission to write the laws from the god of justice, the sun god Shamash. Many years later the stele was carried off to Susa by an Elamite raider, sometime between 1207 and 1171 B.C., as a trophy of war. It was discovered in modern times by a French archaeologist in 1901-1902 and was taken to the Louvre in Paris as a trophy of archaeology. Many of the laws were chiseled off by the Elamites, but these have been preserved by other copies.

Hammurabi and his dynasty were foreigners to Babylon, but due to his influence, Babylon rose to world fame for the first time. The laws of Hammurabi had penetrated society far and wide by the time Abraham and his family made their pilgrimage, as directed by God, from southern Mesopotamia around the fertile crescent to the northwest and then southward into Palestine.

Many of the laws of Hammurabi deal with subjects that are common to the Law of Moses. Because of some of the similarities some historians have concluded that the Law of Moses came from the code of Hammurabi. However, this cannot be substantiated.

Before comparing some of the Mesopotamian laws with the Law of Moses, one other set of laws should be alluded to. They are the Middle Assyrian Laws. After the downfall of the old Babylonian Empire, 155 years after Hammurabi's death, the next major empire, known as the Middle Assyrian Empire, shifted power back to the north about 1390 B.C. This period lasted about 200 years, during which time Middle Assyrian Laws were committed to tablets, extant copies of which date from the time of Tiglath-Pilezer I in the twelfth century B.C. However, the laws may go back to the fifteenth century B.C.

Brief Comparison of the Babylonian
and Assyrian Laws with the Laws of Moses

A few of the laws which are similar and often compared are these: The Code of Hammurabi (CH) #8 states: "If a man stole either an ox, or a sheep, or an ass, or a pig, or a goat, if it belonged to the temple, if it belonged to the state, he shall make restitution 30 fold; if it belonged to a private citizen, he shall make good 10 fold. If the thief does not have sufficient to make restitution, he shall be put to death."

Laws in the Bible concerning theft may be found in Exodus 20:15; 22:1-4; Leviticus 19:11, 13.

CH #14—"If a man has stolen the young son of another man, he shall be put to death."

Compare Exodus 21:16; Deuteronomy 24:7. CH #195—"If a son has struck his father, they shall cut off his hand."

CH #196—"If a man has destroyed the eye of another man, they shall destroy his eye."

CH #197—"If he has broken another man's bone, they shall break his bone."

CH #198—"If he has destroyed the eye of a commoner or broken the bone of a commoner, he shall pay one mina of silver."

Exodus 21:12-27 deals with the same subject and in a similar way. It may be that some of the Laws of Moses were incorporated in that body of law because they were generally in practice over the land prior to the time of Moses and were generally accepted by the Israelites living in that environment. However, it could also be that these laws are similar simply because they are dealing with a similar subject and the basic concept of justice in the Near East among Semites decreed similar punishments. At any rate, there are too many differences to draw the rash and hasty conclusion that the Law of Moses was copied from the Code of Hammurabi. All over the land the concept of law and justice and the dignity of citizens in a basically democratic society (in contrast to the law of Egypt) was prevalent.

The Middle Assyrian Laws are harsh and cruel, and there are some subjects which are dealt with in a way similar to the Law of Moses, but there are other wide divergencies. The differences are far greater than the similarities. Once again we may draw some tentative conclusions by comparing the laws of the Bible with the laws of the land, and in so doing we will see a greater affinity to the Biblical system than to the laws of the Babylonians and Assyrians. We would say that our concept of justice is most suited to the laws of Moses.

The People of the Land—The Patriarchs

The Life and Times of Abraham

Until recent times many Biblical scholars have considered the patriarchs as myths. They were looked upon as being eponymous ancestors from the shadowy world of tradition. One reason for this was that there was no external evidence for the existence of such characters. Another reason was that such men as Terah, Nahor, and Haran bore the same names as cities.[22] However, in the last thirty-five years thousands of documents have turned up to show that there were many peoples like those described in Bible references, such as the Western Semites at Mari, Syria, Nuzi, Ugarit, and so forth. We now know something about the customs, life, laws, and problems of the people of this time. Archaeological discoveries have not only authenticated the background of Abraham and his descendants, but even the name Abraham itself has appeared on cuneiform tablets in a variety of spellings.

The time that Abraham lived has been the subject of much discussion. He has been dated all the way from 2000 to 1500 B.C., with the more likely period being somewhere between 2000 and 1700 B.C.

The place of Abraham's origin has also been the subject of much discussion. Genesis 11:28 refers to the point of origin as Ur-Kasdim.[23] However, when Abraham referred to the land of his nativity, the land of Haran, is meant (Gen. 27:43; 28:10; 29:4). Perhaps the explanation which takes into account all of these issues is that which accords with the references in the Bible, indicating that Terah and his family left Ur-Kasdim in the south and journeyed toward Canaan by way of Haran, which would be the logical route of travel.

Some scholars have looked for the location of Ur in northern Mesopotamia, but this is very unlikely. Excavation of Ur in 1922-29, shed a great deal of light on the history of the city. Settlements in this area go back to a period earlier than 3000 B.C. and the area was inhabited by Sumerians. The Third Dynasty of Ur was the greatest period of Ur's history, when it was the capital of the Sumerian Empire from 2079 to 1960 B.C. Further details of Terah's home-town will be discussed later in this chapter.

At the time that Terah made his journey, many peoples were shifting about. Amorite (western) chieftains occupied much of the northern Mesopotamian area. Amorite names were prevalent. Trade was widespread. A number of people were referred to as "Hebrews." This name has been variously interpreted, but it seems to means "Caravaneer." Terah's band must have been fairly typical of this group and Abraham has even been called "the Hebrew."

Abraham wandered from Mesopotamia, northwestward to Haran, to Canaan, to Egypt, and back to Canaan, an area in which others were also traveling a great deal. Palestine during this period was under the control of Egypt, and the hill country and desert Negeb were thinly populated at this time—mostly with nomads. Because of what we have learned of Egyptian domination of the area, the Biblical record of Abraham's sojourn is very realistic.

The Customs of the Patriarchal Period

Due to the customs alluded to in the Bible, there is justification for concluding that Abraham lived under the law code of Hammurabi. If so, this would place his date in the period around 1700. On the other hand, the practices and customs codified by Hammurabi must have been in practice prior to their codification. Thus Abraham could have lived under these practices as early as 1900 B.C., which is the date often given for his period.

One of the customs that was widespread in the area at this time had to do with a childless wife giving a foreign handmaid to her husband. According to the custom (or law), if the handmaid bore children she could not be sent away. Also, it was the wife who selected the handmaid.

It is interesting to note that CH #145 and #146 describe the legal conditions of the day.

> If a man married a wife and she did not bring forth children and that man decides to marry a lay priestess, he may marry the lay priestess and bring her to his house, but she shall not share equal rights with the wife.

> If a man married a wife and she gives a maid servant to her husband who afterwards bears children, this maid shall share equal rights with her mistress. Since she has borne children her mistress shall not sell her for money. A slave mark shall be placed on her and she is reckoned among the servants.

From the excavations at Nuzi, actual marriage contracts have come to light where this practice was carried out.

> Tablet of adoption of Mr. Zigi, son of Akkuia. (Zigi's) son, (named) Shennima, is herewith given to Mr. Shurihilu. As far as Shennima is concerned all these lands, earnings, etc. shall have one portion given to him. If Shurihuilu should later have his own natural son, the natural son shall receive the inheritance rights of the firstborn son and Shennima shall be considered second in inheritance. As long as Shurihilu is alive Shennima shall serve him. When Shurililu dies, then Shennima will be made his heir.

> If Miss Gilimninu is given to Shennima as a wife and she bears him children, Shennima shall not take a second wife. But if Gilimninu does not bear a child, then she shall give a woman of the Lullu to Shennima.

These documents date from earlier than 1700 B.C. and give us a vivid picture of life in Mesopotamia at the time. Now read Genesis 16:1 ff. This gives us exactly the same picture.[24] Sarai is barren so she relies upon the custom of the times and takes the initiative in presenting her handmaid, Hagar, who significantly enough is a foreigner (Egyptian). According to the plan, Hagar would bear a child in behalf of Sarai and thus an heir would be presented to the aging patriarch. Although the law of the land would not permit Sarai to cast out the woman, Sarai violated this principle by acting in such a manner that Hagar left. But an angel rectifies the situation and sends Hagar back to the household where she belongs.

It is significant that such accounts as this were at one time considered fable. Now, thanks to archaeological discoveries in the land of Abraham, the minute details live again as vividly as if we had a newspaper account. There are other circumstances which are just as vivid, such as the "cutting of a covenant." The principle of the covenant as described in Genesis 15:10 is something that we can see portrayed time and again from the legal documents of the day.

Another such example is the record of Abram and Sarai going to Egypt (Gen. 12:10 ff.) where Sarai is referred to as his sister.[25] Legal contracts from Nuzi commonly referred to as "my sister acts" would seem to indicate that Abram could have been relying upon certain legal loopholes when he referred to Sarai as his sister in the presence of the Pharoah.

A further example of how the Biblical record fits with the customs of the time is in the last will and testament of Isaac (Gen. 27:2) whereby the solemn declaration of the last words of a man on the threshold of death are awesome. The formula "behold now, I am old . . ." was the correct legal phrase for a legal testament, and not just the chance words of an old man.[26]

In summary, therefore, we can see that when the Bible gives us the incidental details of the lives of the patriarchs from the earliest chapters of the Bible, there is an authenticity not heretofore recognized by many scholars. The early Biblical record is supported by the records and laws of the people who lived at the time these events transpired. No longer do higher critics have this crutch to lean on.

The Cities of the Land

Of the many areas where archaeologists have found materials shedding light on the Bible, naturally the uncovering of the cities gives the most impressive records from which the history of the land can be reconstructed. There are a number of sites where people have lived, more or less continuously, throughout historic times. The remains left by the inhabitants, layer upon layer, tell the story of the rise and fall of empires. The changes of ethnic groups, the destruction and the rebuilding of the cities; artifacts which betray the nationality of the dominating power all go to make up the details of the history of the land. Abraham's city of Ur is just such a place; many others could be cited. The city of Lachish furnishes us with a good example.

On the basis of the probable location and size, W. F. Albright suggested that Tell Ed-Duweir is the site of the Biblical Lachish. Lachish, located about twenty-eight miles southwest of Jerusalem, was excavated in 1933. Artifacts uncovered at one level of this city indicate it was occupied by cave dwellers in the Early Bronze Age.[27] A city of the Late Bronze Age was standing when the Israelites came (Josh. 10:31). Egyptian domination of the city until the thirteenth century has been indicated by Egyptian scarabs found at the site. A broken bowl inscribed with Egyptian writing by an Egyptian tax collector was dated in the fourth year of Mereneptah's reign, or about 1230 B.C.

The period at Lachish which holds the greatest fascination for the student of the Bible is the period of the fall of Judah to the Neo-Babylonian Empire. You will recall that when Jerusalem first fell to the Babylonians in 606, the puppet king, Jehoiakim, was put on the throne in Jerusalem. He later rebelled and his son, Jehoiachin, was put on the throne in his place. His rebellion and punishment—another invasion of the Babylonians in 598 B.C.—is recorded in II Kings 24:1-17. After this, Zedekiah was placed on the throne but, like his predecessors, did not remain loyal to Babylon. So Nebuchadnezzar II advanced on Judah and laid seige to Jerusalem for eighteen months (587 B.C.). Its walls were broken down, the houses and the temple were burned with fire. All of the people, except the poorest of the land, were carried into exile (II Kings 25:1-12). Jeremiah preached in this period "when Babylon's army was fighting against Jerusalem and against the cities of Judah, against Lachish, against Azekah" (Jer. 34:7).[28] Located as it is on part of a limestone ridge, the area lends itself to protective fortifications.

The excavations at Lachish show that it was destroyed by fire twice within a short time,[29] first probably around 598 and second probably 588. A series of letters has been found on a level from Lachish at this period of time. A clay seal was found which showed the mark of the fibers of a papyrus document on its back with the inscription "the property of Gedaliah who is over the house." It is interesting to note that this is the name of the governor of Judah in 587 (II Kings 25:22; Jer. 40:5 f.; 41:2). The room where guards must have been quartered was discovered in 1935. In it were a great many ostraca in Hebrew, with a Phoenician script. These proved to be dispatches written by Hoshaiah, (cf. Jer. 42:1; 43:2) who was at some military outpost, to one Joash, who must have been a high commanding officer at Lachish.[30] It could have been a warning from this Hoshaiah that led to the flight to Egypt (cf. Jer. 43:1-7). Because they were found in the ashes of the second destruction of the city, these letters have been dated 588. In one letter part of a prophet's name survives. Some scholars believe the name is that of Uriah who is referred to by Jeremiah as having been executed by Jehoiakim (26:20 ff.) and another letter has been interpreted as a plea to spare his life. On the other hand, some scholars have identified this reference in the letter to Jeremiah himself. This illustrates the tenuous nature of some archaeological material due to difficulty reading some texts. Nonetheless, the language, phraseology, spelling and style of these Lachish letters is very similar to that of Jeremiah. Jeremiah 34 indicates that Jerusalem, Lachish, and Azekah were the three towns to hold out the longest against Nebuchadnezzar. This is corroborated by these letters. One letter may indicate that Azekah had already fallen; it states:

> We are watching for the signal stations of Lachish according to all the signals which my lord gives, because we cannot see the signals of Azekah.

Many names appear in the letters which are also found in Jeremiah. They may or may not refer to the same persons. The name of God, Yahweh, is referred to several times. Other names that are mentioned are Gemariah (cf. Jer. 29:3; 36:10, 12, 25); and Jaazaniah (cf. Jer. 35:3). Mibtahiah is referred to as a son of Jeremiah. Neriah was the name of the father of Baruch (Jer. 32:12); the same name appears in the letters. One letter refers to the "weakening of the hands of the people" which is the same phrase used in Jeremiah 38:4. These words were used by a prince in the letter. Apparently a military mission was on the way to Egypt to ask for help. It stopped at a small garrison to secure provisions. The officer of the outpost who sends his reports to Lachish defends himself against the charges of negligence made against him by a superior. Although this material may not be considered revolutionary, it certainly adds a touch of realism and authenticity to a catastrophic scene at a critical juncture in Israel's history.

Many other cities could be listed as examples of this same principle. But "Ur of the Chaldees" is a picturesque example. Sir Leonard Woolley, in his characteristically colorful manner, describes the discovery and history of the city in laymen's terms.[31] Space does not permit a summary of every period of this ancient city but it is interesting to note a description of the city as it was at the time of Abraham.

The ancient Babylonian city of Uru was found beneath the ruins of the more recently named el-Mukayyar on the right bank of the Euphrates, twenty-five miles southeast of Erech. This Uru is the only city by that name known to modern man but the Biblical use of "Chaldees" (or Kasdim) suggests there must have been others known to Israel.

Clay tablets found in excavating the city indicate that Hammurabi conquered Ur. In the eleventh year of Hammurabi's reign the southern cities rebelled and the twelfth year is designated "that year in which the king destroyed the walls of Ur." In 1674 B.C., Hammurabi's army destroyed the city, burning at least sections of it, and looted the temple of Nin-Gal.

The houses destroyed at that time must have been the type Abraham and Terah inhabited. They were constructed of burnt brick in the lower part and with mud brick in the upper levels, with an overlay of plaster or whitewash hiding the change in brick. Usually they were two stories high and contained as many as thirteen or fourteen rooms around a central paved court which supplied light and air to the dwelling.

The streets were narrow, winding and unpaved, with blank walls without windows on both sides. Donkeys would have been used for transportation and freight.

As one entered the house through the front door, he would pass into a tiny lobby with a drain in the floor where the visitor could wash his feet. From the lobby he would pass into the central courtyard. On one side of the court against the wall there were stairs leading to the upper floor. Behind the stairs was a lavatory with its terra-cotta drain.

On the ground level there would be found a kitchen with fireplace and stone grinders. Ceilings were over ten feet high which would probably be helpful in the hot climate.

Likely, there was a gallery or open porch around the open court.

The people, seemingly, were very religious because typically each residence had its private chapel. It would have a niche in the wall for an image and under the "nave" floor would be a brick tomb for each member of the family. There was a feeling that the dead man continued to inhabit the house and his heirs dwelt on in the rooms above his grave. Such arrangements indicate that there was prevalent a strong feeling of family continuity.

As you can see, Abraham was a citizen of a great city in a highly organized civilization. The houses give evidence of comfort and luxury, and the culture was advanced. Copies of hymns, mathematical tables ranging from plain sums in addition to formulae for extraction of square and cube roots, and many other written texts have been found.

Truly, it must have been difficult for Abraham to leave his father's house and make the long journey into a strange and foreign land. It is no wonder that he is known as a man of great faith.

Conclusion

Archaeology is one of the new sciences, but it has developed rapidly and has earned its place among the scholars of society. It is significant that as the science progresses and develops, it adds immeasurably to our knowledge of the setting and customs of the Biblical period, and hence, confirms what we read in the Bible. There are still problems and apparent conflicts among archaeologists as well as among Biblical scholars, but as research continues these problems are solved and conflicts reconciled. Just as surely as we see inconsistencies between the interpretations of the archaeologists, we have to admit problems in our interpretation of the Scriptures. Being human, we are not infallible. No student of the Bible would dare say he knows it all.

Thus, generally speaking, where the results of archaeological research meet the Bible we find a basis for the renewal and strengthening of our faith.

But beyond this, I must confess, that although the search for continued evidence of inspiration is intriguing, the fact remains that in the last analysis we cannot expect everything to be proved. There comes a time when we must "take the leap of faith"—otherwise we would be walking by sight and not by faith.

1. Robert J. Braidwood, *The Near East and the Foundations for Civilization*, (Eugene, Ore.: University of Oregon Press, 1962), p. 2 f.
2. E. A. Speiser, *Oriental and Biblical Studies*, eds. J. J. Finkelstein and Moshe Greenberg (Philadelphia: University of Pennsylvania Press, 1967), p. 23 ff.
3. E. A. Speiser, "The Ancient Near East: Cradle of History," *Mid-East: World Center*, Vol. VII, *Science and Culture Series*, ed. Ruth Nanda Anshen (New York: Harper and Brothers, 1956). Robert J. Braidwood, *op. cit.*
4. V. Gordon Childe, *New Light on the Most Ancient East* (New York: F. A. Prager, 1968), p. 1 ff.
5. Dorothy A. E. Garrod, *Primitive Man in Egypt, Western Asia and Europe*, *The Cambridge Ancient History Series*, eds. I. E. S. Edwards, C. J. Gadd, N. G. L. Hammond (Cambridge: Cambridge University Press, 1965), p. 8 ff. William Foxwell Albright, *From Stone Age to Christianity* (Baltimore: Johns Hopkins Press, 1946), Chap. III, p. 88 ff.

6. E. A. Speiser, "The Ancient Near East: Cradle of History," p. 31.

7. J. Mellaart, *The Earliest Settlements in Western Asia, The Cambridge Ancient History Series*, eds. I. E. S. Edwards, C. J. Gadd, N. G. L. Hammond (Cambridge: University Press, 1967).

8. V. Gordon Childe, *What Happened in History* (London: Penguin Books, 1948), p. 91.

9. M. E. L. Mallowan, *The Development of Cities, The Cambridge Ancient History Series*.

10. V. Gordon Childe, *What Happened in History*, p. 104. G. Maspero, *The Dawn of Civilization* (New York: F. Ungar, 1968), Vol. II, p. 725 ff. M. E. L. Mallowan, *Early Mesopotamia and Iran* (London: Thames and Hudson, 1965), p. 59 ff. A. Leo Oppenheim, *Ancient Mesopotamia* (Chicago: University of Chicago Press, 1964), p. 228 f. S. N. Kramer, *From the Tablets of Sumer* (Indian Hills, Colo.: Falcon's Wing Press, 1956), p. xix ff.

11. E. A. Speiser, "The Ancient Near East: Cradle of History," p. 35.

12. Thorkild Jacobsen, "Primitive Democracy in Ancient Mesopotamia," *Journal of Near Eastern Studies*, Vol. II, 3, 1943, p. 159 ff.

13. V. Gordon Childe, *New Light on the Most Ancient East*, p. 9. A. Leo Oppenheim, *Letters from Mesopotamia* (Chicago: University of Chicago Press, 1967), p. v. ———, *Ancient Mesopotamia*, p. 153 f, 335 f.

14. Millar Burrows, *What Mean These Stones?* (New Haven: American Schools of Oriental Research, 1941), p. 68.

15. *Ibid.*, p. 11 f.

16. E. A. Speiser, *Ancient Near Eastern Texts*, ed: James B. Pritchard (Princeton: Princeton University Press, 1950), p. 60 ff.

17. Cf. G. R. Driver and John C. Miles, *The Babylonian Laws* (London: Oxford, 1952). E. A. Speiser, *Oriental and Biblical Studies*, p. 534 f.

18. S. N. Kramer, *Ancient Near Eastern Texts*, p. 159.

19. Albrecht Goetze, p. 161.

20. T. J. Meek, *Hebrew Origins* (New York: Harper, 1936), p. 163. S. R. Driver, *The Book of Exodus* (Cambridge: Cambridge University Press, 1953), p. 418 ff.

21. Cf. A. Leo Oppenheim, *Ancient Mesopotamia*, p. 154 for variant date of 1792-1750 B.C.

22. E. A. Speiser, *Genesis*, "Anchor Bible Commentary," Vol. I, (New York: Doubleday, 1964), p. 79 f.

23. *Ibid.*, p. 80.

24. *Ibid.*, p. 119.

25. Speiser, *Oriental and Biblical Studies*, p. 62 ff.

26. *Ibid.*, 89 ff.

27. W. F. Albright, *Stone Age to Christianity*, p. 26, 194, 212.

28. Sir Charles Marston, *The Bible Comes Alive* (New York: Fleming H. Revell, 1938), p. 109n164. H. H. Rowley, *The Re-Discovery of the Old Testament* (London: James Clarke, 1946), p. 30 f.

29. Millar Burrows, *op. cit.*, p. 107, 252 f.

30. *Ibid.*, p. 65, 76 f.

31. Sir Leonard Woolley, *Ur of the Chaldees* (Harmondsworth-Middlesex, Great Britain, 1952).

4

THE PAST UNFOLDS THE ANSWER

Joseph F. Jones

Rationale, Definitions, Assumptions

The inclusion of an essay on history in a major work on Biblical apologetics obviously assumes that history relates to God and His activities in the sphere of time and space, dimensions characterizing history; and, further, that in history man may find the presence and working of the Creator, fulfilling His redemptive purpose for the creature.[1] It is, therefore, essentially this assumption that historical process is known by a God who purposed and created the process and the human participants in it which provides the rationale for this essay.[2] And it is the task of this paper to demonstrate that such an assumption provides the most reasonable interpretation of the drama of human existence, man's agonies and achievements, an answer to the haunting question of life's purpose and the direction of historical process.[3] Elaborating on this basic Christian assumption, better affirmation, Montgomery writes that

> God did enter human life—in the person of Jesus the Christ—and did reveal to man the nature and significance of history and human life, and did bring men into contact with eternal values. "God was in Christ," says the Christian proclamation, "reconciling the world unto himself."[4]

Any Biblical interpretation of history rests upon this belief in the historical involvement of God for the exercise of His purposeful will and redemptive activity toward man. This conception of history views God as involved in creation, manifested in historical event, and pointing toward the culmination of history with the judgment of God and the realization of His eternal kingdom (Gen. 1; John 1:1-18; I Cor. 15:24, 25; Rev. 1:56-7).[5] Fuller treatment of this conception

71

will be given subsequently in contrast with other philosophies of history, in particular the ancient Greek view, reviewed periodically through the centuries, of a hopeless cyclical repetition through the ages.

With the rationale of the present essay laid, some attempt must be made to define the term *history,* and to provide a frame of reference for its use as related to the Christian conception of history. Definitions of history are without end, and much study of them is a "weariness to the flesh" (cf. Solomon's reference to books). Recognizing the difficulty of precise agreement in definition of the concept, Norman F. Cantor and Richard I. Schneider have attempted to extrapolate three distinct but related definitions. They write:

> (1) History is the study of what men have done and said and thought in the past. (2) History is biography, that is, a work of the creative imagination in which the author attempts to recreate the life and thoughts of particular men who actually lived at a certain time. (3) History is the study of man in his social aspects both past and present.[6]

Within these broad definitions scholars with varying philosophical persuasions and historical methods attempt to interpret the significance of the past to our contemporary setting.[7] While each of the definitions has validity and obvious functional advantages, none of them seems to provide adequately for the Biblical view of history as that sphere in which God acts upon men and nations. Still pursuing their effort to ascertain an acceptable definition of history, Cantor and Schneider conclude that "the only acceptable definition of history has to be that *history is what the historian does.*"[8] And what any historian does is to select information about the past, and then attempt value judgments upon its meaning, significance, and relatedness to the present. Such "historical judgments involve assumptions about what is important and real in human affairs and about what is ephemeral and unreal."[9]

It is readily seen now that every historical approach has its basic philosophical stance; and from this vantage point the historian may proceed to gather his information and to make his value judgments.[10] The Bible itself opens with the assumption, "In the beginning God." If the historian can assume a God and, subsequently, that this God is not indifferent to the world of men and nations but in some way related, then he may direct his historical inquiry toward those sources which purport to interpret historical process. But the historian's philosophical world view *(Weltanschauung)* obviously determines both his definition of history and his treatment of historical sources. The historian, for instance, who has ruled out *a priori* the possibility of the miraculous in nature and history, must find "reasonable" and "acceptable" explanation for the purported miraculous events recorded in historical documents when those literary sources appear to have met the criteria of historical criticism as authentic and reliable. And this is precisely what happened when theologians who accepted the naturalistic assumptions of liberalism could not accept the concept of the miraculous as event *(historie)*, and were forced into a demythologizing or de-historicizing of Biblical revelation in historical happening. Fuller treatment of this problem will be given in the section where Bultmann's views of the historicity of Christian events are considered.

"Meaning" in History

Since the time of Herodotus and Thucydides (perhaps even before), men have sought to understand the nature of history, asking the perplexing query of meaning, direction, and goal. Men and nations of men, clustered about a given time and geophysical setting, have asked of themselves, "What is the meaning of our existence?" And to this stubborn and often haunting question have come various responses, speculative ideas, and theoretical expositions.

History is a succession of cycles or spirals, comparable to the ups and downs of a fast Ferris wheel;[11] or it is the sphere of God working out His purposes from creation to some eschatological goal at the end of man's ventures.[12] With the Renaissance and the breaking away of history from theology, came new "meanings" in the historical interpretations of Machiavelli and Guicciardini, followed later in the eighteenth century by the historical and philosophical works of such thinkers as Voltaire, Hume, and Gibbon. The writing and interpreting of history at one time employed rational, not religious concepts; it might well be an autonomous, self-sufficient sphere, predominantly immanent, not transcendent.[13] According to Herder history might be only a natural process of human actions, forces, and instincts within any given time and space;[14] whereas Hegel saw the essence of the human existence and social process as a dialectic.[15] With the emerging of the scientific spirit and era, and the concept of natural laws which were so vital in explaining natural phenomena, one would also expect the historians to develop their own philosophies of history wherein certain ironclad laws could be seen in historical process. With such historical laws not only could the past be examined and explained, but more accurate projections (if not prophecies) could be rendered toward the future course of history. Thus emerged added modern attempts to find meaning in history with the laws of inevitable evolutionary progress, flowering and decline, "challenge and response," or even a new face on the old Greek concept of the "eternal return of the same."

But whether from the apostle Paul to Augustine, or from Hegel to Toynbee, regardless of the particular approach and the presuppositions undergirding it, one certain strand emerges: all of these historians, philosophers, and theologians have sought to find meaning in the actions of men and nations; and Myerhoff asserts that in all of them there is "a strong teleological component as well."[16] But once this unifying search for meaning has been pointed out, the essence of what is historically significant becomes as varied as the historians and their particular philosophical stance.

While no definitive effort concerning historical studies and their influence, positively or negatively, on Biblical studies and Christian faith is intended here, several of the more significant historical interpretations in the past two centuries will be mentioned and briefly discussed. And in these limited references, we may look with interest for the two perennial foci earlier mentioned by Myerhoff, since they are indeed Biblical emphases: the feeling that history has meaning, and the teleological element. For serious-minded men cannot divorce themselves from the thought that human actions within the sphere of time and space have some purpose and design (otherwise, one might well query if there were any worth in being a historian, or a philosopher of history!).

Modern Historical Studies and the Bible

The nineteenth century witnessed some of the most significant events and movements in the entire historical span of the Western world. The industrial revolution came of age, modern socialism with its varying doctrinal forms was born, and the scientific revolution moved toward completion. Politically, some nations moved closer to the establishment of democracy, while others at least achieved national unification. Viewing the interaction of political and cultural forces, the clash of ideologies, the challenges and responses among men and nations, the century might accurately be characterized as an era of reaction and counterreaction.

Hegel and Dialectical Process

With traditional concepts of the Hebrew-Christian tradition toward God and history somewhat overthrown, men sought for new explanations of the meaning of human existence. Significant in this "modern" approach to find purpose for mankind was George Hegel's philosophy of the dialectic. For Hegel (1770-1831), follower of Kant and professor at the University of Berlin, the history of mankind is the realization of the good, and the good is the unfolding of God's plan. And where there is good in the world, there is also its opposite, evil—and the two are in conflict.[17]

Hence, for Hegel, history is dialectical process, a series of inevitable conflicts. In this conflict there is always the thesis, the established prevailing order of life; and there is antithesis, the challenge of the old. Out of the clash between thesis and antithesis emerges synthesis, not merely a compromised position blending the thesis and antithesis, but a new order of life. Another plateau toward the slow but ever-certain progressive goal of human attainment is reached; but soon the synthesis becomes a thesis, destined to be challenged by another antithesis, and the dialectic process continues. This pattern of dialectic, according to Hegel, is not mere chance, but a necessary part of God's design for history.[18] That the dialectical philosophy of history was the direct antecedent of the dialectical materialism of Karl Marx is unquestioned by historians, and the treatment of that system of historical interpretation with its influence on Biblical faith will be subsequently pursued.

Brief reflection, however, on the dialectical philosophy of Hegel and the Biblical viewpoint at this juncture may prove helpful. For Hegel, God was the ideal in reality, the ultimate in understanding nature. In the challenge and counter-challenge of imperfect movements in historical process, mankind climbs ever gradually closer to the Ideal, to the Perfect Idea, or God Himself. Whether or not one chooses to employ the term *dialectic* as Hegel understood it, the Biblical revelation certainly portrays God as working among men and movements to accomplish His will. Nation is pitted against nation for divine discipline purposes, only to see the ruler or nation who was the instrument for such discipline soon subjected to God's punishment. For example, the Assyrian onslaught against Israel of the eighth century B.C. was used of God for just punishment on the nation guilty of breach of covenant; while soon the cruel and merciless Assyrians were themselves overpowered by the Neo-Babylonians (II Kings 17:1-23; 18:9-12; Isa. 44:28—45:7).[19] Whether one can always identify the three elements of Hegel's dialectic in Biblical history, there seems to be the presence of movement and counter movement, all under the providential working toward God's purposes in history and beyond history. Hegel's dialectical views may be justly criticized, however, for finding historical goals in reason, or for its singling out of great men in the crises of nations and through a metaethical evaluation appear to justify either national imperialism or the unprincipled actions of such individuals in human crises.[20]

Marx and Economic Determinism

Karl Marx (1818-1883), labelled as the "Red Prussian" because of his intolerance, unquestioned self-confidence, and dogmatism, and the most revolutionary socialist of the nineteenth century, was confident that communism was the answer to man's historical questioning and searching. Influenced strongly by the concept of Hegel's dialectic, he thought Hegel wrong in identifying God as the Ideal or Ultimate toward which this whole process was moving. To Marx, not God (Idea) but matter was the ultimate, and the Ideal was, in his thinking, identified with the material processes of history. Crane Brinton has accurately captured the Marxian view when writing, "The Marxist God is the omnipotent if impersonal force of dialectical materialism."[21]

Marx believed that he had found the essential laws of history which explain the pattern of human behavior. Three in number, these laws were *economic determinism,* the *class struggle,* and the *inevitability of communism.* Economic conditions basically determined the direction of all human institutions, whether art or religion, political or social. When antagonistic economic groups clashed, the dialectical process could be seen at work, those without material goods confronting those with material goods. Out of the struggle would come the triumphant victory of proletariat over the bourgeoisie, and the establishing of a higher, more advanced social order—communism.[22] Marx's faith in the natural working of economic determinism and the class struggle was but the God-less application of Hegel's philosophical dialectic, a view of history totally rooted in materialism. Thus Marx borrowed Hegel's concept of the dialectic and, substituting matter with all its limitations and change for Hegel's Idea, concocted the philosophy of dialectical materialism. Brinton sums up this Marxian notion succinctly in his intellectual history, *Ideas and Men,* when writing,

> Change for Marx takes place according to a plan, but the plan of Hegel's silly world-spirit. Change takes place in matter, in the sense world that surrounds us, of which we too are wholly a part, just like all other animals. The changes in this material world—it can be called simply our environment—determine our whole lives, our physical well-being, our institutions, our ideas of right and wrong, our cosmology. The key word here is "determine," a favorite of Marx, for whom "dialectical materialism" and "historical materialism" were almost equivalent phrases.[23]

While some of these environmentally determining factors of Marx had long been recognized by philosophers and historians, the essential factor in his entire historical interpretation is a historicism which attempts to answer all of man's questioning—the daily practical and the ultimate queries—in terms of history itself. He believed that the answers to all human concerns were found within the framework of historical process. Let the right combination of deterministic factors emerge, and the "summum bonum" would be realized.

Since the days of its inception, Marxianism has posited a most serious challenge to the Christian faith. Such a philosophy of history, including its notion of man and purpose, denies the Biblical revelation of God in history from creation to culmination. The Marxist system has matter for its God; history is reduced to economic determinism, indeed "man is what he eats." Earle Cairns, writing with intensity, concludes,

> This system is abhorrent to the Evangelical because it has no room for love or faith in history and also denies God as an ultimate. Neither the historical facts of sin in the world nor the sacredness of personality inherent in Christianity is given any room in this theory. Its repellent atheistic materialism blinds it to any higher force in history.[24]

Brinton again suggests that while it might be possible for a non-Marxist Leftist to accept some measures of traditional Christianity, and even to consider himself Christian, Marxianism as a rigid creed of life "can hardly make any open compromise with Christianity or any theistic religion, but must remain firmly positivist and materialist."[25] The challenge and threat of the Marxian philosophy of history is obvious for those who desire the Biblical interpretation of men and nations in the stream of historical process.

Spengler: Decay and Disolution

Just after the close of World War I, the German historian and philosopher Oswald Spengler (1880-1936) published his now famous *The Decline of the West*. Thoroughly pessimistic in its approach to history, the work is yet another example of that historicism characterized by rejection of any reality beyond time and space. A culture, not the class division of Marx, was the essential unit of history, according to Spengler. From historical records, Spengler found these cultures, very much like biological organisms, to go through a life cycle, without progress, goal, or meaning. Although several such cultures have existed in human history, each approximating a "lifespan" of a thousand years or so, the story of each is essentially a monotonous cycle from primitive historyless existence to culture, to an urban democracy and money economy, to a universal state, followed by wars and dictatorial rule, and a return to its primitive state.[26]

While his influence in intellectual history and historiography are more far reaching than this brief critique may indicate, the essential point for the present essay is to note another case of closed-history interpretation, a circular or spiral look at the on-going process of humanity in time. "Force" for Spengler was the dominant note in history;[27] a "cyclical pattern of degenerative determinism" which is oblivious to man's responsibility to God and the freedom of man's choices which affect the course of history. Inasmuch as force is the dominant characteristic of history, Spengler emerged with a relativism in truth and ethics which denies the Biblical revelation of absolutes. Perhaps the man of Biblical faith needs to read again Augustine's retort to circular historians that the only circular fact of history is the circular maze of cyclical interpreters.[28]

Toynbee: Challenge and Response

The name of Arnold J. Toynbee (1889-) is perhaps a household word in both English and American society, and his many-volume opus may very likely be much more discussed than read, even by historians. Toynbee's philosophy, although spelled out in great detail through several volumes, is reasonably well summarized in his *Civilization on Trial,* and is in actuality another version of historicism. Opposed to Spengler's view of historical cultures numbering six or eight, Toynbee sees the pattern of history in terms of cycles of civilizations, numbering twenty-one. But in contrast to Spengler's pessimistic outlook on history, Toynbee's Christian background allows him to provide for a note of hope, if man of the Western world particularly can return to the faith of his fathers.[29]

The story of civilizations for Toynbee is told in their pattern of "challenge and response," and this broad pattern has several integral aspects. Civilizations are born by overcoming obstacles when a creative minority leads a people through effective response to challenges, whether physical, social, moral, or economic in nature. Arriving at a successful position in history through meaningful acceptance of any challenge, a civilization may try to maintain itself through force. But the seeds of destruction are inherent in such a philosophy of man and nations, thus leading to the deterioration of that civilization. Not material advantage but the rousing of the spirit to meet challenges in a moral and spiritual way constitutes the hope of civilization.[30]

For the Christian historian, Toynbee's view of what constitutes a hope for our present civilization is significant. Man may survive if he "develops a synthetic religion of Christianity and Mahayana Buddhism, a more collectivistic society, and a democratic world order.

Then earth will become a province of the Kingdom of God."[31] The
hope of present Christian civilization may lie in

> an infusion of Chinese philosophy into Christianity. . . . It is even
> possible that as, under the Roman Empire, Christianity drew of
> and inherited from the other Oriental religions the heart of what
> was best in them, so the present religions of India and the form
> of Buddhism that is practised today in the Far East may con-
> tribute new elements to be grafted onto Christianity in days to
> come . . .What may happen is that Christianity may be left as the
> spiritual heir of all the other higher religions. . . .[32]

Because of Toynbee's vast influence and impact upon the world of
intellectual thought, the student of the Scriptures needs to acquaint
himself thoroughly with his philosophy. Heralded, on one hand, for
his brilliant analysis of historical process and what appears to some as
a realistic possibility of a new and better social order based upon
revival of the forgotten fundamentals of faith and religion, Toynbee
has also been deplored for his views of our "post-Christian" era, his
idea of a syncretistic higher religion (even though the core is Christian), and his reduction of sin primarily to bad environment. As the
Christian believer reads Toynbee to any degree, he may well be
driven back to the Hebrew-Christian Scriptures for a clearer grasp of
what constitutes the essence of both Biblical faith and its philosophy
of history.

Modern Theological Views of History

The relationship of faith and history raises an inevitable question
for the Christian believer, since Christianity is essentially a historical
faith. In contrast with mystical Eastern religions, which seem indifferent to the historical concepts of time and space, the Christian
religion roots in a thoroughly historical past. Its antecedent, the
people of Israel, had their undeniable history traceable to the mighty
acts of God.[33] The calling of Abraham, Egyptian oppression and
divine deliverance, revelation and response at Sinai, the conquest of
Canaan and the amphictyony of tribes, the kingdom—both united
and divided, exiles and return constitute Israel's historical heritage.[34]
And out of this deeply historical religion came Jesus of Nazareth,
who made claims, called disciples, died and was purported to have
been raised by God in vindication of the divine purposes.[35] "Whereas other religions have looked to nature and mystical or rational
experience to find the revelation of God," writes Hordern, "the
Biblical faith finds revelation primarily in certain historical
events."[36] And Biblical revelation includes not only the events of
God in history, but the inspired interpretation of these events.[37]

With limited exceptions, reputable scholars of the twentieth century have made no serious efforts to deny the historical personage of Jesus; but with this admission made the views about Jesus range over an unbelievable gamut of perspectives. Avrum Stroll, now of the University of California (San Diego Campus), represents one extreme in the continuum in his supposedly academic summary of those who have attempted their quests of the historical Jesus, by concluding that "the existence of Jesus is beyond question; but the information we have about Him is a composite of fact and legend which cannot reliably be untangled."[38] The scholarly opinion to which he refers in such a summary includes well-known names in their critical studies of the life of Jesus: Albert Schweitzer, Rudolf Bultmann, James Robinson, Gunter Bornkamm, Shubert Ogden, and the more radical theologian of the nineteenth century who explicitly denied the existence of Jesus, Bruno Bauer.

While Stroll gives voice to the view that there was a Jesus, although beyond that acknowledgment very little can be reliably asserted of a historical nature, there are other scholars who affirm that the Jesus of history may be better known than many, perhaps all of His contemporaries, through the knowledge of the New Testament documents coupled with limited extra-Bibilical references; and this assertion rests not upon a naive assumption of inspiration or infallibility of the Biblical documents, but upon "the tests of reliability employed in general historiography and literary criticism."[39] Between these two poles of the theological continuum rests the debate of the twentieth century about the nature of the historical Jesus, and in fact, the entire historical problem of *Historie* and *Geschichte*.

The Neo-orthodox and Biblical History

Rationalistic liberalism, dominant during the first part of our century, and stemming from the thought of Schleiermacher, Ritschl, and Troeltsch, was met with serious reaction in Europe with the work of Karl Barth. While recognizing the validity in part of liberalism's stress on the divine immanence in historical process, stress on the immanentalism of God ruled out special revelation, miracle, and the special redemptive character of God in history. Against such reasoning Barth appeared with a new emphasis on God's transcendental working, and the divine initiative in human redemption. God's wrath against sin, miraculous revelation and divine redemption were once again emphasized. And this new "theology of crisis," with weaknesses yet to be noted, seemed as a messiah to the Christian church of Europe. The death knell seemed to have struck immanental philosophy.[40] But what of Barth's theology of history? How truly Biblical was it even with his saving impact on the churches of Europe?

Barth and History

While numerous references to Barth's voluminous works might be cited at this juncture, the discussion of Adam and Christ in his epoch-making work *Römerbrief* (Commentary on Romans) serves most adequately to illustrate his distinction between *Historie* and *Geschichte,* i.e., the facts of history discoverable by historical research, and revelational events which are never discoverable through historical inquiry but contingent upon faith. Barth wrote:

> Adam is the one through whom death entered the world. . . . But the Adam who did this is not Adam in his historical unrelatedness, but Adam in his non-historical relation to Christ. . . . Adam has no existence on the plane of history and of psychological analysis. . . . The entrance of sin into the world through Adam is in no strict sense an historical or psychological happening. . . . The sin which entered the world through Adam is, like the righteousness manifested to the world in Christ, timeless and transcendental.[41]

Barth is impatient with those who hold to an Adam who sinned in history, to a Christ who died as an historical event, and through whose bodily resurrection men are justified. While employing Biblical terminology, Barth seems to modify its meaning from historical fact to symbolic or mythical significance. Faith must rest upon what Barth calls the "Christ-Event"; and this is not to be understood as a happening in historical process, as one event follows another in sequence, but rather through the believer's subjective response to the event. The Biblical affirmation that the Word became flesh (a real fleshly human being), that men saw Him and touched Him, is not the Christ-Event which Barth sets forth as the objective revelation of God in history.[42] The crucified and risen Jesus, seen by many after His resurrection, is for the apostle Paul the source and object for our salvation, since He "was delivered for our offenses and raised again for our justification" (Rom. 4:25). Not only does Barth's depreciation of the facticity of sin and the saving death of Jesus need correction, but other serious weaknesses in his views of theology and history have come in for sharp criticism. In evaluating total history, Barth makes a sweeping judgment by referring to "the obviously outstanding feature of world history" as its "all conquering monotony." And this monotony roots in man's pride which always works detriment to himself and his neighbor. Indeed the Scriptures witness to man's sinful pride and its consequences; but to conclude that the Scriptures only and obviously set forth this pessismistic view of man and history is to be blinded to the conviction that the "earth is the Lord's and the fullness thereof; the world and they that dwell in it."[43]

Barth's theology, carried to its logical conclusion by Bultmann's principle of "circularity," comes in for incisive criticism by Montgomery. He writes:

> When Bultmann relativizes and existentializes both general history (by saying that "always in your present lies the meaning in history") and Heilsgeschichte (by saying that "Jesus rose in the kerygma"), he is simply carrying Barth's position to its appropriate conclusion. A dualism between earth and heaven—between history and theology—between Jesus and the Christ—between the Bible and Revelation—becomes essential; and with it, inevitably, comes a denial of incarnation, the Word actually made flesh.[44]

Such duality in interpretation of Biblical revelation leads not to clarity and communication, but to doubt for the believer and confusion for the unbeliever. The layman certainly may wonder what one can believe in the Bible, if indeed history is not history, sin is not really sin, and resurrection is not actually rising from physical death. Barth's position in regard to history does little to aid the believer in his faith in Biblical revelation; but it may well confuse and harm.

Bultmann and History

During the Second World War the New Testament scholar Rudolph Bultmann stirred the theological world with an article entitled, "New Testament and Mythology," published as a part of the greater volume edited by Hans Werner Bartsch, *Kerygma and Myth: A Theological Debate.* The impact of Bultmann spread from the continent to the American scene, and during the fifties was widely accepted in American theological circles. Bultmann's writings are difficult to read and understand, and it has been the habit of his disciples to accuse each other and critics that they have not adequately understood the Marburg professor and theologian. While it is not the purpose of this paper to do other than present only the essence of Bultmann's view on history (or the theology of history), diligence will be exercised to present him accurately and clearly.

In a concise volume entitled *New Directions in Theology Today,* William Hordern has attempted to abstract several theses from Bultmann's article which seem to have stirred the theological fires.[45] The reader will do well to study Hordern's incisive analysis of Bultmann's thought as it relates to the New Testament message, and the form which this message has assumed throughout the centuries. Bultmann believes that the New Testament message was set within an ancient framework of myth; and that while this myth was acceptable in ancient times, it is certainly incredible to modern scientific man. Insistence upon such prescientific myth in its literal form can only "turn off" modern man.[46]

Such myth was never intended to portray accurately the cosmos, but to express man's understanding of himself. Often these mythical positions are self-contradictory, and demand demythologizing if modern man is to find genuine meaning in the Scriptures. Liberal theology, Bultmann insists, in trying to eliminate myth completely from the Biblical record also eliminated the heart of its message, the kergyma; thus to "demythologize" is not to discard myth, but to interpret myth from an existential perspective.

For Bultmann the Christian faith rests upon the proclamation of the Word of God and not on historical facts. At this juncture he employs two well-known terms, *Historie* (from the Greek) and *Geschichte*, to illustrate his theological stance. *Historie* is that actual series of happenings which scientific historians, using the standard criteria of historiography, may study, impartially and objectively, to determine what actually happened. *Geschichte* is seen as the past, interpreted by the person as he lives today and enters into the past with sympathy, antipathy, derision. From this viewpoint, it is the historian who makes history, and gives meaning to it—no historian, no history. Hordern well summarizes the obvious end of such logic by writing, "For Bultmann the truth of Christian faith does not depend upon what Historie can verify; it is a matter of man's personal response to the church's preaching of Christ."[47]

The force of Bultmann's position has challenged the church to face anew the objective basis for its faith. In so doing, the concept of myth has of necessity been restudied and, subsequently, the nature of revelation and divine communication. In the study of myth and revelation, discussion has centered again on the objective character of Jesus of Nazareth. And here Bultmann is clear that the resurrection is not an event of past history.[48] The use of post-resurrection appearances of Jesus by Paul in I Corinthians bothers Bultmann as "proofs" of the kerygma, although when studied carefully it becomes clear that Paul is not adducing proofs of the resurrection, but asserting a self-contradiction in the position of some of his readers—believing in Jesus on the one hand while denying bodily resurrection on the other. But what Bultmann wishes to do, and this is significant, is to relate the believer's faith now to the meaningful event of the kerygma, and not to idolize isolated past events. (And there is an element of truth and need in this concern for modern man.)

Bultmann has made Christians restudy the concept of history, indeed Biblical history, and to face more squarely the problem of relating event and interpretation of event. That Biblical revelation is seen in the mighty acts of God is acknowledged; but that these events need interpretation is equally essential, and this raises the question of historical hermeneutics.[49] How has God made Himself known to man? Who has the final word of interpretation of these events? How does the believer distinguish between the eternal and the temporal in Scripture? How should the church take the message of "God in Christ reconciling the world to himself" and proclaim it to a world which has "sinned and come short of his glory"? At least Bultmann has awakened a lethargic church to more sensitive concern about both kerygma and proclamation.

Existentialism and Biblical History

While brief attention has been focused on Bultmann, who may be classed generally with the existential movement between the two World Wars, some effort must be made to summarize the existential stance as it relates to the present essay on history.

Existentialism insists that the truth most worth attaining is not that of propositional truth or carefully defined positions, but that with which one can be personally, passionately involved in his own existence.[50] While existence can be encountered and apprehended by faith, one cannot find the ultimate answers in rational investigation, objective knowledge, and historical sources.[51] Origins for this rather strange philosophy may be traced to Søren Kierkegaard, Danish theologian (1813-1855), Fëdor Dostoevski, nineteenth century Russian novelist; and Friedrich Nietzsche (1884-1900), German atheist, philosopher.[52] All three were reacting sharply to what seemed terribly superficial in their social structure, whether in religion or the new industrial society. Whatever hampers the restless, surging, creative nature of man's free spirit must be thrown off. During the two World Wars, when the awfulness of man's predicament became only too evident, existentialism began to receive, rather belatedly, its appropriate recognition. Names representing a cross section of political and religious positions both in Europe and America, need only be mentioned at this point: Martin Heidegger, Jean-Paul Sartre; Martin Buber and Karl Jaspers; Nicolas Berdyaev, Gabriel Marcel, Rudolf Bultmann and Paul Tillich.[53]

While recognizing the shortcomings of attempted summaries and syntheses of thinkers in such a movement, nevertheless, only that can be done in this essay. The existentialist use of myth and symbol has enabled many Christian believers, who found difficulty in literal interpretations of ancient doctrines and dogmas, to hold to some form of meaningful Christian faith. Tillich has been instrumental in demonstrating to believers that they can engage in meaningful prayer without feeling the necessity for clearly formulated doctrines about God which create honest doubt; while at the same time he has forced such believers to see the need for ultimate concern without which doctrines have little religious value.[54] Existentialism has, according to its adherents, likewise contributed to the Christian church by providing a powerful stimulus to the conforming believer, who accepts secondhand ideas and parrots them without meaning through conventional religious forms. It has dared suggest that all reasoning rests upon some presuppositions of faith; and that the choices of man are not actually between a rational life or faith life, but between a choice of faiths.[55]

But while the devotees of existentialism herald their contributions, Christians who feel otherwise point out serious inadequacies. Pertinent to this essay is the stress on myth and symbol, and the result of thinking and writing such as that of Tillich, Marcel, and Jaspers. The treatment of language as a historically verified means of communication, which these men make leads one to wonder about their basic desire to help or hinder mankind in his quest for the ultimate and good in life. For instance, reference to terms such as the resurrection, when one actually believes that death is the end, hardly seems designed to assist man in any meaningful search for life's answers. Harold DeWolf, in a popularly written little volume for laymen, suggests that

> Much existentialist use of myth and symbol looks perilously like an effort to deny the meaning of historic Christian doctrines, while seeking so to entertain them in imagination as to indulge the emotional effects of believing them.[56]

It becomes quite clear upon reading the existentialists that such a philosophy, with its variant position in all the disciplines of knowledge, holds serious threat to the Biblical views of history. But the Christian needs to recognize the service which this bold and daring movement has done in purging the church of much unnecessary dross, awakening believers to personal, dynamic faith, and challenging the Christian church to a vital retrospection of its own understanding of life's meaning and goals.

Evangelicals and Biblical History

The older fundamentalism of the early part of the twentieth century was oriented against classical liberalism with its destructive

criticism of the Scriptures, and the doctrine of inevitable progress
which saw its flowering in the social gospel movement. But such
fundamentalism, while championed by competent Biblical leaders,
and resulting in appreciable response from the common people,
seemed to make little headway in theological circles. It remained for
a new school of Christian scholars to emerge on the theological field
of battle just prior to mid-century who would seriously challenge
both liberal and neoorthodox stances.[57] It is noteworthy that the
movement in America received the support of such Europeans as
Berkouwer and Bromiley; and while several literary journals have
emerged as representative of the neofundamental or evangelical
school of thought, perhaps the most influential and widely read is
Christianity Today.[58]

Evangelicals reacted sharply to the variously prevailing views of
history at mid-century.[59] Schools of interpretation which found the
explanation of historical purpose in terms of one single factor were
obviously inadequate, said the Biblically oriented evangelicals. Neither economic determinism nor the geographical, environmental situation of a nation could fully explain history's existence and direction; and while great personalities played significant roles in the life
of nations, they were not to be viewed as ultimate causation. For
while recognizing all such immediate variables as economics, environment, and great men as integrally involved in historical process, the
evangelical saw God revealed in the Bible as Lord of both nature and
history.[60]

To the evangelical that view of history which denies man's essential sinful nature and predicament must be rejected; and, similarly,
where historical interpretation had borrowed from biological philosophy the belief of inevitable progress, it seemed too clear to these
new theologians and historians that the events of the first half of the
present century negated such superficial optimism. Two World Wars,
with a devastating depression sandwiched between and a third major
conflict, perhaps global in nature, a definite possibility, and several
wars characterized as "police action" did not appear evidence of
progress in the moral and spiritual dimensions of mankind. Moral
deterioration in family life, crime and the increased population of
penal institutions, growing numbers of persons suffering from mental
and emotional breakdowns only substantiated the need to reject such
optimistic views of history.[61]

While respecting every human effort to restrain evil, improve the
plight of humankind, and to appropriate the benefits of technological advancement to the masses, the evangelicals believed that the
fullness of the kingdom of God would not come by man's ingenuity
and might, but by catastrophic event according to the will of God at

the termination of history.[62] But this critical view by the evangelicals of those who would virtually equate the churches' efforts in
social reform with the kingdom of God should not be interpreted as
an adequate basis for the countercharge that the new movement is
not socially sensitive in its Christian ministry. One of the earliest and
most significant works of Carl Henry, *The Uneasy Conscience of
Modern Fundamentalism* (1947), sharply indicted the existing fundamentalism for its lack of ethical concern and responsibility. And
subsequent leaders and evangelical churches have demonstrated that
the Good News of Jesus must strike at sin manifested in social
ills.[63]

Within the past decade certain evangelicals have postulated what
to them is the Biblical philosophy of history; and while there may be
varying perspectives among the evangelicals, there is unquestionably
a core of essentials to which most of these scholars hold. As with
previously discussed positions, no effort is made here to delineate in
definitive manner what the evangelicals' stance is on their Biblical
view of history, but only a concise summary from which the interested student may initiate more depth study.[64] The evangelical's
basic presupposition is the reality of a self-existent, all-sufficient
God, who has acted in creation in a purposeful and voluntary manner
for his glory and man's good. This God had revealed himself in both
creation and history, in time and space, in various manners and
persons, until the full manifestation of himself in his Son Jesus. This
Jesus was a full-fledged historical personage, through whose life,
death, resurrection, and ascension was brought into reality a historical community, God's church. This community continues to share in
God's purposes, will, and knowledge, as revealed in Jesus through
Holy Scriptures which are the product of God's own creative Spirit.
Such documents are definitely within the historical process, and
through the critical study of these historical sources man has access
to the very working of God's will.[65]

Evangelicals accept the presence of evil in the world, but attribute
it to man's sinful and fallen nature. Carnell voices this view forcefully
when writing "the aggregate movements of history—wars, strife,
punishment, etc.,—can be explained within this pattern of movement
of God toward man, and the movement of man from God."[66] While
there is evil in the world, it is not to be explained in terms of
meaningless circular repetition, but rather as a part of mankind's
movement toward the terminus of history.[67] The ultimate goal of
historical movement is the Rule (Kingdom) of God, wherein all
beings may acknowledge Him and His eternal, self-sufficient Being,
and worship Him in perfect accord to His glory and man's endless
good.[68]

The Biblical Interpretation of History

While Biblical scholars may differ in their own interpretations of the essentials in a Biblical philosophy of history, most agree that for the writers of the Hebrew Scriptures there is no separation of religion and history. H. H. Rowley has rightly concluded that

> religion to them was something that belonged to the whole of life and experience, both individual and corporate. There is, in their view, no aspect of our life from which God is excluded, or in which He is uninterested. Nor is He merely the spectator, watching to approve or to disapprove, to confer or to withhold His favour. He is participator in the drama of all our life, and especially in the drama of history. It is this that gives meaning to history in the eyes of these writers. They find God's hand in it all, and seek to penetrate His purpose and to understand what He is saying through it to men. Some of the profoundest and most fruitful theological ideas were born of Israel's history.[69]

With the strong affirmation of Rowley that Old Testament writers could not conceive of history apart from religion, i.e., without the reality of God, we can begin a more carefully delineated discussion of the essentials in the Biblical philosophy of history.

God Who Is and Acts

Although the Bible opens with the recognition of God's existence and immediately portrays Him as related to history through His creative work, Reinhold Niebuhr argues that the "idea of a divine creation of the temporal world is not a uniquely Biblical concept"; but he hastens to add that such a claim does serve to distinguish "Biblical thought from the modern idea of a self-explanatory temporal order."[70] And Niebuhr continues by asserting that the Biblical idea of a divine sovereignty over historical destiny is not unique, reasoning that from primitive totemism men have believed in the presence of a power exceeding any human potency, and affecting the destiny of the tribe or nation or empire.[71]

But having qualified these two basic ideas which Biblical students have sometimes wished to insert as a unique part of the Biblical doctrine of history, Niebuhr immediately asserts that "the Biblical concept of a divine sovereignty over the individual and collective historical destiny has a unique quality."[72]

For the God who operates in history and in destiny is not seen as a projection of the nation's ideals and purposes, or as dependent upon any nation or men; but He is recognized as independent of the temporal order. Scriptures do proclaim a uniqueness of God, however, in that He is both independent of His world and at the same time integrally involved in it. The divine Being is existent apart from history—from matter, time, space; yet He is far from unrelated to the sphere of man and nations (Gen. 1:26—2:25; Ps. 8:1-8; Rom. 13:1-7; Eph. 6:1-4; Acts 17:22-31, esp. v. 27).

There is a definite distinctiveness in the Genesis account of God's creative work and involvement in the world of time and space. The late Edward J. Young pointed out that the Genesis record of creation asserts at least four distinctive and noteworthy concepts: (1) that God is, independent of temporalness (or temporaneity); (2) that God acts, of His own initiative; (3) that God acts with purpose or design in His creative endeavors; and (4) that God acts to His own divine complacency.[73]

It is the redemptive story of the Old Testament that the same God who has acted in creation, has now called a people into being; first Abraham and his immediate descendants, and now his many progeny, Israel. God has fashioned Israel into a nation in history; it is not that Israel as a nation chose God. Furthermore, the basis for this calling and formation of a people is His own gracious and sovereign doing (Gen. 12:1-9; Deut. 7:7-8; Jer. 31:31-32; Hos. 11:1-4). Now that God has called and covenanted a people, He must be involved in their historical purpose and destiny.[74] Such is Biblical affirmation.

Now the fact that God chose Israel and not vice versa, and the firm declaration of the Decalogue that God is separate from His world and will brook no competition from those which are not gods, makes possible a belief that this God is Lord of all nations and history; He is not the mere possession of one people or nation. And this "idea of a universal history emerges by reason of the fact that the divine sovereignty which overarches all historical destiny is not the possession of any people or the extension of any particular historical power."[75] From the days of Moses through the succession of the prophets this concern and involvement of Israel's God with all other nations is proclaimed. He is indeed Lord of history, and history is His sphere of operation.

A second implication of this Biblical notion of universal history, according to Niebuhr, is the complexity of history. Human agents do not simply conform to or obey His sovereignty; they may reject the Lord God, equating their wisdom with His, at times rebelling against Him. In fact, Niebuhr presses the implications of human freedom so far in this respect as to assert that the final end of history is very dubious. Thus his conclusion that

> if there is a pattern and meaning in the historical drama it must be worked out against this human rebellion, which sows confusion into the order of history and makes its final end dubious.[76]

That history may witness to vigorous encounters between God and man, is well attested. Jesus' cry over the holy city couches this conflict, God's perennial "I will" pitted against man's stubborn, "You will not" (Matt. 23:37). But Niebuhr must contend with Scripture when concluding that the end of historical process is dubious, for the declaration of Bible writers is that the kingdom of God will finally be fully perfected, that the kingdoms of this world will have become the kingdoms of our Lord and His Christ; the time will be when the Son shall deliver the kingdom back to the Father, that "God may be all in all" (Dan. 2:44; I Cor. 15:24-28; Rev. 11:15).

Centrality of Christ

Beginning with the God who is, who has created the temporal order, and who has entered into a special covenant relationship with His people Israel, the Biblical philosophy of history witnesses to centuries of purposeful revelation through both the spoken word of God and in magnanimous events, ever making more clear the character and will of Israel's God. But revelation is not always met with the response of faith; it may be rejected, as many of the prophets rudely experienced.[77] Yet He continues to work through men and nations for the purposeful realization of His sovereign will.

In the inscrutable purpose of God, yet within the dimensions of historical process, God sent forth His Son, born "in the fulness of time, born of a woman, born under the law," and this event of God's revelation in Jesus the Christ is climactic in the divine drama of human redemption.[78] It should be noted, with reference to our earlier discussion of the distinction between *Historie* and *Geschichte,* that the coming of Jesus Christ was surrounded with real historical facts (Historie); for Paul asserts it was within "time," it was "fleshly," and that He as an Israelite who was subject to the "Law." What can be more specifically historical than Jesus' arrival in history?

The Christian Scriptures declare this Jesus to have lived an authentic human life within rather narrow geographical limits; that He proclaimed the message of God's rule as "at hand" and readied men for its actual presence. And the final revelation of God in the Person of Jesus demonstrated not only the character of God, but revealed the utter depths to which man in his freedom (which Niebuhr so strongly affirms) may descend. Now regardless of what stance one may take toward this Man called Jesus, it is fact that history has been radically altered by His coming. The centrality of Jesus Christ in Biblical history pours over into universal history, thus focusing upon Him as the Ultimate in history, in human enterprise (Rom. 11:33-36; Eph. 3:20-21; Phil. 2:5-11; Col. 1:15-20).

Divine Judgment and the End of History

From creation and Calvary, Biblical witness points toward God's judgment upon men and nations. To set divine judgment in an eschatological context at the end of history is not to conclude that He has not been calling men to judgment in the course of human existence; for indeed He has. The Old Testament vividly teaches that God punished Israel and Judah, calling His own into judgment.[79] And He has not ignored the conduct of all nations; at once using them as instruments of His justice while also making them to receive His just judgment (Isa. 45:1-7; Amos 1:1—2:16). Brief recognition can be made in this connection of Herbert Butterfield's brilliant discussion of what he calls the operation of the moral factor in history. Obviously, this principle of personal or corporate responsibility to the God of history is seen more clearly in the distant past (and with Biblical documents to interpret for us) than in the complex interactions of contemporary nations; although Butterfield is brave to see the hand of God at work in judgment upon such evil nations as Nazi Germany during World War II.[80]

But apart from divine judgments within the historical drama, Christian Scriptures point toward the coming again of the risen Lord, calling the nations into judgment, and requiring men to give responsible account for their behavior (Matt. 25:31-46; John 5:25-29; Rev. 1:7; 22:10-21). This is the terminus of history when divine love and divine judgment have been fully extended and perfectly blended. The absolute sovereignty of God will have triumphed, and the "Lord God omnipotent reigns" (Rev. 4:8; 11:16-18; 15:3,4; 19:8).

Biblical history, then, has purposeful linear direction from creation to Christ to judgment. The writers are not confused about some circular spiral of events hopelessly repeating themselves in varying masks, only to breed human despair. For the Biblical philosophy embodies an eschatological hope for those who have fixed their trust in the central figure of history, Jesus the risen Lord.

---

1. John Warwick Montgomery, *Where Is History Going?* (Grand Rapids: Zondervan, 1969), p. 31.

2. The writer is aware of those neutral or anti-Christian historical approaches which imply that man's past can be meaningfully interpreted and understood apart from religion; but the brilliant work of W. F. Albright and other archaeologists has silenced such assertions that cultures ever existed without their own religions.

3. William Foxwell Albright, *History, Archeology and Christian Humanism* (New York, 1964), pp. 46-51, 317-319.

4. Montgomery, p. 31.

5. Also see G. Ernest Wright, *God Who Acts* (London: Allenson, 1954), pp. 21-27; John Bright, *The Kingdom of God* (Nashville: Abingdon, 1953), pp. 18, 26-28; 237-243.

6. *How to Study History* (New York: T. Y. Crowell, 1967), p. 17.

7. Hordern has wrestled vigorously with the difficulty of defining the word *history* and the complexities which escape the more superficial efforts of definition. He suggests at least four different meanings of history all of which are involved in the contemporary theological discussion. Summarized, these meanings are: (1) History is to designate events that have happened; (2) history is not simply all which happened but the "significant events that happened"; (3) history denotes the study and work of professional historians; and (4) the interpretation of events based upon *a priori* assumptions of the historian, theologian, or philosopher. Hordern's treatment of *historia* and *Geschichte* are exceptionally well done and deserving of the student's reading time. (Cf. William Hordern, *New Directions in Theology Today*, Vol. I, *Introduction*, Philadelphia; Westminster, 1966, chapter on "History and Kergyma", pp. 55-73.)

8. *Ibid.*, p. 19.

9. *Ibid.*

10. Historicism, the older approach which assumed the historian could view his materials and task with absolute objectivity, and best embodied in von Ra, is no longer accepted very seriously. The involvement of the historian, and his own philosophical stance, are themselves a part of history. However, to conclude that all of history is purely of the historian's own making is to deny the objective character of historical process—events have and do happen irrespective of either the historian's presence or his presuppositions.

11. Hans Meyerhoff, *The Philosophy of History in Our Time* (New York: Doubleday 1959), p. 1; also see Aurelius Augustine, *The City of God*, trans. Marcus Dods (Edinburgh, 1934), XII, 13.

12. Romans 9-11; I Corinthians 15:24-28; Revelation 1:5b-7; also Augustine, XXII, sec. 29, "Of the Beatific Vision" and sec. 30, "Of the Eternal Felicity of the City of God."

13. Meyerhoff, pp. 4, 5.

14. Patrick Gardiner, *Theories of History* (Glencoe, Ill.: Free Press, 1959), pp. 35, 36. Gardiner includes lengthy excerpts from Herder's *Ideen zur Philosophie der Geschichte der Menscheit*, trans. T. Campbell, 1830.

15. Georg Wilhelm Friedrich Hegel, *The Philosophy of History*, trans. J. Sibree (New York: Peter Smith, 1956) Dover ed.

16. Meyerhoff, pp. 7, 8.

17. Hegel, *Reason in History*, trans. Robert S. Hartman (Indianapolis: 1953). A very readable English translation of Hegel's lectures originally published in German in 1837.

18. *Ibid.*, pp. 14-19; also see Gardiner, *Theories*, pp. 65, 66.

19. See also John Bright, *A History of Israel* (Philadelphia: Westminster, 1959), pp. 288-294; Samuel Schultz, *The Old Testament Speaks* (New York: Harper and Row, 1960), pp. 156-167.

20. Montgomery, *Where is History Going?* pp. 18, 19.

21. Crane Brinton, *Ideas and Men: The Story of Western Thought*, Second Edition (Englewood Cliffs, N.J.: Prentice Hall, 1963), pp. 377-378. For an excellent treatment of Marx in his broader European setting see Eugene Weber, *A Modern History of Europe* (New York: Norton, 1971), pp. 662, 663; 725, 726; 1001-2.

22. Karl Marx and Friedrich Engels, *The Communist Manifesto,* ed. D. Ryazon-off (New York: Russell and Russell, 1930), pp. 25-42.
23. P. 375.
24. Earle E. Cairns "Christian Faith and History," *Christianity and the World of Thought,* ed. Hudson T. Armerding (Chicago: Moody, 1968), p. 157.
25. *Ideas and Men,* p. 372
26. Trans. Charles Atkinson (New York: Knopf, 1926), I, 21-22.
27. *Ibid.,* pp. 412-417.
28. XII, 13.
29. In a radio debate with Pieter Geyl on January 4 and March 7, 1948, Toynbee vigorously denied the charge that he was really a philosopher of doom and pessimism, although frequently so criticized. Rather, he claimed a realistic portrait of the nature of history, and to hold forth a ray of light, a genuine note of hope if Western civilization could return to the faith of the fathers. These two foci in his outlook are well couched in his own words during a retort to Geyl, "Professor Geyl has interpreted me right in telling you that I have some pretty serious misgivings about the state of the world today. . . . Professor Geyl thinks I am a pessimist because I see a way of escape in a reconversion to the faith of our fathers." (See Patrick Gardiner, ed., *Theories of History,* Glencoe, Ill.: The Free Press, pp. 312, 313). For fuller elaboration see Toynbee, *Civilization on Trial* (New York: Oxford, 1958), pp. 3-15; 239-252.
30. Pieter Geyl, Arnold J. Toynbee, and Pitrim A. Sorokin, *The Pattern of the Past* (Boston: Greenwood 1949), p. 13.
31. Cairns, p. 158.
32. Toynbee, *Civilization on Trial,* pp. 239, 240.
33. Bright, *A History of Israel,* pp. 110-127; note also here Ernest Wright, *The Old Testament Against Its Environment* (London, 1950), pp. 9-41.
34. Bright, *The Kingdom of God,* pp. 17-44.
35. Matthew 4:18-22; 5-7; 12:1-8; Luke 4:16-24; John 4:7-26; note the great "I Ams" of John's account; Acts 2:22-36; 3:12-26; Romans 8:31-39; I Corinthians 15:3, 4.
36. William Hordern, *New Directions in Theology Today* (Philadelphia: Westminster, 1966), p. 55.
37. *Ibid.*
38. Montgomery, *Where is History Going?* p. 213.
39. *Ibid.,* p. 44.
40. Carl F. H. Henry, "Cross Currents in Contemporary Theology," *Jesus of Nazareth: Savior and Lord,* ed. Carl F. H. Henry (Grand Rapids: Eerdmans, 1966), pp. 4, 5.
41. Karl Barth, *The Epistle to the Romans,* trans. Edwyn C. Hoskyns, (London, 1932), 6th ed., pp. 170, 171.
42. *Ibid.*
43. Deuteronomy 10:14; Psalm 10:14; 67:1-7; also see Joseph F. Jones, *Studies in Christian Stewardship,* (Austin, 1968), pp. 13-16.
44. Montgomery, p. 110.
45. Pp. 24-27.
46. Gordon H. Clark, "Bultmann's Historiography," *Jesus of Nazareth,* ed. Henry, pp. 216-223.
47. P. 27.
48. Hans Werner Bartsch, ed. *Kerygma and Myth: A Theological Debate,* containing articles by Rudolf Bultmann, et al, and trans. by Reginald H. Fuller (London, 1953), I, p. 42.

49. For a concise summary of Bultmann on exegesis and existential interpretation see Hordern, pp. 42-54.

50. Edward J. Carnell, "Existential, Existentialism," *Baker's Dictionary of Theology*, ed. Everett F. Harrison, et al., (Grand Rapids: Baker, 1960), pp. 205, 206; also Roger Shinn, *The Existentialist Posture* (New York: Doubleday, 1959), pp. 14-24.

51. Will Herberg, *Four Existentialist Theologians* (New York: Doubleday, 1958), pp. 1-27 for a concise summary of the common themes of four of the best-known existentialist theologians, yet representing different religious stances: Jacques Maritain, Nicolas Berdyaev, Martin Buber, Paul Tillich.

52. Shinn, pp. 42-47; also L. Harold DeWolf, *Present Trends in Christian Thought*, (New York: Association Press, 1960), p. 58; and Brinton, pp. 389, 390. A brief though scholarly appraisal of existentialism is Milton D. Hunnex, *Existentialism and Christian Belief* (Chicago: Moody, 1969).

53. DeWolf, pp. 58-69.

54. D. Mackenzie Brown, *Ultimate Concern: Tillich in Dialogue* (New York: Harper and Row, 1965), pp. 1-16; 42-46.

55. Pp. 70, 71.

56. *Ibid.*, p. 73.

57. It is neither necessary nor feasible to attempt any definitive listing of the major names in this new movement of evangelicalism; but certainly the names of Carnell, Henry, Clark, Van Til, Wiley, Linsdell, Ockenga, Montgomery, to mention a few, deserve recognition. In this new conservatism one finds representatives of all the Protestant fundamental denominations. Representative lists of scholars in this new evangelical movement may be found in the following theological volumes edited by Carl F. Henry: *Contemporary Evangelical Thought* (1957), *Revelation and the Bible* (1958), *Basic Christian Doctrines* (1962), *Christian Faith and Modern Theology* (1964), *Jesus of Nazareth: Savior and Lord* (1966).

58. Similiar journals in theological stance, although more scholarly in nature and format, are the *Evangelical Quarterly* and *La Revue Re'formee*, published in England and France, respectively.

59. C. Gregg Singer, "The Nature of History," *Christian Faith and Modern Theology*, ed. Carl F. H. Henry (Grand Rapids: Baker, 1964), p. 233.

60. Cairns, p. 160.

61. Singer, p. 225.

62. No attempt is made in this essay to delineate the three varying views of evangelicals concerning the specific sequence of events associated with the Second Coming of Christ. All agree upon the ultimate realization of the kingdom of God, the goal toward which all history has been moving, and in which "God may be all in all."

63. Hordern, p. 78; and Dirk Jellema, "Ethics," *Contemporary Evangelical Thought*, ed. Carl F. H. Henry (Grand Rapids: Baker, 1957), pp. 130-137.

64. Several evangelical scholars upon whose writings the present writer has relied heavily for this summary should be mentioned: Carl Henry, Edward J. Carnell, Ralph P. Martin, Leon Morris, Merrill C. Tenney, and James Warwick Montgomery.

65. Evangelical scholars will differ in their historical approach to the Biblical documents. Some declare that the historian's basic premise must assume the different, inspired character of such documents, while others boldly approach the Biblical materials through the same principles of historical criticism and historiography as they would "secular" materials. See Montgomery, *op. cit.*, pp. 44-45 and Carnell, *Christian Apologetics*, pp. 201-210.

66. Edward J. Carnell, *An Introduction to Christian Apologetics* (Grand Rapids: Eerdmans, 1948), p. 297.

67. Cairns, p. 161; Carnell, pp. 229, 230.

68. John Warwick Montgomery, "Toward a Christian Philosophy of History," *Jesus of Nazareth*, ed. Henry, pp. 227-240.

69. *The Rediscovery of the Old Testament* (Philadelphia: Attic Press, 1946), pp. 83, 84.

70. *Faith and History* (New York: Scribner, 1949), p. 102.

71. *Ibid.*

72. *Ibid.*

73. *An Introduction to the Old Testament* (Grand Rapids: Eerdmans, 1949).

74. Romans 9-11; and Bright, *The Kingdom of God*, pp. 17-30.

75. Niebuhr, p. 104.

76. *Ibid.*, p. 105.

77. The entire prophetic movement witnesses to the fact that God's revelation, progressive in history and pointing toward ultimate fulfillment of His purpose, met with varied response: kindling faith anew, or meeting with resistance, from His beloved Israel, or warnings to other nations around Israel who were under His Lordship and judgment.

78. Galatians 4:4; also Adolf Köberle, "Jesus Christ, The Center of History," *Jesus of Nazareth*, ed. Henry, pp. 63-70.

79. Amos 2:4-8; 3:1-8:14; Jeremiah 25:1-14; also R. K. Harrison, *Old Testament Times* (Grand Rapids: Eerdmans, 1970), pp. 255-269.

80. Herbert Butterfield, *Christianity and History* (New York: Scribner, 1949), pp. 50-57; and Galatians 6:7, 8.

5

THE RHYME OF SCIENCE AND SCRIPTURE

H. Douglas Dean

"In the beginning God created the heavens and the earth." Thus begins the Genesis account of creation. Up until 1859 this was generally believed by most people, although even as far back as Aristotle ideas of evolution had already been proposed. But within the past 100 years there has been a complete change of attitude toward the Genesis account of creation. Why did all this happen? Perhaps the best answer can be found by noting a quotation in the recent Life Nature Publication *Evolution.*[1] "Darwin did not invent the concept, but when he started his career the doctrine of special creation could be doubted only by heretics. When he finished, the fact of evolution could be denied only by the abandonment of reason." It was not so much what Darwin said that undermined faith in the creation account. Rather, he accumulated what looked like a concrete structure of evidence for evolution and, because no one up until that time had bothered to try documenting the creation account, this "evidence" for evolution simply overwhelmed those unprepared to meet such an onslaught. Many began to think that Darwin was right and almost immediately set about to harmonize the Genesis account of creation with the so-called facts of science. This has led to a tremendous modification of earlier Scriptural interpretations in order to bring them into agreement with scientific theories. Examples of this are seen in the changing of "days" to millions of years; by saying that the first few chapters of Genesis are poetical and allegorical; even by saying that the evolutionists are right, that they have the facts, and evolution was *God's* way of establishing life on earth.

Are all these concessions necessary? Do we have to twist the Genesis account of creation to fit the so-called facts of science? I believe not! Like many others of today, I feel that a literal interpretation of the creation account is as justified today as it was years ago.

Either evolution is true as taught by the scientific world or the Genesis account of creation is true. Both cannot be true. To state, as do some church leaders, that there is no conflict between science theories and the Bible is certainly an abandonment of all reason. Why should the believer in creation have to apologize for his belief or resort to desperation in his attempt to twist the Scripture to fit the facts of science? The *facts* of science support the creation account. In fact, there is more evidence in support of the creation account than there is for the evolutionary account of origins of life.

The basis for believing in the Genesis account of creation is based first on faith; second, on the total lack of any evidence in support of evolution; third, on the harmony of this Biblical view with all the known facts of science. Genesis contradicts none of the facts of science; on the contrary, it contains much helpful information which can help the scientists to solve some of the more difficult problems of science. True science demands that all available sources of information be considered in arriving at a scientific discovery of facts. Science has done much to help us to understand many portions of the Bible. Why should the Bible not be used to help the scientist to arrive at a better understanding of the world in which we live? Genesis should be considered as perfect, historical, and factual. There is no need to attempt to explain portions of it away in the light of scientific discovery. Unlike the theory of evolution, which must retreat as new scientific facts are discovered, the Genesis account of creation can stand comparison with any of these newly discovered facts.

Much of the conflict between men of science and of religion has been due to misunderstandings on the part of both. During the time of Darwin most people believed that the Genesis record taught the "immutability of the species," which means that species have not changed since the original creation. Darwin himself believed Genesis taught that all species were made fixed at the original creation and that there have been no changes since. This was commonly believed in scientific circles and taught by theologians as being what the Bible taught. When Darwin made his famous voyage on the *Beagle,* he discovered that there was evidence of change and variation throughout the world. This led him to believe that the Bible was wrong and caused him to go so far as to insist that there could be change from one kind to another kind. With speculation of this type, he began to formulate his theories of evolution.

In all fairness it should be noted that Darwin made many important discoveries, such as the fact that the many different finches in the Galapagos Islands descended from one or more basic species. Many other important ideas are found in the *Origin of the Species;*

for example: "Animals are descended from, at the most, only four or five progenitors; plants from an equal or lesser number." Darwin says that all forms of life as we know it today have evolved from these basic types and he presents scientific data in support of these theories. Darwin thus concludes that all life has evolved from eight or nine basic types, or possibly fewer. More will be said of this discovery of this later. Darwin, then, did make many important discoveries; but he carried his ideas to the extreme by stating that all forms of life have evolved from a few original simple one-celled forms of life through the natural selection of beneficial variants. Today Darwin's ideas have been extended to the idea of chemical evolution with Oparin's *The Origin of Life* being the commonly accepted concept as to how life began. It is interesting to note that in 1964 Berkner and Marshall proved that life could not have existed in the atmosphere postulated by Oparin.[2]

Since much misunderstanding is prevalent between science and religion, it is important to note what Genesis says and what it does not say. It is unfortunate that Darwin did not consult the Genesis account himself instead of listening to what others said it taught. Had he examined the record himself, he would have seen that the opening chapters do not teach that all life was created in the beginning as we know it today.

Let us examine the Genesis references to the creation. The creative events are recorded as occurring during six days. Although the account does not say that the days were twenty-four hours long, other references would indicate that this was the case. We might point out that not all days have been twenty-four hours long; for example, the long day of Joshua. Immanuel Velikovsky in *Worlds in Collision* points out that our years have not always been 365 days long.[3] There were times when the year was 360 days long, thus indicating a departure from the twenty-four hour day. It is really unimportant to speculate as to how long the days of creation were since an omnipotent *God* could choose to create in twenty-four hours, or He could choose to take a longer time. The truth is that we do not know and the evidence is not available to prove it one way or another.

It is significant to note the importance of the statement *"Let there be light."* The ultimate source of all energy is the sun, as far as the earth is concerned. Yet the creative acts involved energy. The entire universe is one vast system of light and energy. The creative acts involved the conversion of energy into mass. By the fourth day the conversion of energy into mass reached a concentration high enough to activate the various systems of atomic furnaces which we now recognize as the sun and stars. The creation account, in stating that the sun, moon, and stars were not activated until the fourth day of creation, indirectly supports the Copernican system of astronomy. According to the discarded Ptolemaic system the sun in its daily circle around the earth caused night and day. According to this concept, then, there could not have been nights and days before the sun gave light. We now recognize that the earth's rotation gives us our day and night cycles, and this has been true ever since *God* said, *"Let there be light."* The light came directly from Him until the fourth day, the day on which the sun was activated.

It is interesting to note the significance of water in *God's* creation. *". . . and the spirit of God moved upon the face of the waters,"* Genesis 1:2. Water is a unique feature of earth, and evidently it is found in no other place in the universe. Venus was considered the "watery planet" until the data of Explorer II showed that it does not have any water and thus could not support life. Water has played an important role in the fashioning of the earth's surface and today is still the primordial agent in the ever-changing surface of the land. Some speculate whether the Flood of Noah was universal or local. Geological evidence indicates that the earth has been completely submerged beneath water on two occasions. The Genesis account confirms this: once in the originally created state (Gen. 1:2), and again in the days of Noah. There seems no doubt, then, that the Flood of Noah was universal—scientific evidence indicates this was the case.

Biological research reveals that all the phyla of animals are of great antiquity with no evidence of forms of animal life earlier than the basic phyla. Life goes back to Cambrian times, which is the earliest period in the classical geological chronology. All animal phyla are represented in the Cambrian Period and no new phyla have appeared since then. This tends to support the fixity referred to in Genesis. It is also interesting to note that none of the basic forms of life have disappeared nor have any of the basic forms become extinct. According to biology, there is a basic tendency within each phylum for it to increase in variety. According to the evidence the usual pattern for any phylum is to first appear in relatively few forms and later to become vastly diversified.

Let us now examine the creative events of the third, fifth, and sixth days, for it was on these days that the various forms of life were created. Once again, it is important in our examination to note what it definitely stated and what is not stated.

Third Day of Creation

On this day we see that God, having created land and water, commanded the earth to put forth two kinds of vegetation:

A. *"Grass, herbs, yielding seed after their kind."* The Hebrew word from which grass is translated means it to be damp. This probably includes the simplest forms of aquatic plants. The "herbs" include the plants which are commonly used as food by animals and man, as well as most other intermediate plant forms.

B. *"Trees bearing fruit, wherein is the seed thereof, after their kind."* The higher forms of plant life such as the trees and the shrubs are included here.

Botanically speaking, there are only two basic kinds of plants: aquatic and terrestrial, with some so-called in-between forms.

Genesis records the creation of these two kinds of plant life.

Fifth Day of Creation

It is on this day that animal creation begins. On this occasion God commands the waters to bring forth two kinds of animal life.

A. *"Great sea-monsters and every living creature that moveth, wherewith the waters swarmed, after their kind."* Most commentators agree that this refers to the aquatic animals such as fish, amphibians, reptiles, and aquatic mammals.

B. *"Every winged bird after its kind."* This may have included all of the aerial animals, those that fly above the earth.

Sixth Day of Creation

On this day the terrestrial animals were created. In this case God commanded the earth to bring forth three kinds of animals.

A. *"Everything that creepeth on the ground after its own kind."* This may have included all of the small terrestrial animals such as squirrels, rabbits, etc.

B. *"Cattle after their kind."* The word translated here as cattle refers to the domesticated animals which are so useful to man, such as cows, horses, sheep.

C. *"Beasts of the earth after their own kind."* This refers to animals which are not domesticated or easily tamed such as lions, tigers, and perhaps dinosaurs.

On the sixth day of the creative events, God created man from the dust of the ground (Gen. 2:7). Now according to the Genesis record we see that God created seven basic kinds plus man, or a total of eight kinds of life. Remember that Darwin said that all forms of life have descended from eight or nine basic kinds of life. It is unfortunate that Darwin did not realize that his conclusion that all life had descended from some basic kind actually confirmed the Genesis account of creation—Genesis states that there were in the original creation eight basic kinds; and Darwin after his five years of travel concluded that life has come from eight or nine basic kinds. May we emphasize again that the facts of science always support the authenticity of the Genesis account of creation?

The question may be asked as to what kinds were created. This we do not really know; but we do know that there were at least seven kinds of life besides man. Genesis does not teach that God created species or any other man-made categories of life. Neither does the account state as to how many individuals were created to originate each kind. Certainly all the varieties that we know today were not created in the beginning. Notice that in the case of man, only one kind was created. All men of today have descended from that one basic kind. Today we have many variations of the original man. There are many different races, body types, skin colors, etc.; but all are descended from the basic type man. It is probable that all cats have descended from some basic ancestral cat which was created in the beginning. Evolution teaches that all members of the cat family have descended from some ancestral cat and presents evidence to support it. As to the origin of the ancestral cat, evolutionists are unable to answer. The answer lies in the fact that God created the ancestor of the cats of today. God in the beginning created the basic kinds and from those kinds have descended the many varieties which we see in the world today. The varieties have developed *within the kinds* and not from kind *to* kind.

It is interesting to note the number of animals that Noah placed in the ark. Critics of today like to emphasize that the story of the Flood is false because Noah could not have placed all the animals now in existence in the ark. It is true that he could not have placed inside the ark all the varieties that we have today; but here again, let us examine the Genesis account and see what it said. In Genesis 6, Noah is told to take into the ark two of every kind: *"cattle after their kind," "fowl after their kind," "creeping things of the earth after their kind."* The only ones taken into the ark were the kinds that were in existence then, and these are the same described in Genesis 1. In Genesis 7:23, we find that only the terrestrial animals were destroyed. In Genesis 8:17, there come forth from the ark: fowl, cattle, creeping things, *"that they may breed abundantly in the earth and be fruitful and multiply upon the earth."* That this happened is evidenced by the many different varieties which we see on earth today. According to this, Noah could have taken into the ark small lizard-like animals from which the dinosaurs descended after the Flood. Biology teaches that present day lizards are the remnants of the dinosaurs which perished during some cataclysmic event. This event could have been the Flood, with the dinosaurs having lived before the Flood.[4] There is evidence that dinosaurs have lived since the Flood,[5] so it is logical that if lizards descended from dinosaurs, then dinosaurs could have descended from small lizard-like animals.

A number of areas of information have been presented by evolutionists from time to time in support of the evolutionary theories and against the creation account. These are usually submitted as "proof" that evolution occurred and that the Genesis account of creation is inaccurate.

Darwin first introduced the idea of natural selection in support of his evolutionary ideas. Today this concept has been discarded in favor of what the scientist regards as more favorable evidence, indicating that natural selection is not favorable evidence. Darwin also proposed the theory of survival of the fittest. An organism usually produces offspring like itself, unless a mistake which we call a mutation occurs. When this happens, the organism is usually unable to cope with the environment, thus finding itself ill adapted to survive. It thus dies rather than evolving to a new kind. That an organism will produce like itself is one of the fundamental laws of biology and also the fundamental law of God, which says that each was to reproduce "after its kind." If this law is violated, then the organism perishes.

Comparative anatomy is often used as proof of the evolution of life. In this area of science, we have learned many of the similarities between various organisms. Certainly the "seed bearing plants" have much in common. The "fowl that fly in the heavens" have many similar characteristics, as also do all animals that live in water. All have similar structures which are necessary for them to inhabit their place on earth. Reptiles, fish, and mammals which live in the water have similar characteristics which adapt them for aquatic existence.

One of the favorite presentations of the evolutionist is to point out the similarities between man and animals. One recent high school biology book pointed out a number of similarities between apes and man,[6] but failed to mention the three hundred or more distinct differences between man and apes. (They call this science.) In the interest of presenting factual information, there is nothing wrong in comparing men with apes or any other animal and pointing out the similarities, because the Genesis account points out that both animals and man were formed from the ground. Since both were formed from the same substance, one would expect both to have physical and chemical similarities. Science has acknowledged that man is far different from animals; but what is that difference? It is not necessarily physical or chemical; it is not something that can be measured in the test tube or touched with the hands. The difference is: man has spiritual attributes—animals do not. Science is unable to account for the evolution of this obvious distinction. It is true that some, like Teilhard de Chardin, in his book *The Phenomenon of Man*,[7] have tried to account for this evolution, but they fail miserably. Such a book makes good reading for the person who feels that he cannot accept the Genesis account of creation. Genesis presents us with a logical truth as to the origin of man's spiritual attributes. He was made in the "image of God." In the absence of any scientific explanation for the origin of these attributes of man, it is logical to accept the Genesis account.

Blood serology tests have often been used to establish evolutionary lines. The evidence here is that all humans had a common human ancestor. Man's blood is in no way similar to that of his supposed ancestors. Genetic evidence as to how blood types are inherited establish the fact that in the first man and woman were the genes which could produce all four blood types as we know them today, namely A, B, AB and O.

In regard to the origin of the races, the genetic evidence favors the existence of a common racial type from which all 160 or more racial types have emerged. In the creation of the first man and woman, the Creator must have placed genes which would later be selected to produce the many racial types of today. The facts of genetics support this idea. The genetic evidence is that the various racial types became established through adaptation to varying environmental situations.

Anthropological evidence points to the Near East as being the center of the origin of the races. This agrees with the Genesis account of the origin of man. From this part of the world those people who moved eastward became the Oriental races; those who moved into Europe became the Caucasians; and those who moved into Africa became the Negroid races. In each case it was a dispersion of peoples, each adapting to a new environment. In each case the genes were already in the ancestral types, but each selected those that molded it best to fit the environment. No mutations were involved, merely the selection of those genes best adapted to survive. If mutations had occurred, they would have been detrimental, as are all mutations, and thus no races would have developed. Only an all-powerful God could have foreseen this and placed in the original created beings genes which would be selected to produce the various types. In genetics we learn that selection of genes is favorable to the organism as it adapts to the environment, whereas mutations are again detrimental. Today the evolutionist tries to use genetics to support the concept of evolution, but the facts of genetics and the way genetic mechanisms operate give more support to the Biblical teaching of the creation.

The fossil evidence is in support of creation. According to the fossil record all forms of life appeared suddenly. All animal phyla are represented in the supposedly oldest strata of the earth. This sudden appearance of all forms supports the idea of a creation over a brief period of time rather than a progressive creation over eons of time. In answer to questions about the age of the fossils, there is no way to date them as being millions of years old. The actual evidence is that such things as coal and petroleum deposits are not millions of years but only a few thousand years old. There is no evidence that anything is much over six to ten thousand years old. The evolutionist speculates and speaks in terms of millions of years without any evidence to support this concept. Recent evidence indicates that dinosaurs and men walked together, and that dinosaurs died out as recently as 1500 B.C. There is no evidence that they lived millions of years before man appeared on the earth. Genesis teaches that all life is of recent origin. Fossil evidence leads one to believe that life appeared suddenly and in relatively recent times.

In order to further show that scientific facts support Genesis, we will note that three of the most basic laws of all science are seen operating in the Genesis account of creation. These laws are: The First Law of Thermodynamics, the Law of Biogenesis, and the Second Law of Thermodynamics.

> The First Law of Thermodynamics is also known as the Law of Conservation of Mass-Energy. It states that energy may have different forms, including mass, and that it is possible to change from one form to another, but the total energy remains constant. The Law of Biogenesis states that life comes from preexisting life.

> The Second Law of Thermodynamics states that there is an irreversible tendency for processes in a self-contained system to go towards a lower order. There is thus an increase in randomness, decay, and disorder if the whole system is considered.

No laws of science are more firmly established than these laws. There are no known violations of these laws. It is obvious that the evolutionist has nothing to gain by using the second law. According to these laws, matter and energy cannot be created while the first law of thermodynamics is in effect. Life cannot be created out of the inanimate while the Law of Biogenesis is in effect and an increase in orderly-complexity cannot happen while the Second Law of Thermodynamics is in effect. All of these are observable phenomena. There is a logical time sequence which these laws must have followed. The sequence is as follows:[8]

1. The First Law of Thermodynamics began after the origin of mass and energy.
2. The Law of Biogenesis began after the origin of life.
3. The Second Law of Thermodynamics began after the existence of the fully wound-up system with living maturity.

Certainly no one would maintain that our present laws can be employed to explain the beginnings of the physical universe. The processes involved in origins lie outside the realm of science. Speculations and indeterminacy become very common at this point.

It is interesting to note how the Genesis account of creation makes the above time sequence of the three laws consistent. This is as follows:

1. The creation of the physical universe preceded the First Law of Thermodynamics.
2. A creation of life preceded the Law of Biogenesis. The law began with the command to reproduce after its kind.
3. A fully wound up biophysical world preceded the Second Law of Thermodynamics.

All of the processes that we see in effect today are consistent with this type of beginning.

It is not necessary for the Christian to try to make peace with science by giving in or trying to harmonize the Genesis story of creation with science because in actuality, science is now proving the Genesis account to be correct. Science does not know the age of the earth. Methods used to date the age of the earth are not valid. Radioisotopic dating is the most commonly used method today but even this has descrepancies. If Rhenium 187 is used to date the earth, the age is given as close to 4.5 billion years old. If the potassium argon method is used, however, the date is 9.5 billion years—an uncomfortable difference.

The doctrine of uniformitarianism, the foundation of the evolutionary theory, is gradually crumbling. It is now apparent that the earth has been subjected to numerous cataclysmic events which have played important roles in the development of plant and animal life. Consequently, geologists, realizing that it is necessary to explain previously unexplained evidence in the earth's surface, are beginning to revive the idea of cataclysmic events. The explosion of the first atomic bomb brought the realization that catastrophic events are not only possible but probable. Further atomic experimentation has exposed the earth to so much radiation that biologists are warning that unless these tests in the atmosphere are brought to a halt the possibilities of mutations occurring are very real. But why fear mutations if it was through the process of mutation that man progressed from a primitive animal state to his advanced present state? Their fear is an admission that mutations are mistakes and are in all cases detrimental . . . further proof that evolution by mutation could not possibly have occurred.

It is heart-warming to know that science is now proving the Genesis account of creation to be correct and to know that this account can withstand any critical examination by any area of science or other human "wisdom."

In our quest for knowledge may we always be able to say the words found in Revelation 4:11, *"Thou art worthy, O Lord, to receive glory and honor and power: For thou hast created all things, and for thy pleasure they are and were created."* (K.J.V.)

1. Life Nature Library, *Evolution*, (New York: Time Incorporated, 1964) *
2. L. V. Berkner and L. C. Marshall, *The History of the Earth's Atmosphere*, "The Origin and Evolution of Atmosphere and Oceans," New York: John Wiley and Sons, 1964.
3. (New York: Dell, 1965).
4. Ibid.
5. Roland Bird, "Thunder in His Footsteps," *Natural History*, May 1939.
6. BSCS Green Version *High School Biology*, (Chicago: Rand McNally, 1963).
7. Teilhard de Chardin, *The Phenomenon of Man*. (New York: Harper and Row, 1961).
8. Dr. Thomas G. Barnes, "A Scientific Alternative to Evolution," Address delivered to Los Angeles Creation Seminar, November 5, 1965.

6

THE CASE FOR CHRISTIAN MIRACLES

Arlie H. Hoover

"Rabbi," said Nicodemus to Christ, "we know that you are a
teacher come from God; for no one can do these signs that you do,
unless God is with him" (John 3:2). Nicodemus gives us the proper
theme of a discussion of miracles by focusing on the proper interpretation of them. Miracles, signs, wonders—these have a vital function
in the Biblical story. Since we cannot see God directly (John 1:18),
it is only what God says or does that gives us any real knowledge of
Him. If there were no miraculous events, God would not be revealed.
As John Klotz says, "science can make deists, it cannot make
Christians."[1] To become a Christian one must believe in the miracles
of Biblical history.

It doesn't take long to prove that Biblical miracles are integral, not
incidental, to God's revelation. They occur throughout the entire
Bible, from the exodus to the church. At a critical juncture in Israel's
history God told Moses to answer Pharaoh's challenge, "prove yourself by working a miracle" (Exod. 7:9). Christ made special appeal to
His workers to authenticate His message. To His disciples He said,
"Believe me for the sake of the works" (John 14:11). To a crowd
questioning His messiahship He said, "The works that I do in my
Father's name, they bear witness to me" (John 10:25). To prove His
messiahship to His cousin, John, He pointed to the fact that "the
blind see, the lame walk, the lepers are clean, the deaf hear, the dead
are raised to life" (Luke 7:22). The strongest statement of all is in
John 15:24, "If I had not done among them the works which no one
else did, they would not have sin; but now they have seen and hated
both me and my Father." His miracles were so clear that an unbelieving eyewitness hated both Him and God!

It would not be wrong, therefore, to say that the truth of the
Christian faith stands or falls with the historicity of its miracles.

109

Those who deny this historicity have no right to use the term "Christian" in its historic meaning, any more than a Marxist has a right to call himself a Platonist.

Definition of a Miracle

It is important that one properly define a miracle before our investigation begins. Those who define a miracle as a *violation, interruption, transgression,* or *contradition* of natural law prejudge the question before the examination can even start. It is far more honest to define miracles so that their historical possibility is left an open question. Your definition, that is, should not have any metaphysical implications. It is a curious species of logical knavery that defines something as impossible and then concludes from the definition that there is no evidence for it.

We offer as a neutral definition of *miracle* the following: "an event, occurring in history, which is so different from a well-known natural law that it arrests the attention of the spectator and deserves to be considered a special intervention of a supernatural agent." Notice that we haven't concluded that a miracle is a sign of God, only that it is so different from the regular order that it *might* be interpreted as a divine sign.

You may expand this definition in the interests of precision by saying that a miracle is a "non-repeatable counterinstance of a law of nature."[2] If the event did not run counter to natural law it would not be considered a miracle at all, for a wonder must have a background of uniform activity to stand out as unique. By "non-repeatable" we mean, not that the miracle occurred only once in history, but that ordinary men can not duplicate it at will, as they could if it were a law of nature. If men could cause a regular, repeatable counter-instance of an alleged law to occur, we would then change the law the miracles were countering; the miracles would become regular and not unique and the original law would have to be revised.

Therefore, miracles and laws are different, but it is wrong to define a miracle with words like "violate," "transgress," or "contradict," for these words conjure up a misleading analogy between nature's laws and laws of society. Our definition is neutral; it identifies the event we're looking for while leaving open the possibility of its actual occurrence.

Objections to Miracles

You might think that all we have to do now is to present historical evidence for Christian miracles. Actually, we must wait until Section

III for that; first, we must remove a host of objections. After surveying them all you can see that they fall into two major groups, philosophical and historical.

A. Philosophical Objections

The essence of a philosophical objection is the assumption that the universe is so structured that miracles are impossible by definition. This objection comes from two major systems: naturalism and philosophical theism.

1. **Naturalism.** The objection from naturalism is essentially deductive, strange as it may sound for scientists to use *a priori* reasoning. It rules out miracles by an *a priori* metaphysical assumption and relieves the objector of the hard task of examining the alleged miracles in history. This objection is usually voiced in the name of scientific humanism. It says, in short: "There is no God, only nature, only matter, mechanically determined matter, ruled by uniform, unchanging, physical laws. Miracles are obviously impossible in such a cosmos."

I have stated it rather baldly to bring out the subtle bias in the position. Such a dogmatic statement needs a lot of proof before you can use it as an *a priori* club. Has this person carefully surveyed the theistic arguments and ruled—beyond all doubt—that all of them are totally worthless? What arrogant human would say this? But this is what you must say to use naturalism as an *a priori* club against miracles. You say, it seems: "I know what all is possible in this universe, and I know that non-repeatable counterinstances to natural laws are impossible."

Do you really know all that? As a matter of fact, many who have carefully and systematically examined the theistic proofs have come away from the experience actual believers, or at least "reverent agnostics." You cannot say the proofs are totally worthless. In their total, cumulative effect they are rather impressive, one might say probable, certainly possible, maybe plausible. But you cannot viciously rule out miracles with the certainty of their worthlessness.

Suppose for the moment that there *was* strong proof for a miracle. How would this objector react to it? He would just classify it as a "random malfunction" of nature, a strange phenomenon to be explained someday as we uncover more laws. But what if the event were so unusual and the law it countered so well-established that this rationalization would not satisfy his inquiring intellect? Could it not make the objector wonder if such events were indeed miracles and if such a causitive agent really existed? Yes, it could, and it has, all through history.

This question reminds you of the man who asserted that "in theory, a bumblebee can't fly." Why? His body violates some fundamental rules of aerodynamics (wings are too short, body is the wrong size, weight is wrongly proportioned). Now, that's fine, but have you ever seen a bumblebee fly? I have—and I therefore strongly suspect any theory that says he cannot. Now, if miracles really happened, I strongly suspect a world view that says they are impossible. Especially if it says it *before* I am even allowed to look at the historical evidence.

Philosophical naturalism is thus a prejudice, a world view assumed *a priori* by a man who has made up his mind beforehand not to even look at evidence. You should construct your world view from the facts of history and not use your world view to rewrite history. Or, you could at least hold your world view with a certain critical flexibility, realizing that your inability to "see" miracles in history *could* be caused by your "glasses" (your world view) and not a defect in the historical evidence.[3]

What I am saying is that people can encounter miracles in a variety of ways: (1) you can first change your rigid world view so that you can see them, or (2) you can look at the alleged miracles and let them change your flexible world view. A third method is employed by (3) those who already believe in the Agent (God) being able to cause miracles. When such people receive good historical testimony they naturally accept the miracles. In the history of the Christian faith people have accepted miracles by all three methods. Also, in all three cases the data is the same: the historical evidence of Biblical miracles (see Section III).

But the naturalistic objection to miracles takes a subtler form than this. Instead of the dogmatic statement we have just analyzed, you more often will hear it like this: "Science is not friendly to miracles. A universe in which miracles occurred would be completely capricious, whimsical, unpredictable. It would destroy science, which must have uniform laws."[4] Stated this way, the objection is harder to answer.

I suggest first that scientific laws are not rigid regulations like the laws of society. Scientists do not "pass" laws, they discover them. Often the law they discover is more of a choice among possibles, rather than something forced on the investigator. Furthermore, a scientific law is usually contingent; it can be modified or even completely rejected in the future. Hence, scientists are more like historians than legislators. They *describe* how nature acts; they can not *prescribe* how nature must act. For most reflective thinkers David Hume took the logical necessity out of scientific laws. Thus, when you complain that a miracle "breaks" a law of nature, you need to realize that the word *breaks* implies an extensive knowledge of nature that no mortal has.

Science usually opposes miracles by appealing to the principle of the uniformity of nature, the first premise of every natural law. This principle allows you to say that an event, which you have observed in only one time and space, can be predicated of many times and spaces. But the problem is this: there is no way to prove the principle of uniformity of nature. The idea that the future will be like the past is just hope, expectation, "blind, animal faith" (B. Russell). A scientist merely assumes it on pragmatic grounds. But if the principle is grounded pragmatically and cannot be proved to be "in the nature of things," then you surely cannot use it to brutally exclude the possibility of miracles.

Verifications that are merely pragmatic leave open the possibility that situations will occur in which the principle does not hold. This does not prove miracles have occurred (you need historical testimony for that), but it shows that you cannot arbitrarily rule them out before looking at the testimony of eyewitnesses.

For instance, you may say, if you wish: (1) "I have never personally observed water becoming wine by just standing in stone jars." Fine, neither have I. You may even add: (2) "And furthermore, modern science has never observed it." Fine again, you're probably correct. But here's the rub: you have no right to press on and say: (3) "Therefore, water can never become wine by this method." Your first two statements are historical, empirical, descriptive, inductive, and humble. Your third statement is normative, metaphysical, deductive, and arrogant. It is really bad form for you to pass from the empirical to the normative without admitting that you cease to be a scientist and become a metaphysician. You can make this leap from (1) and (2) to (3) but do not call it science, because it is sheer metaphysics and what is more, it may be bad metaphysics.

Please do not misunderstand me: Christians do not argue for a complete lack of order in the universe. We, too, believe in a cosmos, not a chaos. But what is the precise type of order that obtains? The scientific naturalist believes in a mechanical system; he thinks that nature is a closed, autonomous system in which there is fundamentally only one type of causal sequence, that found in mechanical systems.

The Christian believes in order, but in purposive, teleological order. He is convinced that nature cannot be explained except as the activity of Mind expressing itself through purpose. To the Christian, nature is not a self-operating machine but a subsidiary system created and sustained for a reason. This reason imparts as much dependability to nature's behavior as any scientist could want, for purpose is just as much opposed to chance as is mechanism.[5]

Thus, the world is rational, not because it is a system of natural laws, but because it is the expression of a Transcendent Reason. The regularity of natural laws is explained if God is self-consistent in character and if His actions are not capricious. Exceptions to natural laws (miracles) occur for a good reason, i.e., to authenticate God's revelation. Understood properly, therefore, miracles would never be looked upon as "breaks" in a purposive order but rather as demonstrations of that order. Miracles, when interpreted by Christian theism, would appear to be necessary, not at all embarrassing.

2. **Philosophical Theism.** Naturalists oppose miracles because they want a totally determined universe. Strangely, some theists oppose them for the same reason. Even though such people believe in a Rational Agent powerful enough to work miracles, they still reject them. "God would never do it that way," they insist. "Miracles are embarrassing; it is easier to believe in God without them. They are cheap parlor tricks, performed by old deities, or, better, ascribed by ignorant people to the true deity." Max Born, a famous German physicist, argues:

> Something which is against natural laws seems to me rather out of the question because it would be a depressive idea about God. It would make God smaller than he must be assumed. When he stated that these laws hold, then they hold, and he wouldn't make exceptions. This is too human an idea. Humans do such things, but not God.[6]

Dr. Born resembles the deists of the Enlightenment, who claimed that God revealed Himself perfectly through the order and harmony of the creation. That this is false is seen by the fact that many observers who admire the order and harmony of the universe are not driven to theism. The deist is really not unlike the naturalist—he values the order of the cosmos so much that he is perplexed by a disturbance of that order.

My chief question for the deist is this: How does he know God would never suspend one of His laws? Did God inform him personally of this? Or does the deist just have a personal preference for uniformity and order? What is the evidence that this preference defines what really happened in history or what God has truly done?

Ask yourself: How could God make His presence known better than by temporarily suspending or reversing the regular pattern of nature? Would this not arrest the attention of the observer? Would it not dazzle the mind and draw attention to the miracle worker and His message? Would the regular behavior of nature do this? Once you see nature acting in a regular way you tend to take it for granted. Natural law would not convince you of God's presence nearly as well as a sudden suspension of natural law.

I can understand why the objector dislikes the notion of God disturbing the order He created, and therefore I offer this parable to help make the point. Imagine a king, looking out his window one day, gazing down on the main street of his capital city. Suddenly he notices an emergency; a truck loaded with dynamite starts to roll downhill because its brakes have failed. The king instantly rushes to a big switchboard and pulls a special switch that turns all the traffic lights on that street green. The truck rolls down the hill and coasts to safety and no collision occurs with cross-traffic because the king made all the lights green. No explosion, no one injured, hundreds of lives saved . . . but a law was suspended . . . for a brief time.

Please . . . what king in his right mind would *not* have suspended his law for a brief time in such an emergency? In this situation, wouldn't we consider it a *moral obligation* to suspend the law? Is there any virtue in maintaining uniformity when lives are at stake? In our view, lives are at stake. God uses miracles to attest to his revelation, to save lives eternally as well as temporally. We feel that if you understand the proper function and purpose of a miracle you can see that revelatory pressures justify occasional miracles to call attention to the word of God. "The Gospel message," claimed the writer of Hebrews, "was attested to us by those who heard him, while God also bore witness by signs and wonders and various miracles and by gifts of the Holy Spirit" (Heb. 2:4).

Hence, both forms of determinism, naturalism, and philosophical theism, have no right to rule out miracles before we can examine historical evidence. Yet, so certain are some thinkers of this determinism, that they attribute all possible miracle stories to ignorance and credulity. For example, Arthur B. Komar, Dean of the Belfer Graduate School of Science, Yeshivah University, New York, insists that miracles always occur when people are ignorant of science. "Why isn't there a density of miracles today proportional to the density of miracles reported thousands of years ago? Quite clearly because people are more critical today."[7]

Dr. Komar assumes that people never believe in miracles when they know the laws of nature. This is not true and it overlooks the fact that an age of science is not always the opposite of an age of ignorance. Those who live in the modern era have no monopoly on knowledge of how nature works in her macroscopic behavior. Most of the Biblical miracles are violations of such well-known laws of nature that they would have been recognized as "wonders" in any part of the world at any time in history.

Joseph, for example, knew how babies got started in the womb. That is why he was tempted to put Mary away secretly when he found her pregnant during their bethrothal (Matt. 1:19). If this objection is true, we might wonder why he did not instantly attribute her pregnancy to a visitation of the deity—so credulous were folks in those days! No, the Jews of the first century Palestine were not that ignorant; it took a special visit from an angel to explain the origin of the child in Mary's uterus (Matt. 1:20, 21).

The same goes for most Biblical miracles. It doesn't take an M.I.T. graduate to know that water does not usually become wine standing in stone jars, that men do not come back from the grave, that five loaves and two fishes will not feed five thousand people, that mud will not cure congenital blindness. The person making this objection needs to remember that the first century was the heart of the *Pax Romana* and that Palestine was right in the heart of the empire, not on the fringes. This was one of the most cultured, secular, affluent, educated, skeptical periods in human history before the modern era. It hardly qualifies as an age of ignorance.

Dr. Komar also expresses a common complaint—that there is a density of miracles in Biblical history and very few since that time. This is easily accounted for by the purpose of miracles. Miracles occur in "revelatory clusters"; they are not spread out in perfect proportion throughout the Bible. The two big clusters are (1) the exodus from Egypt and (2) the time of Christ and the church. These periods witnessed the two most important revelations God ever gave—the law and the gospel. If miracles accompany and attest to revelation, these clusters are exactly where we would expect to find them in Biblical history.

The fact that there are few miracles since Biblical times proves nothing in particular, except perhaps the objector's preference. Instead of complaining about miracles being in clusters and in past times we should face the real issue: is there any historical evidence for them, regardless of where or when they occurred? If our reasoning in this section is sound, we can assert that no philosophical objection which argues from material or spiritual determinism can relieve one of the duty of examining the historical data. We pass, then, to the historical objections.

B. Historical Objections

If a person stops making philosophical objections to miracles, like those above, he then admits that miracles are possible. The essence of a historical objection is the assertion that there are insuperable difficulties with observing and/or reporting a miracle that actually happened. Even if one occurred, it is argued, you could never really prove it. Why?

1. First, the objector may assail the very ability of any human to observe and accurately describe *any* event. He may argue that human beings are all poor reporters. Experimental situations have been constructed where spectators all contradict each other after viewing a staged event. The objector, therefore, takes refuge in historical agnosticism; he doubts all of the past.

It does not take long to see that this doubt thrown on miracles also destroys all human reporting. This objection will kill all history; it will close all law courts; it will stop all newspapers. The objector should not even trust his own memory since it too is not "immediate" enough. It is one thing to prove that human testimony is not infallible; it is another thing to prove that it is totally worthless. There is a middle ground: human testimony is basically reliable provided certain procedural canons are observed. This middle ground has satisfied most people for a long time.

Furthermore, the man making this objection is apt to contradict himself. If he sets up an experimental situation and then shows that all observers see the event differently, one must ask, how did he see it accurately? Why doesn't the same disability he attributes to the observer affect him also? If all human observation is faulty, why shouldn't we be skeptical of the proposition, "all human observation is faulty," since it was established by observation?

Any good lawyer will tell you that not only can human testimony be reliable, but also that discrepancy among witnesses is often a good sign of authenticity, since differences that do not result in outright contradiction can be harmonized and may demonstrate that each witness remembered an individual portion of the event and reported his portion accurately. We need only combine all the portions to see the event in its fullness. This happens in court almost every day.[8]

This objector also overlooks the fact that there is more than just eyewitness testimony to most historical events.[9] Every big historical event (e.g., the Resurrection) leaves "scars" on history that supplement the eyewitness accounts. Sherlock Holmes did not need eyewitnesses; he could often tell by the arrangement of the furniture in a room what had happened there the day before. Even if eyewitnesses differ on the event you can often check their testimony with the circumstantial evidence left after the event. For example, the Resurrection is established, not only by eyewitness testimony, but also by the circumstantial evidence of an empty tomb, the transformed lives of the apostles, the rapid growth of the church, and the unusual conversion of Saul of Tarsus.

2. After attacking human testimony *per se,* the objector may

attack specifically man's ability to observe and report a miracle, a counter-instance to natural law. It is argued that we would not be able to apprehend a miracle if we saw one; its sheer novelty would make it incomprehensible.

Following the cue of Hume, this objector takes the essence of a miracle and uses it against the miracle—to startle, to dazzle, to sting, to upset, if necessary. Miracles are signs that a new age is dawning, as in the exodus and with Jesus Christ. If a new era is to be inaugurated, it may require some unusual interruptions to accomplish such a difficult breakthrough of nature's structure. Perhaps only a startling event could induce a transformation in man, causing him to "repent and believe the gospel" (Matt. 1:15).[10]

Surely you cannot argue that all startling experiences are to be rejected as unreliable! How then could a man in the tropics ever believe in ice? How could man ever accept the appearance of a "miracle drug"? How could startling new discoveries in science be accepted? Glorifying the ordinary is certainly no path to scientific progress. Galileo asked a skeptical monk to look into his telescope to see the moons of Jupiter but the monk refused; whoever makes this objection is just as reprehensible as that monk.

I can see why one might be suspicious when he first saw a miracle. That is why we have so many miracles of Christ repeated over a period of three years and performed in several different situations. When you see this Man performing the same wonders over and over again, your suspicions grow into wonder and your wonder gradually blossoms into conviction of His divinity. Christ's miracles never lost their quality of being nonrepeatable counter-instances of nature's laws, but they did tend to become "normal" or "natural" for Him. The people of the time felt so: "When the Christ appears," they asked, "will he do more signs than this man has done?" (John 7:31).

3. It has been said many times that the Bible books recording miracles are historically inaccurate. They contain errors, it is argued, and these errors destroy them as good witness to miracles.

This type of objection cannot possibly be answered in detail. It must be answered one-on-one, in specifics. Where, for example, is an error in the Bible? When one is pinpointed, we can go to work on it. Space prohibits us from giving a long argument for the historical accuracy of the entire Bible. We can only say in general that it is just not very learned today to ridicule the Bible as "that old collection of worthless folk legends." That may have been possible in the last century but not in this one. We have too much evidence, mainly archaeological, that shows the Bible to be basically accurate.

I can only recommend that one read some good, general accounts of Biblical archaeology before he generalizes too much about the historical worth of the Bible. To be sure, there are difficulites, but these do not make a document worthless; if they did, we would have no dependable history.[11]

Which means that our hypothetical objector still has the duty, if he's honest, of examining the documents purporting to describe miracles and telling me why he does not accept them. So far, none of the objections, philosophical or historical, relieves him of his duty. But there are a few miscellaneous objections we must consider.

Other Objections

1. One favorite position today is to say that Christ was just a super faith healer, a skilled practitioner of psychotherapy.[12] Many of His cures do have a superficial resemblance to modern psychotherapy. This view has the virtue of accepting many of Christ's miracles and explaining them in a natural way, a way that can be duplicated and checked by modern psychology. In principle, any good psychotherapist could copy the cures of Christ. Even the most avid, however, admit that Christ was probably the most magnetic, charismatic psychotherapist in history.

The prime difficulty with this theory is it cannot possibly explain all the miracles of Christ. It explains only those that have human psychology as a factor in the event. It cannot even explain all the cures; it has trouble with congenital blindness, leprosy, restoring amputated ears and withered limbs, and it is especially weak in explaining how Christ could raise people from the dead!

This view also fails to provide any natural explanation of Christ's nature miracles, such as stilling the storm, multiplying bread, and walking on water. You need a subtheory to explain all the wonders left over from your main theory and this always weakens the main theory. Furthermore, the subtheory leaves someone in a very bad light because it has the Gospels attributing nature miracles to Christ, when He, on this theory, performed only faith cures. The whole matter leaves Christ in a bad light for He interpreted His miracles in a way different from this simple theory of psychotherapy (John 14:11; Mark 2:9, 10).

2. Another favorite dodge today is to say that the very existence of several world religions with miracles disproves the miracles of Christianity. If they all happened it would confirm several, contradictory religious systems.

First, the person making this objection usually does not know much about world religions. There really aren't as many miracles in other religions as you think. Islam has very few, as Thomas Aquinas complained.[13] Hinduism has some, but they hardly constitute the philosophical basis of the religion; they are accepted because one accepts the religion already.[14] In their original forms, Buddhism and Confucianism were so humanistic that a miracle would have been a scandal. Buddhism, Confucianism, and Taoism, all three, are more like social and psychological moral systems than they are religions. The miraculous element is very weak in all three of them.

The fact is that only in the Hebrew-Christian religion do you find miracles put on a stand, offered as the decisive proof of the whole system. If Christ did not rise from the dead, argued Paul, our faith is futile, we are still in our sins, those who died in Christ died without hope, and we are the most pitiful group in the world (I Cor. 15:12-19). Remove the linchpin of Christ's resurrection and the entire structure falls apart.

Second, the objector has missed the proper procedure. You do not prove the Biblical miracles false by just showing that the world's religions are full of miracles (though they are not), any more than you prove all diamonds fake by proving that we have a few imitations. The logical procedure is to ask: which group of miracles has the *best* historical evidence?

In summing up the objections to miracles, I must report that, in my experience, the most general objection to miracles is a kind of inarticulate historical agnosticism, or, better, historical apathy. There is abroad in the land a general ho-hum attitude toward history, toward miracles, toward anything that occurred long ago. Since we must suspect everything over thirty years of age, miracles so far back, even if true, could hardly be material for a current, objective world view.

The idea that only the present has meaning is one of the most vulgar fallacies of our time. If a person applied it seriously he would have to doubt his own memory, since it is not totally "immediate." This modern idol called "relevance" has feet of clay; men cannot live without history. I have found that part of my job in arguing for miracles boils down to simply arguing for the value of history, for the reality of the past. C. S. Lewis told of how people in his experience looked upon history as subscientific, yet would talk of prehistory (where the data is vastly inferior) as if it were a science as certain as chemistry!

Historical apathy is just another facet of the scientific argument against miracles, the complaint that they are not currently repeatable. What it finally amounts to is this: "Work a miracle for me and I'll believe, but do not ask me to accept one two thousand years old." If one insists on this peculiar form of blindness it would be difficult to dissuade him, but if he once gives up this peephole view of reality, and opens up his heart and his mind to the dimension of the past, we feel that the high quality of Christ's miracles will make a profound impact on him.

The Quality of Christ's Miracles

When space is limited it suffices to focus only on the miracles of Jesus Christ. We can forget for the moment the remainder of Biblical miracles. If Christ worked His miracles and if He arose from the dead He is the divine son of God (Rom. 1:4), and since He confirmed the Old Testament retrospectively (Luke 24:44) and the New Testament prospectively (John 14:26) He, in His divine person, ties the entire Bible together into one neat apologetic package. If we can break through the naturalist's defenses at this juncture his entire front will collapse. If the miracles and the resurrection of Christ are established then the whole Biblical revelation falls into your lap, because Jesus Christ is the son of the same God who spoke and acted from Genesis to Malachi. What, then, are the features of His miracles that commend them to rational men?

1. First, Christ's miracles had unusual publicity. Paul told Festus that the facts of Christ's career were not "done in a corner" (Acts 26:26). Actually they *were* done in a corner of sorts, one of the best-known corners of the globe, the eastern Mediterranean, the hearth of several great civilizations for three millennia. Palestine was right on the world's crossroads; it would have been difficult for God to select a more public area in which to stage an incarnation. If Christ's career had taken place in Iceland or Ireland or on the fringes of the Roman Empire we would have a problem; but there's no problem with Palestine.

Even inside Palestine we are fortunate that Jesus performed wonders in the very thick of things, in crowded cities, at busy street corners, around market places, while discoursing with multitudes, in and around the Jerusalem temple, surrounded by crowds as large as four and five thousand. He did not perform miracles in one place or in a special staging area where His colleagues could control the event in any way. His wonders could literally "happen anywhere." (See, for example, the following passages which speak of "great multitudes" and "entire" cities witnessing the miracles: Matt. 15:30, 31; 19:1, 2; Mark 1:32-34; 6:53-56; Luke 6:17-19).

2. Christ's miracles have the necessary variety we would expect of a divine agent. If one claims divinity I would expect him to demonstrate the power and control a creator would have over his creation (Heb. 1:3; John 1:3; Col. 1:6). I would demand a variety of wonders to demonstrate the role of creator. Pseudo-saviors sometimes show a

limited control over a part of reality, but Christ displayed power over all aspects of reality.

He often exhibited powers of knowledge and insight as when He divined the evil thoughts of His enemies (Mark 2:8), or when He knew that Nathanael was under a fig tree (John 1:48), or when He told the Samaritan woman about her previous marital life (John 4:17, 18).

In seventeen recorded miracles Christ showed complete control over a great variety of physical diseases—palsy, leprosy, fever, blindness, deafness, mutism, blood hemorrhaging, lameness, withered limbs, paralysis, dropsy, and amputated ears.

Most of all, Christ showed power over the greatest enemy of all, death. He raised at least three people from the dead, the daughter of Jairus in Capernaum (Matt. 9:18-26), the widow's son at Nain (Luke 7:11-15), and His friend, Lazarus, of Bethany (John 11:1-44). The first had just died, the second was already on the bier, and the third had lain in the tomb four days.

Christ also had power over nature. He could stop a storm, make a fig tree dry up, create wine, cause fish to swim into a net, walk on water, and make food increase in volume. Nature, mind, body—none of these could resist His power. There have been many alleged miracle workers in history but none have approached Christ in this comprehensive control over the whole of creation.[15]

3. Christ's miracles have consistency. I mean that the quality of power we are describing was maintained during a ministry of over three years and over a sufficiently wide spatial area. Jesus performed wonders at such varied times and places that you could not ascribe any naturalistic explanation to them that would depend on space or time. The power never varied or waned. Every*where* He went and every *time* He worked a miracle it was consistently the same power. He performed wonders in Galilee and Judea, in Capernaum, Jerusalem, Nazareth, Jericho, Cana, and Nain. He worked miracles in summer, winter, spring, fall, morning, noon, and night. He even worked miracles among the non-Jewish areas occasionally (John 4:46-53; Mark 7:24-30) so that one could not say that only His compatriots believed in Him.

4. Christ's miracles have ethical propriety. By this I mean that His miracles were chaste, reasonable, dignified, and benevolent. They were never grotesque, childish, amateurish, or selfish, and they never had the quality of the magician's act. Read through the thirty-five recorded miracles and you will not encounter a single one done for personal glory or self-aggrandizement. His miracles are in themselves a revelation of the loving, benevolent, kind, and generous character

of God. There are no card tricks, no flying carpets, no Aladdin's lamps, no genies creeping out of bottles.

This point can be seen more graphically if you contrast Christ's miracles with some of those attributed to Him by Apocryphal gospels written later than the first century, when the pious imagination of some Christians had been given time to work on the life of Christ. In these works we are told that Christ as a boy made a snail shell on the Sea of Galilee suddenly grow to the size of Mount Tabor and then as suddenly shrink back to its original form; that He impressed His friends by having six birds recite the Old Testament in six different languages; that He would fashion birds of clay and make them fly; and that He could, in a fit of rage, transform His friends into stones and animals. Nothing so puerile occurs in the canonical miracles of the four Gospels.[16]

The chaste, benevolent character of Christ's miracles fits the tenor of His teachings. We expect such merciful and helpful acts from the one who taught us that mercy is a prime moral obligation. If a brutal man like Nero or Hitler were to work miracles for three years it would distress me; if a saintly man like St. Francis couldn't perform them it would arouse pity in me; but notice how natural it is for One who claimed so much, who taught such lessons of wisdom, to have at the same time such power! I judge the New Testament miracles to be canonical not only because they occur in the Canonical Gospels, but also because they fit together by this rule of chastity. I say to myself: "God would do it just that way."

5. Most important, Christ's miracles have sufficient testimony from competent witnesses. We have eyewitness testimony from several groups who observed the career of Christ.

a. We have the testimony of those who were beneficiaries of the miracles, especially of those who were cured of their infirmities. In some cases the person healed went everywhere telling about the miracle even after Christ cautioned him against it (Luke 5:15). Other outstanding cases were the blind man of John 9, the Samaritan leper (Luke 17:11-19), the infirm man of Jerusalem (John 5:11), and the five thousand who were fed (John 6:14).

b. We have the testimony of observers who were not beneficiaries of the miracles. Several passages in the Gospels speak of the wonder and amazement experienced by the crowds that saw His miracles (Matt. 15:30, 31; 21:28; Mark 2:12; Luke 4:36; 9:43). Mark 2 is a typical case. When Jesus healed the paralytic the men around were all amazed and glorified God saying, "We never saw anything like this!"

c. We even have the witness of the disobedient and the skeptical, though it is often indirect and oblique. For instance, John tells us that many of the Jewish leaders believed in Jesus but for fear of the

124   *Is the Bible Scientifically Reliable?*

others they would not confess Him (John 12:42, 43). The Jerusalem scribes obliquely testified to Christ's power of exorcism by charging that "he is possessed by Beelzebub, and by the prince of demons he casts out demons" (Mark 3:22).

d. Though the argument from silence is never conclusive, we must add that there is no contrary evidence from the first century concerning the miracles of Christ. One can usually find an exposé of alleged miracle workers; if not an exposé, then an "explanation" of their wonders. But none exists for the Christian miracles. On the contrary, they were trumpeted abroad from about A.D. 30 onward and soon felled the Roman Empire's traditional religions. Significant also is the fact that many of the opponents of the faith (e.g., Celsus, Hierocles, and Julian the Apostate) admitted that Christ worked miracles during His ministry.[17]

e. Finally, we should repeat that when all the eyewitness testimony has been covered there is still the circumstantial evidence that supplements and corroborates it. The lives of the apostles, the rapid growth and permanence of the Christian church—all these things complement the witnesses and help to prove that Christian miracles really happened.

Conclusion

If the reasoning of this chapter has been sound, there is no sufficient reason why a rational man cannot assent to the miracles of Jesus Christ. I realize that miracles alone will not convert a man, that miracles are not the total argument of the Christian faith. They are vital but they must not be studied in isolation from the rest of Christian apologetics.

I hope the reader will supplement his investigation of miracles with a comprehensive examination of the totality of Christian evidences. The Samaritan woman was so impressed with Christ's supernatural knowledge that she convinced many of her friends that they should believe in Him, just on the basis of her brief encounter. "He told me everything I ever did," she said. Other people in town, however, needed a fuller testimony. After Christ stayed in Sychar for two days, John tells us: "Many more became believers because of what they heard from his own lips. They told the woman, 'It is no longer because of what you said that we believe, for we have heard him ourselves; and we know this is in truth the savior of the world' " (John 4:40-42).

1. *Modern Science in the Christian Life* (St. Louis: Concordia, 1961), p. 80.
2. Part of this definition is borrowed from R. G. Swinburn's paper, "Miracles,"

in *Philosophy of Religion: Selected Readings,* edited by Rowe and Wainwright (New York: Harcourt Brace Jovanovich, 1973), p. 403.

3. For good statements of this point see: B. Ramm, *Protestant Christian Evidences* (Chicago: Moody, 1954), pp. 129-133; E. J. Carnell, *Introduction to Christian Apologetics* (Grand Rapids: Eerdmans, 1948), pp. 250-260.

4. See e.g. several of the scientists interviewed by F. E. Trinklein, *The God of Science* (Grand Rapids: Eerdmans, 1971), pp. 78-93.

5. See Elton Trueblood, *Philosophy of Religion* (New York: Harper and Row, 1957), pp. 215-218.

6. Trinklein, *God of Science,* p. 80.

7. Ibid., p. 79.

8. For a good discussion of how practising historians handle the problem of alleged contradictions in historical witnesses see Jacques Barzun and Henry F. Graff, *The Modern Researcher* (New York: Harcourt, Brace and World, 1970), pp. 146-173.

9. Ibid., pp. 146-148. Barzun and Graff discuss the distinction between "verbal" and "mute" testimony.

10. See Frederick Sontag, *How Philosophy Shapes Theology: Problems in the Philosophy of Religion* (New York: Harper and Row, 1971), pp. 328-330.

11. One can begin with just about anything ever written by the "old masters," Albright, Glueck, and Ramsey. Some of the older books by Joseph Free and George Barton are still very useful. Newer treatments should also be consulted such as G. E. Wright, *Introduction to Biblical Archaeology* (1960), and *The Biblical Archaeologist Reader* (1961); M. F. Unger, *Archaeology and the Old Testament* (1954), *Archaeology and the New Testament* (1962); F. F. Bruce, *The New Testament Documents: Are They Reliable?* (1960); J. A. Thompson, *The Bible and Archaeology* (1968), and others.

12. John B. Noss, *Man's Religions* (New York: Macmillan, 1963), p. 599. Noss calls this view of Jesus a "minimum view" of His powers, to which much could be added.

13. Alan Richardson, *Christian Apologetics* (New York: Harper & Row, 1947), p. 162.

14. C. S. Lewis, *Miracles: A Preliminary Study* (London, publ. 1947), p. 83 *et. passim.*

15. Of Christ's 35 recorded miracles, 17 are bodily cures, 9 are miracles over nature, 6 are cures of demoniacs, and 3 are resurrections. For an official list see any good Bible handbook or dictionary, e.g., Halley's *Bible Handbook* (21st edition, 1957), pp. 416, 417.

16. See Wilbur M. Smith, *The Supernaturalness of Christ: Can We Still Believe in It?* (Boston: Wilde, 1941), pp. 115, 116.

17. Ramm, *Protestant Christian Evidences,* p. 144.

PART THREE

CAN FAITH SURVIVE
IN AN AGE OF DOUBT?

INTRODUCTION

In the foreword we indicated some of the problems of maintaining faith in God's Word in an age essentially rationalistic and skeptical. As every informed person knows, the Bible has been subjected to a great variety of critical tests: Are its records in accord with the findings of history, archaeology, geology, and other sciences? Has its text been preserved without major changes or corruptions? How can the supernatural events be reconciled with known phenomena?

Honest seekers of truth have faced, rather than evaded, these problems. They have spent many years and large sums in trying to verify the accuracy of Biblical history, place names, and natural events, and to test the revelations of the Book against the best sources known to man. They have studied the ancient languages used in the Bible and have tried to understand also the meaning of "inspiration" as applied to it.

The essays in this section offer the findings of several scholars on these important topics.

7

THE AUTHENTICITY
OF THE SCRIPTURES

J. W. Roberts

If man is to trust the message of the Bible, he must have confidence that it is a reliable book. Enduring faith cannot long survive doubts about the trustworthiness of the documents that convey the message claiming to be God's revelation.

Fortunately the Bible is rooted in history, and its history is part of the events in a time and region which can be checked by the modern archaeologist and historian. Its historical claims can and have been verified.

But the Bible not only arose in a historical situation, it has also come down to us through a process which is verifiable. Its transmission is a part of its history. Nothing is more certain today than the Bible is a real, historical revelation of God's action in history and that it is the same Bible as that which the ancient Israelites received, collected, and passed on to us.

If this is true, it follows that the Bible is not a fraud which could have been written at some later time, the product of imagination, passed off as divine revelation; neither are the modern versions subject to the charge that they have been changed in process of transmission so that one cannot know whether he possesses the substance of the original message or not.

In this chapter we shall consider the double question of the authenticity or trustworthiness of the Bible and the question of the preservation of its contents through the centuries.

We are not concerned here with the questions of inspiration and infallibility. This writer is committed to the divine inspiration of the Bible and to the doctrine of Biblical inerrancy. But those are theological subjects and are related to the Bible's own claim to being the Word of God. These topics are treated elsewhere in this volume. We are here to deal with the historical trustworthiness of the Book.

131

The Bible as History

Higher criticism has long insisted that the Bible should be sub-jected to the regular canons of historical criticism, that is, it is claimed that where the Bible records events which purport to have been enacted at a certain time and place in history, they should be able to stand the test of reliability from contemporary records, monuments, and documents. This is a perfectly reasonable conten-tion and a challenge undertaken gladly and ably, for example, for the New Testament by J. W. McGarvey at an earlier period.[1]

Unfortunately, many of those who have been the leading critics of the Bible from this point of view did not merely insist that the Bible meet empricial tests of reliability. They were also uncritically con-trolled by presuppositions which led to conclusions about the nature of Biblical origins which today appear strange. The nineteenth cen-tury was dominated by a closed world (mechanistic) point of view, along with a naturalistic evolutionary supposition. This eliminated any suggestion of supernaturalism for the origins of both the Old and New Testament religions and demanded evolution from simple to higher and more complex systems.

This assumption of evolution or optimism C. S. Lewis has called the "Great Myth of the nineteenth and early twentieth centuries."[2] It led critics of the Old Testament (the Graf-Wellhausen school) to doubt the history underlying the early records of the Old Testament. In like manner is caused the Tuebingen school, led by F. C. Baur, to posit a naturalistic development and late dating for New Testament documents which ruled out historicity.

The Old Testament

In the Graf-Wellhausen theory the early Old Testament records were believed to have been put together out of some earlier docu-ments but largely out of imagination only after the religion had reached the apex of its evolution in the ethical monotheism of the eighth-century prophets. The documents were rejected as the authen-tic products of contemporary writers. In fact, the picture of races, cultures, and so forth, set forth was considered fictitious, the theo-logical products of later times and peoples who wrote to create from fancy a setting for a supposed divine origin!

The school claimed great "objectivity" for its studies, but how different the facts have proved to be. The entire fabric of the Old Testament history has been placed upon a historical basis by the work of Old Testament archaeology. Beginning in the late nineteenth century, archaeologists, led by the brilliant American, William Foxwell Albright of the American School of Oriental Research, systematically excavated the ancient occupation sites or tells of Palestine and the ancient Near East. The results of this development may well be stated in the words of Albright himself:

> Until recently it was the fashion among biblical historians to treat the patriarchal sagas of Genesis as though they were artificial creations of Israelite scribes of the Divided Monarchy or tales told by imaginative rhapsodists around Israelite campfires during the centuries following their occupation of the country. Eminent names among scholars can be cited for regarding every item of Gen. 11-50 as reflecting late invention, or at least retrojection of events and conditions under the Monarchy into the remote past, about which nothing was thought to have been really known to the writers of later days.

> Archaeological discoveries since 1925 have changed all this. Aside from a few die-hards among old scholars, there is scarcely a single biblical historian who has not been impressed by the rapid accumulation of data supporting the substantial historicity of patriarchal tradition.[3]

Albright goes on in his chapter on the Patriarchal Period to pile up the evidence supporting this claim. The immigration of the Semites from the region of Ur to Haran, the donkey nomadic life, the similarity of local names to Biblical names, the worship of family deities, and the covenant rituals, are a part of that evidence. Albright concludes:

> As a whole the picture in Genesis is historical, and there is no reason to doubt the general accuracy of the biographical details and the sketches of personality which make the Patriarchs come alive with a vividness unknown to a single extrabiblical character in the whole vast literature of the ancient Near East.[4]

What is done for the Patriarchal Period can be repeated with even greater emphasis for later periods of the Old Testament. Thus the basic historic nature of these documents is established by the hard facts of scientific investigation. Compare, for example, the furor created by the work of the great archaeologist Nelson Glueck in his work in surveying the Trans-Jordan and Negev areas of Palestine. Glueck found the data in the Biblical documents so accurate and helpful in locating sites that he spoke of the "wonderful memory of the Bible." It was charged by some that Glueck was unscientific and trying to "prove the Bible right." Glueck, a liberal Jewish scholar and not a fundamentalist, declared that the facts speak for themselves.[5]

The New Testament

The Christian situation was very similar. Here, too, nineteenth- and twentieth-century liberal scholarship, starting from humanistic and evolutionary presuppositions doubted the historicity of New Testament documents. Using Hegelian dialectic, F. C. Baur constructed a situation of a Hellenistic and Jewish opposition which gradually evolved into a more complex theology. Only four of the epistles ascribed to Paul were considered genuine. Acts was thought to be unhistorical, a piece of irenic or compromise literature to cover up the original situation. Most of the rest of the New Testament documents were given a very late date, with the Johannine literature given a date as late as the fourth century A.D. because of its higher Christology.

There was, of course, a conservative rebuttal. In Germany such scholars as T. Zahn denied this reconstruction;[6] and, when it was introducted into England, the great trio of J. B. Lightfoot, B. F. Westcott, and Anthony Hort undertook the systematic investigation of the historical background of the New Testament. Westcott wrote of the Palestine Jewish situation,[7] Lightfoot of the Acts and John and the Apostolic Fathers,[8] and Hort (collaborating with Westcott) on the Greek text and its transmission.[9] Harnack in Germany also defended Acts.[10] Somewhat later Sir William Ramsay fell into a situation which led to the survey and publication of the historical and geographical background of Asia Minor and the journeys of Paul.[11] The details would occupy too much space. I have attempted to tell part of the story in an introductory article to the study of Acts in *Restoration Quarterly*.[12] The results are similar to those of the Old Testament and just as conclusive. The value of Acts, for example, as a historical document has been recently upheld by such scholars as G. H. C. McGregor,[13] the great German historian Eduard Meyer,[14] B. H. Streeter,[15] A. H. McNeile,[16] C. H. Turner,[17] and the great Harvard liberal scholar Henry J. Cadbury. This writer heard Cadbury deliver at Southern Methodist University the lectures which went to make up *The Book of Acts in History*.[18] He gives the Acts accounts high value and describes them as accurate in the known historical context of the first century A.D. He prefaced his first lecture by the statement that if he were a conservative he would consider the lectures as having high apologetic value.

Note: It is not here contended that all archaeological discoveries have supported and confirmed the Biblical narratives. Such has been the case in an overwhelming majority of instances. The Bible is shown to be a historical book, worthy of high regard in its own right in any dispute of testimony. Its high accuracy entitles it to be given equal, if not greater, weight in conflicting testimony with secular monuments and records, which, it must be remembered, are themselves highly subject to the human margin of error. The Christian's faith in the inerrancy of the Biblical records rests on a solid foundation substantiated by scientific investigation.

The Genuineness of New Testament Documents

What is the current view of the genuineness of the New Testament documents? What is the evidence that the documents were written in the time and place and by the men to whom they are ascribed? We have already seen that the tendency to late date these books was characteristic of earlier schools of Biblical study and that their claims proved embarrassing to them. What about modern scholarship?

Of the thirteen Pauline Epistles, the greater part have never been seriously questioned. Even the most radical school of the nineteenth century (Baur's) admitted that the four great letters—I and II Corinthians, Galatians, and Romans—were genuine. In the rehabilitation which was forced by the archaeological discoveries at the turn of the century, the two Thessalonian Epistles, Colossians, Philippians, and Philemon were almost universally acknowledged. This leaves only Ephesians (which some have concluded to be a cover epistle written as an introduction to the collected epistles when they were first published together later) and the Pastoral Epistles about which there is any question. Today the arguments against these have lost most of their force. The discovery of the new Gnostic documents has mitigated against the argument that the heresy of the Pastorals is Second Century Gnosticism,[19] and the linguistic arguments raised by P. N. Harrison's[20] work have been shown to be vastly overdrawn.[21] Such a scholar as E. F. Scott[22] is singularly unimpressed with the arguments against Ephesians. The results are that there is almost universal agreement that in the body of the Pauline Epistles we have authentic records of genuine New Testament Christianity. If that were all we had, we could reconstruct the gospel from these documents.

The situation is much the same for the literature attributed to John. Baur thought all these documents to be very late. But the study of the early tradition of the literature's origin at Ephesus and especially the discovery of very early manuscript remains [P^{52} , P^{66} P^{75}] have reestablished them.[23] Because of linguistic differences between Revelation and the other Johannine literature some still doubt that the apostle John wrote both parts of the corpus, and they postulate another John living late in the century at Ephesus as the author. But it should be remembered that the literature does not specifically say that John was an apostle, and the inspiration does not depend upon apostolic authorship. However, there are other explanations for the linguistic differences.[24] Today there is nearly unanimous agreement that (even if this material is not of apostolic origin) these documents enshrine authentic first-century tradition, even it if may be independent of that lying behind the first three Gospels.[25] Interesting, too, is the admission of a well-known scholar, John A. T. Robinson, that the presuppositions a scholar brings to the study of the problems are decisive for the conclusions he reaches; [26] the conservatives can make a solid historical case for their position.

With this much acknowledged, less stress has to be put upon the Snyoptics and the remainder of the books. The problems raised by the interrelation of the material in the parallel Gospels has led to many proposed solutions for the so-called Synoptic problem. The most common is supposed early documents: Mark and a sayings source, called Q. This documentary source theory was once said to be a "sure result" of critical efforts. But today the scholars are not so sure. Many have returned to the hypothesis of Griesbach which represents the opinion of the early church that Matthew's Gospel is the earliest.[27] Too, there has been a revival of the position of Alford and Westcott (on a much more scientific basis) of an early oral formulation of the common material in these documents.[28]

Some well-known New Testament scholars like T. W. Manson [29] and F. F. Bruce[30] take the position that documentary sources, if combined with a belief in divine inspiration, can strengthen the belief in the historical reliability of the material since it furnishes even earlier foundations for the apostolic traditions than the finished Gospels, whose origins cannot be fixed earler than the 60s. Even Form Criticism in the hands of believing critics like Vincent Taylor is put to use in the service of historical credibility as demonstrating the existence of material passed on orally in the churches before it was embodied in the documents.[31] Overall, then, it is only the very radical schools such as that of Bultmann that doubt the essential reliability of the material in the Gospels. As for genuineness, there is little ground today for doubting that Mark (his Gospel held to be a recording of Peter's sermons) and Luke (Paul's companion) are personally responsible for the books bearing their names. The tendency is to consider Matthew the result of a "school" operating in the church at Antioch in the name of the apostle Matthew and writing to Jewish Christians in dialogue with non-Christian Judaism (Jamnia). This leaves only the two Epistles of Peter and Jude for discussion of the signed epistles. Here the tendency is to accredit the First Epistle to the apostle and to consider the Second Epistle a rewriting by a later disciple of the epistle of Jude. The internal evidence of II Peter-Jude really favors just the reverse of this.

Hebrews is anonymous. The early attributing of this to Paul is not likely to be correct. But there is no reason to doubt that it is a document by a Christian of the first century operating within the framework of Hellenistic Christian Judaism.

We are faced today, then, with a general acknowledgment of documents arising out of the historical framework of early Christianity. They were canonized by the church as Scripture because they could claim to be authentic documents for the apostles and their circles.

Some Special Problem Areas

There are some areas which are often considered special problem areas with respect to the credibility of the Bible. We shall discuss a few of these briefly, giving some modern bibliography where the sincere seeker may find additional help.

The Modern World View, Science, and the Bible. One of these areas is modern physical science and the Bible. It is sometimes claimed that the Bible sets forth a three-tiered world view at variance with our modern understanding of the universe. One well-known theologian said that he could never be a conservative in Biblical faith because he could never believe in a literal three-storied universe. The radical Bultmann school claims that the Bible must be demythologized to be acceptable to modern man. Other equally "modern" but more conservative-minded students of the Bible believe that the vestiges of terminology which support such a view of the world are already demythologized in the Bible. Thus W. F. Albright said concerning the terminology of creation which retains vestiges of this language,

> The process of demythologization has already taken place. There are only a few traces of earlier mythology in the first chapter of Genesis, and all have been thoroughly demythologized.[32]

So G. B. Caird speaking of the way the Book of Revelation presents the structure of the universe in its visions says, "In the biblical account of creation in Genesis 1 the pagan story has been demythologized in the interests of a thoroughgoing monotheism."[33] Again,

> If we imagine that he [the author of Revelation] was the naive inhabitant of a three-story universe, who believed that bodily locomotion upwards would bring him to the floor above where God lived, and that bodily locomotion downwards would bring him to the floor below with its less desirable tenants, we shall find ourselves constantly in difficulties of our own making. The three-story universe belongs to spiritual, not physical geography,

as the author of Solomon's prayer had made abundantly plain [I Kings viii.27].[34]

It is wrong to consider the Bible a textbook on science. It may be that the Bible contains pre-science as some have tried to argue. But most of these attempts probably claim too much. It may well be that some students of the Bible and also some scientists by claiming too much for their respective disciplines have created difficulties where none actually exist. If the Bible is not written in scientific language, at the same time it may be confidently claimed that all it contains may be squared with anything which can and has actually been demonstrated by science. If the student needs special help in such areas as creation vs. organic evolution, the age of the world and man, the flood, and the chronology of the Bible, he may find that help in some of the following books: Bernard Ramm, *The Christian View of Science and Scripture* (Grand Rapids, Eerdmans 1954); R. E. D. Clark, *Creation* (London,1958); Russel L. Mixter, *Evolution and Christian Thought Today* (Grand Rapids, Eerdmans 1959); J. D. Thomas, *The Doctrine of Evolution and the Antiquity of Man* (Abilene, 1963); J. G. Machen, *The Virgin Birth of Christ* (New York, 1930).

The Biblical Miracles. Some stumble at the miraculous actions of especially chosen prophets and apostles of God and Jesus, and of Jesus Himself. They say that it is not possible for a modern man to believe in these stories. Every man must answer this question according to his world view. A completely closed or mechanistic world view which excludes the possibility of a miraculous occurrence is Deism. This is a question of philosophical presupposition and not of science or fact. If one's metaphysical viewpoint is completely mechanistic, there is no place for miracle. But modern quantum physics has called such a view into question. Few scientists today will affirm that science supports such a world view. Certainly the possibility of a supernatural origin of the universe and the belief in a power higher than man and the universe has much to commend it in a world of uncertainties.

Given the possibility of miracles, the accounts of the Biblical miracles become plausible. They are stated in moderate language and have the characteristics of eyewitness accounts (in contrast, for example, to the Apocryphal Gospels). For the most part, the crux is belief in the deity of Jesus Christ, with the Resurrection the supreme wonder. If these are credible, the miracles are believable. A great twentieth-century scholar has said about the doubts concerning the miracle of Jesus' stilling the tempest:

Let us examine our doubts. Why do some of us who accept Christ's healing miracles boggle at a nature miracle like this? One reason, no doubt, is that, while we can believe that Jesus influenced men's bodies through their minds, we can see no mental bridge between Jesus and the storm. Another is that we tacitly accept "the steel-and-concrete" conception of the universe as a fixed and closed system (though that so-called scientific dogma is fast dissolving in our time). Before, however, we reject this nature miracle, let me suggest three considerations which seem to me to weigh down the scales in the direction of acceptance. First, when we Christians pray God, as we do, to deliver "those in peril on the sea," are we not in fact praying for a nature miracle to happen? Second, if we grant, as most Christians do, that God raised Jesus from the tomb—and a dead body is as much a part of the material order as the winds and waves of Galilee—why should we reluct at the idea that Christ with God's help, was able to control the elements? Third, and most important, if we accept, as most Christians do, the truth of the Incarnation (i.e., if we believe that the divine Spirit was uniquely incarnate in Jesus Christ), we have no right to lay down the limits of what Jesus could or could not do.[35]

No, in reality it is a question of faith in God and in Jesus, God's Son.

This writer has found the following helpful: C. S. Lewis, *Miracles* (New York, Macmillan, 1955); Frank O. Green, "Can We Believe in the Miraculous?" in *Can I Trust My Bible?* (Chicago, 1963); E. J. Cornell, *An Introduction to Christian Apologetics* (Grand Rapids, 1948); James Martin, *Did Jesus Rise from the Dead?* (New York, 1956).

The Scope of Faith Today

Since there are many people for whom the consensus of "modern," "educated," "scholarly," or "scientific" men is important, it may be pertinent to inquire, "Where does the weight of scholarship lie?" It was once common for college and university students to hear their humanist instructors in nearly all fields of scientific and liberal arts disciplines say that no educated or informed people any longer believed the Bible. With the great change in the intellectual and philosophic climate of the twentieth century, with the advent of modern physics (which has called the mechanistic or closed world view into question), and with the general diffusion of the information concerning the historical investigations of the Bible's background, this is less common today. Indeed, such a statement from a professor today would indicate that he is not relevant and up to date. However, it may be well to document this fact. It should be remembered, as we have already pointed out, that even at the heydey of old-line liberalism there were outstanding voices of dissent (recall the names of Schlatter and Zahn in Germany, Westcott, Hort, and Lightfoot in England, and such as Benjamin Warfield and James G. Machen in America).

The mid-twentieth century has seen a real rehabilitation of the Holy Scriptures. The phenomenon may be represented by the example of C. S. Lewis. Mr. Lewis was a great humanist scholar, the world's leading expert on the works of John Milton. His own wrestling with the intellectual difficulties of his atheism led to his conversion: (read the story in *Surprised by Joy,* his autobiography, New York: Harcourt, Brace, World, 1956). Lewis became a conservative in the Christian faith, a preacher of great ability, and a prolific writer of books, articles, and lectures supporting the Christian faith. Anyone who has read his interplanetary novels, his popular presentations of apologia such as *The Screwtape Letters* (New York: Macmillan, 1942), *Mere Christianity* (New York: Macmillan, 1952), and *Pilgrim's Regress* (London, 1950) cannot help being impressed with the formidable logic of such attempts to defend the Christian alternative and with the questions and doubts raised against skepticism.

Other recent examples of this simple but scholarly apologia might include:

The Servant Messiah by T. W. Manson (New York: Cambridge University Press, 1953). This small, erudite work by a Manchester University professor demonstrates that Judaism's expectation of a Messianic deliverer just prior to and contemporary with Jesus and the apostles is accurately portrayed in the four Gospels. It is seen in the picture drawn by the evangelists as they contrast Jesus' own view of the Messianic hope with that of the contemporary Jewish leaders. Manson argues that only by a correct understanding of this situation can the Gospels be read intelligently and that they are thereby shown to be historically reliable.

The Phenomenon of the New Testament by C. F. D. Moule (London: SCM, 1967). This little work by the Lady Margaret Professor of Divinity at Cambridge University shows that there is no suspicious motivation—"neither ideological nor sentimental" which may explain Christian origins to the discerning historian. He further argues that the "birth and rapid rise of the Christian church therefore remain an unsolved enigma for any historian who refuses to take seriously" the resurrection of Jesus Christ as the ground for the church's origin. By appealing to the original Aramaic formulations lying behind the Gospels, to the existence of the Christain community with its consciousness of having been called into being by the death and resurrection of Jesus, Moule lays out some forms of investigation open to the modern student of Christian origins.

The Bible in an Age of Science by Alan Richardson (Philadelphia: Westminister, 1961). This work surveys the rise and fall of the scientific method and its effect on belief in the Bible. The author traces the development of critical unbelief toward the Bible and shows how events of the twentieth century have revealed its inadequacy. Though Richardson's own theology is colored by his existential point of view, the book opens vistas to the inquiring student.

The Dead Sea Scrolls

The 1940s also produced two significant discoveries which have shed great light on the New Testament and added significantly to its credibility.[36] They were the discoveries of quantities of Jewish sectarian materials from the region of Khirbet Qumran and the discovery of Gnostic documents at Nag Hammadi near Chenoboskin in Upper Egypt. We will comment briefly on the significance of each discovery.

When a shepherd boy followed his runaway goat into a cave in the bank of a wadi or ravine near the northwestern edge of the Dead Sea in the Jordan Valley in 1945, he touched off discoveries of far-reaching consequence. In addition to the eleven documents of the original Dead Sea Scrolls, fifteen caves in the region and the ruins of the communal dwelling to which the documents were related have yielded fantastic results. Biblical manuscripts from every book in the Old Testament except Esther have been found. Community materials such as discipline manuals and hymnals are added. Midrashic commentary material showing interpretative methods are there. In fact, the list is long, and discoveries are still being made.

Some scholars (e.g., A. Powell Davies,[37] and cf. the Edmund Wilson article in the *New Yorker*) jumped to conclusions. Pointing to certain parallels in the thought of this group (probably a Jewish Essene group) and Christian thought and practice, Davies boldly proclaimed that here was the answer to the origin of Christianity. John the Baptist, Jesus, and some of His disciples had belonged to this sect and had merely borrowed and adapted these notions. Wilson noted the slow process of publication and suspected that Christian and Jewish scholars were "sitting on the evidence" lest it affect their previously held conclusions.

On the contrary, full publication and discussions have proceeded. The evidence continues to mount that, though there are similarities due naturally to similar roots in the contemporary milieu, the differences are also great; there is much here to explain facets of Christianity, but nothing to account for its origin, dramatic growth, and dynamic as a movement. The principal contribution continues to be in the exposing of elements in the thought world and literary expression of Christianity to a comparision with the Jewish people of the times. Formerly, for example, certain symbolic use of terms like "light" and "darkness," the personification of good and evil, were thought to show the lateness of the writings of John, thus arguing a late date for these books. Now some have argued that John could have been the first of the four Gospels to be written.[38] Also, the Qumran discoveries have shown the accuracy with which the traditional Hebrew texts of the Old Testament have been handed down. The so-called Massoretic Texts of the Jewish Bible in our earliest manuscripts (from late Medieval times), despite the centuries of copying, are shown to be amazingly accurate. The translators of the Book of Isaiah in the Revised Standard Version say that in only some thirteen places did they find any significant variation in the Scroll of Isaiah from Cave I and the traditional text. The discoveries do show that this type of text was only one type of rescension existing at the time. But once it was chosen over the others, it has been transcribed with great accuracy.

The Gnostic Documents from Nag Hammadi

The Gnostic Documents from Nag Hammadi were discovered about the same year as the Dead Sea Scrolls, though they are less well known.[39] They consist of some forty volumes which make up a library of a Gnostic group in Upper Egypt. They are written in a subdialect of Sahidic. They are, however, translations of earlier Greek documents. Among them one is able to read for the first time books which the Christian writers wrote against the Gnostic heresy such as the Gospel of Truth by Valentinus.

The rise and development of docetism and gnosticism have long been clouded in mystery. Whether the cluster of ideas, so-called, developed out of Greek philosophy, from fringe Jewish and Christian groups, or is of Samaritan or Persian origins is still not clear. The documents do show, however, that the Christian heresiologists were not fighting straw men, as has often been claimed. More importantly, they show that the roots of Sectarian Gnosticism go back much further than some have been willing to allow. This has important implications for the historicity and credibility of some New Testament documents. For example, it has often been claimed that the heresy combatted by Paul's Epistles to Timothy and Titus must be placed deep in the second century because of its similarity to the ideas of the heretics Marcion and Valentinus.[40] No longer is such a claim plausible. Such Gnostic ideas as theological dualism, overrealized eschatology, and libertinism reach back into Paul's day and provide the background to much of the controversy of his later epistles. Soon, with the more adequate publication and discussion of this group of records, we shall be better able to assess the authentic background against which much of the later New Testament was written.

Another important implication of the Gnostic writings, indeed the whole history of this movement from Marcion on, is on the canon. They show that by the middle of the second century the books commonly recognized by the Gnostics were known to them in the form which the canon was later to take historically.[41]

The Discovery of the Palestine Targum of the Pentateuch

Another recent discovery which helps to show the antiquity and credibility of the New Testament documents is the recently discovered Palestine Targum of the Pentateuch.[42] It has long been known that the Jews of New Testament times who were wedded to their Hebrew background held onto their Hebrew Scriptures and continued to have them read in their synagogues rather than the Greek translation (the Septuagint). To accompany the reading of the Hebrew, which could no longer be understood by the people, there developed a paraphrase or translation in to the Aramaic which would be recited. Our modern copies of these targums (the Onquelos and Pseudo-Jonathan of the Pentateuch and Jonathan Targum for the Prophets) have been much worked over in later times and cannot be relied on to give us information contemporary with the New Testament.

In 1956 Neofiti I, a previously miscataloged document, was discovered in the Vatican Museum which seems to be an authentic copy of the first-century Targum. Its publication is in process.[43]

This Targum throws much light on the New Testament. Many early Jewish Christians, even the apostles themselves, were accustomed to hearing the Bible read and quoted in this Targum. Since it was a paraphrase, it contained many explanations woven into the translation. Many passages in Paul and John, for example, which have heretofore been a puzzle, since they do not correspond exactly to either the original Hebrew or the Greek translation, are now shown to rest upon authentic contemporary material. This is quite natural, since the Targum was the Bible to these early Christians. When this material is fully published and digested by the commentators, it will bring much enlightenment. Meanwhile it already gives another clue to the authenticity of the New Testament records.

Can We Be Sure We Have the Original Text?

Even if it is conceded, as we have argued in Part I, that the Bible was reliable when written, some will argue that one cannot have confidence that we still possess what existed at the beginning. After all, so the reasoning goes, the documents have been in existence for nearly two thousand years; they have been copied thousands of times and there are many variations in the manuscripts or copies of the Greek text which we possess. Furthermore, we do not have any of the originals by which the existing texts may be corrected. How then may we be sure that what we read today is true to the original?

This criticism, though actually arising from lack of information about the nature of the transmission of the text and of the nature of the evidence for its restoration to its original state, is frequently voiced. Sometimes it is a tool of agnosticism which merely wishes to raise doubts. Sometimes novices in the subject matter of textual criticism, such as reporters in magazines, learning that variations exist, will play up the "errors" in the Biblical manuscripts. For example, a few years ago a popular American weekly magazine assigned a reporter to do a story on the beginning of the project for a new critical apparatus. When he learned that the purpose was to collect the variants in many MSS into one volume, he wrote about the "fifty thousand errors" in the Bible which the experts were going to "correct"! He did not know the difference between a transcriptional variation of late scribes (a difference between copies) and a variation between what we have as the consensus text today and what the original said (a difference between the evidence as a whole today and what was originally written).

It is true that we do not possess any of the original manuscripts. Perhaps this is just as well, since the history of Christianity has shown a tendency to worship ancient relics. But this does not mean that we are any less certain about the original text. This writer is not aware that we have the original text (called autographs) of any important ancient document. But if an original was widely circulated early, was copied, was quoted, and was translated into different languages, it can be reconstructed by a comparison of the different witnesses. Actually, if only one witness had been kept by itself, that one source might have been stolen and replaced by a substitute, whereas many independent witnesses, even if they are secondary, cannot be fabricated.

It is also true that there is some confusion in the English translations as to what the original readings were. This is because the first English translations were made from the first published Greek text set in type (that of Erasmus in 1516). Unfortunately, this text was made up by consulting a few very late and inferior Greek manuscripts. But as years went by, better manuscripts from earlier times, along with evidence from early translations and quotations, came to light and were incorporated into later editions of the Greek New Testament. Hence the succession of English translations has merely kept pace with the advancing knowledge which God's providence has made known, thus offering English readers a progressively more accurate text. It ought to be pointed out that any questionable readings that had crept into the text were not of such nature as to obscure or change any item of doctrine or belief of the Christian faith.

Three Types of Evidence

As we have already mentioned, there are three types of evidence from which one may ascertain the original text: Greek manuscripts, early versions or translations, and quotations from early Christian writers (called Church Fathers). We shall discuss these sources briefly.

The Greek Manuscripts. We possess, according to a recent counting (1964), nearly 5,000 different copies in whole or part. They date all the way from the time of the invention of printing (when copying ceased) back to the very early part of the second century. The latest of these are cursive or minuscule (written in a running or connected script, a style of writing which became popular after the invention of paper in the ninth century). We have 2,646 *cursives or minuscules.* The next oldest are *uncial* MSS on vellum (made between A.D. 350 and the ninth century), of which there are 250. And the oldest MSS are on *papyrus,* the early writing material preserved only in Egypt (it deteriorates in other climates), of which we have 76. *Lectionaries* are mixed manuscripts copied from different books according to the calendars of church readings. We have 1,997 of these. In addition, there are some 25 known portions of Scripture on bits of pottery (ostraca) and 9 talismans (bits of Scripture written on "Good Luck" charms).[44]

When this is compared with the evidence for any other writer of antiquity, the evidence for the Christian Scriptures is, as it has been said, "embarrassing by its wealth." For example, the most important writing of antiquity—Homer (the so-called Bible of the Greeks)—was represented, before the discovery of the papyri, by only two known uncial MSS and some 188 later cursive ones. To date there have been found from Egypt 457 fragments of papyri of Homer. What a contrast! Of the important Latin historian Tacitus there exists only one MS of the ninth century, with later copies made from it. This means that we have no copy of Tacitus within some eight hundred years of the time he wrote. However, incidentally, from early quotations and other means of checking, we are quite sure that on the whole we have a fairly accurate text of this author's works. For Demosthenes, the gap lengthens to more than one thousand years.

This evidence has accumulated impressively through the years (since Deism of the eighteenth century) as skepticism has raised its questions. Beginning with the sixteenth-century texts published by Erasmus and Ximenes, more and earlier manuscripts began to be discovered. Great names such as Lachmann, Tregelles, Griesbach, and Tischendorf made contributions, both in discovery of copies and in the principles of restoration (textual or lower criticism). By the publication of the great text of Westcott and Hort in 1881 the MS evidence rested solidly upon the great Greek Bibles of the fourth and fifth century (such as the Vatican, the Sinaitic, the Alexandrian, and the Ephraemi). Too, scholars had discovered that the manuscripts had existed in recensions, or text-types made in different localities in the great centers of Christian learning. This meant that manuscripts could be classified and assessed according to the relative merit of the type to which each belonged. Of course, the evidence from quotations and the early translations were used in this process. But no one dreamed that the evidence, at that time considered very strong, could become even stronger.

But then came the discovery of the papyri in Egypt, and the evidence for the text was carried back in some cases two hundred years earlier to within a few short years of its origin. For example, in the 1930s the Chester Beaty Papyri were found and published. These were remains of three ancient collections: one (P45) of the four Gospels and Acts (first half of the third century), the second (P46) Paul's Epistles (first half of the third century), and the third (P47) text of Revelation 9-17 (latter part of the third century).

In 1935 a small portion of the Gospel of John was published (P52 of the John Rylands Library) which is dated by experts in ancient handwriting within the first half of the second century. This means that a copy of John's Gospel existed in Egypt, many miles from its place of publication (presumably Ephesus) within some thirty years of its writing!

But this is only the beginning. The Bodmer Library of Geneva has acquired and since 1956 published an entire copy of the Gospel of John (P66) dating from A.D. 200, the earliest known copy of Jude and I & II Peter (P72) dating from the third century, another manuscript (P75) containing the entire text of the Gospel of Luke and the Gospel of John, dating from between A.D. 175 and 225. No one knows what other treasures are already discovered and awaiting publication.

It is true that many of these copies are fragmentary. But when available points are checked and prove accurate, they confirm the whole. As someone has said, from only one footprint Robinson Crusoe knew that there was another man on his island and knew much about him.

The Versions. We can now discuss the versions and quotations in much less space.

From early times, missionaries desired copies of the New Testament translated into other languages. So from the early part of the second century, translations were made into Syraic or Aramaic, of which the Curetonian and the Sinaitic manuscripts are the most important. Later a revision, the Peshitta (around 411) was made of this ancient version. Very early the New Testament was translated into the Old Latin for preaching in North Africa and Italy. Of these early translations (for there were many) we possess excellent and early copies. Later the Latin Bible was revised by Jerome. A third ancient version was in the dialects of Coptic, the language of Egypt: the Sahidic (Southern or Upper Egypt), and the Bohairic (Northern or Lower Egypt). These translations date from around A.D. 200.

There are problems in reconstructing the text from translations. Admittedly many idioms cannot be translated. But for checking the absence or presence of a given reading in the text being used by the translators, these versions are especially helpful. There is no portion of the Greek New Testament which cannot be checked "from the mouth of two or three witnesses" by these three old translations.

The Greek Quotations of the Fathers. Modern investigations (e.g., the work of J. B. Lightfoot on the Church Fathers) have demonstrated the historicity of the corpus or body of documents from the second century written by Christians. These quote the Bible constantly. For example, Lightfoot demonstrated against the contentions of the Baur school that at least seven of the eleven epistles which go under the name of Ignatius are genuine. Ignatius was martyred at Rome under Trajan, who himself died in A.D. 117. Hence the Greek form of many verses of Scripture can be verified by these epistles, all written within a very few decades and in some cases a very few years of the original publication. There are less than a dozen verses of the entire New Testament which cannot be paralleled in the writings of the Church Fathers! There are problems, of course, sometimes quotations were from memory, or loose (paraphrases), yet on the whole, by duplication of testimony, the entire New Testament could be recovered even if we did not have the manuscripts and translations as additional witnesses.

Much can be said about the differences in theory among the scholars as to the best means of using this evidence. It is only fair to say that in a few instances certainty is not possible. At the most, these have to do with a word, a short phrase, transposition of words in a sentence, the spelling of a name or word, etc. Again, in no instance is any doctrine or item of information necessary to the Christian faith at stake. As one eminent critic has said,

> The interval then between the dates of original composition and the earliest extant evidence becomes so small as to be in fact negligible, and the last foundation for any doubt that the Scriptures have come down to us substantially as they were written has now been removed. Both the authenticity and the general integrity of the books of the New Testament may be regarded as finally established.[45]

When all is said and done, we do know that we have the Word of God today.

1. *Evidences of Christianity,* especially Part III, "The Credibility of the New Testament Books" (Cincinnati, reprint from the 1891 edition).
2. "The Funeral of a Great Myth" in *Christian Reflections* ed., W. Hooper (Grand Rapids: Eerdmans, 1967), pp. 82ff.
3. *The Biblical Period from Abraham to Ezra* (New York: Harper & Row, 1963), 1.
4. Ibid, p. 5.
5. *The Other Side of Jordan* (New York: Norton, 1940); *Rivers in the Desert* (New York: Norton, 1968); "The Negev" in *Biblical Archaeologist,* 22 (1959), 82-97; cf. *"Is* Glueck's Aim to Prove the Bible True?", G. Ernest Wright, *Biblical Archeology* XXII, pp. 101-108.
6. Zahn's great three-volume work, *The Introduction to the New Testament* (Edinburgh, 1909, reprinted 1953) is still a valuable work.
7. *An Introduction to the Study of the Gospels* (London, 1895).
8. See especially his great work *The Apostolic Fathers* (2nd ed. London, 1912).
9. *The New Testament in the Original Greek.* Vol. I, The Text; Vol. II, Introduction and Appendix, (Cambridge and London, 1881).
10. *Luke the Physician; The Acts of Apostles,* tr. Wilkinson, (London, 1909).
11. *The Historical Geography of Asia Minor* (1890); *The Church in the Roman Empire before A.D. 170* (1893); *St. Paul the Traveller and Roman Citizen* (1895); *Historical Commentary on St. Paul's Epistle to the Galatians* (1899) and numerous articles in *The Expositor.* Ramsay's work has been described as "among the three or four best things done by an Englishman in the field of Scientific scholarship in this generation" by Hunkin, *The Expositor* (1891), 232f.
12. "The Study of Acts of Apostles Yesterday and Today," in *Restoration Quarterly,* 4 (1960), 173-189.

13. *Interpreter's Bible*, Vol. IX (Nashville, Abingdon, 1954).

14. *Ursprung und Anfange des Christentums*, 3 Vols. (Berlin, 1921-23). It is very interesting that great authorities in the field of Ancient History like Dr. Meyer, Prof. Olmsted of the University of Chicago, and William Ramsay, who have given particular attention to the history of New Testament times in the light of the Bible, have been much more impressed with the trustworthiness of these documents than have New Testament scholars in general. Theological suppositions play a great role in scholars' conclusions!

15. *The Four Gospels*, Rev. ed. (London, 1930).

16. *Introduction to the New Testament* (Oxford, 1927, recently revised).

17. "Chronology" in *Hastings' Dictionary of the Bible*.

18. (London, 1955).

19. Compare below, p. 142.

20. *The problem of the Pastoral Epistles* (Oxford, 1921).

21. Of the many treatments compare J. N. D. Kelley, *The Pastoral Epistles* (London, 1963); and John McRay, "The Authorship of the Pastoral Epistles, *Restoration Quarterly*, 7 (1963), 2-18.

22. *The Epistles of Paul to the Colossians, to Philemon, and to the Ephesians* (Moffatt Commentaries, London, 1930).

23. See discussion on textual criticism below, esp. p. 144.

24. For example, some would put Revelation early and the Gospel and the Epistle later after there was time for John's Greek to improve. Others minimize the linguistic differences, solecisms, etc., pointing to their Hebraistic nature and to the ecstatic situation in which Revelation was written late in John's life.

25. Cf. C. H. Dodd in *The Interpretation of the Fourth Gospel* (Cambridge, 1953) and *Historical Tradition in the Fourth Gospel* (Cambridge, 1963).

26. "The New Look on the Fourth Gospel," *The Gospels Reconsidered* (Oxford, 1960), p. 164.

27. W. R. Farmer, *The Synoptic Problem* (New York: Macmillan, 1964); D. L. Dungan, "Mark—The Abridgment of Matthew and Luke" in *Jesus and Man's Hope* (Pittsburgh, 1970).

28. B. Gerhardsson, *Memory and Manuscript. Oral Tradition and Written Transmission in Rabbinic Judaism and Early Christianity* (Minneapolis: Lund, 1961).

29. *Studies in the Gospels and Epistles* (Philadelphia: Westminster, 1962).

30. *The New Testament Documents—Are They Reliable?* (Grand Rapids: Eerdmans, 1943, revised 1960), pp. 37 ff.

31. *The Formation of the Gospel Tradition*. 2nd ed. (London, 1935).

32. *New Horizons in Biblical Research* (New York: Oxford University Press, 1966), p. 33.

33. *The Revelation of Saint John the Divine. Harper's New Testament Commentaries* (New York: Harper & Row), p. 66.

34. Ibid., p. 62.

35. A. M. Hunter, *The Gospel According to Saint Mark* (Torch Bible Commentaries, New York, 1962).

36. See G. Vermes, *The Dead Sea Scrolls in English* (Baltimore, Penguin, 1962). This Pelican paperback has a good introduction and English translation.

37. *The Meaning of the Dead Sea Scrolls* (New York, 1956).

38. Cf. W. F. Albright's article on the Johannine literature in *The Background of the New Testament and Its Eschatology* (Cambridge, 1956).

39. Jean Doresse, *Secret Books of Egyptian Gnostics* (New York, 1960).

40. Cf. Fred Gealy, *Commentary on the Pastoral Epistles* in *Interpreter's Bible*, Vol XI (Nashville: Abingdon 1955).

41. Cf. Bruce, *New Testament Documents*, p. 99.

42. Cf. Martin McNamara, *The New Testament and the Palestinian Targum to the Pentateuch* (Rome, 1966).

43. Text of *Deuteronomy I, Biblica Polyglotta Matritensia* (Madrid, 1965); Neophyte I: *Targum Palestinense,* Tome 1 Genesis (Madrid, 1968).

44. These totals are from today's standard treatment of the textual criticism of the New Testament by Bruce M. Metzger: *The Text of the New Testament* (New York, Oxford University Press: 1964), pp. 31-35.

45. Frederic Kenyon, *The Bible and Archaeology* (New York, 1940), pp. 288 f.

8

THE WORD OF PROPHECY MADE SURE

Jack P. Lewis

What Is Prophecy?

Ancient man sought to know the will of the Divine in a multitude of ways. Of these, the trade of the diviner, the soothsayer, the magician, and the like (all prominent in ancient Palestine, but all forbidden activities in Israel—Deut. 18:9 ff.; Lev. 20:6; 27; Isa. 65:4), were techniques to be learned. These activities are all to be distinguished from prophecy and are denounced by the prophets (cf. Zech. 10:2). The prophet is also to be distinguished from other legitimate functionaries in Israel such as the wise man, the priest, the elder, and the king. The wise man had a wisdom gained from native ability, divine endowment (I Kings 4:29; Prov. 2:6; Dan. 2:23), and long experience. The priest inherited his position from his father and learned his professional function from those who went before. The elder earned his place by age and reputation. The king's position was hereditary.

In contrast to all of these activities, prophecy in ancient Israel was a special gift from God (Amos 2:11; cf. I Cor. 12:10). Called of God and qualified by God, the prophets spoke by a compulsion from without which is described not only by the promise to Jeremiah, "I have put my words in your mouth" (Jer. 1:9), but also in such phrases as: "The word of the Lord came to me," "Thus saith the Lord," "The Lord God has spoken; who can but prophesy?" (Amos 3:8), and "Men moved by the Holy Spirit spoke from God" (II Peter 1:21). The prophet became the mouthpiece and the interpreter of God (Exod. 4:15-16; 7:1) imparting religious instruction to His people. "Go, and say to this people . . ." is the Lord's commission to Isaiah (Isa. 6:9).

An unusual mixture of the human race—those who have little in

151

common other than the service of God—make up the goodly fellowship of the prophets. Among them were men like Samuel who had
spent his entire life in religious activity, men like the volunteer
prophet Isaiah and like the reluctant prophet Jonah, and men like
Amos who was called from his shepherding and sycamore tending.
There were men of the northern kingdom like Elijah, Elisha, and
Hosea; men of the south like Isaiah, Micah, and Jeremiah; and men
of Palestine as well as men called in exile like Ezekiel. Surprisingly
enough, even characters in the New Testament like the Cretan poet
(Titus 1:12) and Caiaphas (John 11:51) are said to have prophesied
truly though we are sure that the last figure was unconscious of the
larger import of his words.

The prophet in Israel was designated by the terms: "seer" *(rō'eh),*
"seer" *(ḥōzeh),* "man of God" *('ish 'elohim),* "man of the spirit"
('ish hā-ruāh), and "prophet" *(nābi').* While various shades of meaning can be seen in these terms, absolute distinctions in activity
cannot be maintained. "Prophet" *(nābi')* with 400 occurrences as a
noun (and 110 occurrences in verbal form) is the most common of
the terms and "prophets of Baal," "false prophets," "early prophets," and "canonical prophets" are all designated by it. Prophetic
study regularly draws a clear line of distinction between the early
prophets and the writing (classical or reforming) prophets and de-
lights in heaping contempt upon the former while praising the latter.
A linguistic justification for this distinction cannot be maintained; all
categories of prophets are called *"nābi'."*

While it is readily recognized that early prophets did not leave
collections of oracles, some are said to have done writing (allusion is
made to material written in the vision of Iddo the seer (II Chron.
9:29; 12:15; 13:22), in the respective chronicles of Samuel the seer,
of Nathan the prophet, and of Gad the seer (I Chron. 29:29) and in
the prophecy of Ahijah the Shilonite (II Chron. 9:29). The distinction between the early and the late is likely not as clear-cut as some
would represent it. The principal contrasts between the two may be
summarized as follows: first, the stories concerning the early prophets center on their activities while for the latter prophets we have
chiefly their oracles. Other than Jeremiah, we know little of their
personalities. Second, the early prophets were wonder-workers
whereas we have no example—apart from the signs announced by
Isaiah to Ahaz (Isa. 7) and to Hezekiah (Isa. 37-39)—of miracles
wrought by a canonical prophet. Third, some element of ecstasy
seems to be in early prophecy, but no example can be found of a
canonical prophet speaking in an ecstatic state. Beyond these few
points, a distinction is hard to maintain.

The message came to the prophet in a number of ways (Heb. 1:1) the more prominent of which are: the vision (Jer. 1:13; Joel 2:28), the dream (Deut. 13:1; Num. 12:6), the voice of the angel (I Kings 13:18; 19:5), and the small voice (I Kings 19:12 f.; cf. Job 4:12 ff.). No distinction can be made in the relative significance of these various means of revelation; nor is it likely that Jeremiah is denouncing in a blanket way one form of revelation as compared with others when he denounces dreamers and calls for faithfulness with God's Word (Jer. 23:28). The message came with a compulsive force which led the prophet Jeremiah to speak despite an inclination to do otherwise (Jer. 20:9; cf. I Cor. 9:16). The prophet's foresight was not his own, for God revealed His secrets to His servants (Amos 3:7). The true prophet had stood in the council of the Lord (Jer. 23:18, 22) and did not confuse his own dreams with the true Word of God. It was God who "spoke to the prophets, who multiplied visions, and who through the prophets gave parables" (Hos. 12:10). The Servant in Isaiah declares, "Morning by morning he wakens . . . my ear to listen as those who are taught. The Lord has opened my ear" (Isa. 50:4). Again the prophet says, "What I have heard from the Lord of hosts the God of Israel, I announce to you" (Isa. 21:10). Balaam claims to deliver "the oracle of the man whose eye is opened, the oracle of him who hears the words of God, and who knows the knowledge of the Most High" (Num. 24:15, 16). As a consequence of this conviction of receiving revelation, the prophetic oracle is most often issued under the form, "Thus saith the Lord." A force inhered in the true prophetic utterance. That word sent forth from Jehovah will not return void but will accomplish that for which it was sent forth (Isa. 55:10, 11).

Nevertheless, not all prophets were true to their vocation. In addition to prophets like the prophets of Baal and of Asherah (I Kings 18; cf. Deut. 13:1, 2) who exalted other gods, there were also in Israel those men who spoke in the name of Jehovah but whose words were contrary to the warnings uttered by such men as Micaiah ben Imlah (I Kings 22), Micah (Micah 3), and Jeremiah (Jer. 27-29). A unique case is that of the old prophet who first lied and then shortly thereafter delivered a true oracle (I Kings 13:18, 21).

The difference between the false prophet and the true is not a matter of externals. The messages of both were delivered by word of mouth, by symbolic acts, and by letter. Plain speech, poetic figure, parable, and allegory were used by both. Even the ability to work a sign is not an infallible distinction for the Bible readily grants that signs can be wrought by deceivers (Deut. 13:1f; II Thess. 2:9). Not only so, but external verification carries little weight anyway with the man who does not want to be convinced.

There was no easy, infallible way to distinguish between the prophets. The test of time is proposed in Deuteronomy 18:21 f.; but in a tight situation like that confronting Ahab (I Kings 22), one could not wait to see who was telling the truth. Jeremiah suggests that in general warnings are more readily to be accepted than are promises of good (28:8, 9), but this statement should not be carried to the extreme of denying that true prophets were prophets of weal as well as of woe. Men listened to the false prophets because of a defect within themselves (5:30, 31). The life fully dedicated to God and the heart attuned to His will were for the hearers the safeguards from deception: "If any man's will is to do his will, he shall know whether the teaching is from God or whether I am speaking on my own authority" (John 7:17).

Were the Prophet's Messages Limited to Their Own Age?

An earlier generation drew a false antithesis between the prophets as foretellers and as forthtellers. The often-cited words of R. H. Charles are typical of this attitude:

> Prophecy is a declaration, a forthtelling, of the will of God—not a foretelling. Prediction is not in any sense an essential element of prophecy, though it may intervene as an accident—whether it be a justifiable accident is another question.[1]

Under such presuppositions, Old Testament study experienced an extended period in which the concept of prophetic prediction was either severely renounced or was neglected and the prophets were exalted chiefly as social and moral reformers.

Fortunately, this one-sidedness is now passé in prophetic study. Even interest in Messianic prophecy, though supported on a different basis than formerly, has experienced a new birth.[2] While it is still widely and correctly affirmed that the prophet had a primary mission to his own generation, and that his message arose out of the circumstances in which he lived, it is recognized that his preaching was not restricted to his original audience. Most recent treatments of the prophets include sections on the eschatological element in prophetic thought. W. Zimmerli[3] argues that the basic form of prophetic word is the address of the messenger who brings news of that which is to come. He is the forerunner of that which he announces. The new atmosphere has been summarized by H. H. Rowley:

> There is no reason to deny that they also spoke of that more distant future, and uttered prophecies of things not causally related to the events of their own day, and the general relegation to a later age of every such prophecy is no longer in vogue amongst scholars.[4]

T. H. Robinson also asserted: "Biblical scholarship is coming more and more to recognize that prediction was an, perhaps the, essential element in Old Testament prophecy."[5] In this connection, one should note that Isaiah is commanded to write down his oracles "that it may be for the time to come as a witness for ever" (30:8).

Nonetheless, because of a persisting widespread popular misconception about the nature of prophecy which would go to an opposite extreme from that of Charles, a word of explanation and caution is in order. One is not at all to assume that the new attitude in prophetic study which recognizes that the prophet also spoke for other days than his own, is at the same time granting that the prophets are properly used as crystal balls out of which to read tomorrow's news. The prophets did not write the history of the world in advance;[6] their statements are much too spotty for that. It is regrettable that in some fundamentalist circles "to study prophecy" still automatically means to focus on prediction, for such a concept narrows the work of the prophet far too much to be valid. In bulk, prediction is only a small part of prophetic oracles. As one who spoke for another, the prophet was not chiefly one who spoke beforehand nor does the word "prophesy" chiefly signify "to predict." Concerned with Jehovah's role in Israel's past, His activities in the present, and His ultimate purpose in the future, the prophets had a great deal to say that under no definition of the term could be considered prediction. As watchmen of the people (Hos. 9:8; Ezek. 3:16 ff.; 33:1 ff.), warning about and denunication of sin was a major task of the prophets (cf. Micah 3:8). But when concerned with the future, the prophets made clear that the activities of God were conditioned upon Israel's behavior. Unlike the later apocalypses (cf. I Enoch 81:1, 2, etc.), which neither Jew nor Christian considers to be inspired, the prophets did not conceive of the history of the world as written in advance on the heavenly tablets just waiting to be read off.

Is There Such a Thing as Predictive Prophecy?

That the prophet, through the power of God, has the ability to predict the future is an assumption woven into the very fabric of both the Old and New Testaments. At no stage of the prophetic movement is the predictive element absent. In fact, the Epistle of Jude traces prophecy back as early as Enoch (14) and Paul would remind us of promises made to Abraham (Gal. 3:8). There is some prediction in every prophetic book of the Old Testament.[7]

Hebrew prophecy consists neither of vague generalizations like: "It shall rain next year," nor of equivocation that can be taken in either of two ways. The false prophets said, "Go up to Ramoth

Gilead. The Lord will give it into the hand of the king" (I Kings 22:6, 15). Which king, however, was not specified; but Micaiah ben Imlah said, "I saw Israel scattered as sheep that have no shepherd" (I Kings 22:17), and Ahab died in the battle. The stress upon prediction in the Old Testament is too striking to be ignored: Deuteronomy asserts that the prophet whose oracles do not come to pass has spoken presumptuously (Deut. 18:22). Of Samuel it is said, "All that he says come true" (I Sam. 9:6), and God allows none of Samuel's words to "fall to the ground" (I Sam. 3:19). Isaiah promises Hezekiah that Jerusalem would not fall to Sennacherib and the promise was fulfilled (Isa. 37:33 ff.). Isaiah at length develops, as an argument for the existence of God, that God has predicted the future and has accomplished it; while the idols can neither tell of the past nor of the future (Isa. 41:21-26; 42:9; 45:21; 46:8-10). He challenges the idol to tell what is yet to be (Isa. 44:7, 8). He argues that God's purpose and the events of history correspond with each other. God is He who declares "the end from the beginning and from ancient times things not yet done" (Isa. 46:10). "The former things have come to pass and new things I now declare; before they spring forth I tell you of them," declares the prophet (Isa. 42:9; cf. 48:4-5). Jeremiah argues with opposing prophets, "When the word of that prophet comes to pass, it will be known that the Lord has truly sent the prophet" (Jer. 28:9). Ezekiel warns, "When this comes—and come it will!—then will they know that a prophet has been among them" (Ezek. 33:33). So predominant is this concept of prophecy that after the calamity of the exile, a late prophet calls attention to the fact that the threats of the earlier prophets were recognized by his generation to have come to reality (Zech. 1:6; 7:14).

With some frequency one encounters the assertion that Old Testament prophecies were of a general rather than of a specific nature. This allegation does not fit the literature that has come down to us which contains both general and specific prophecies regarding time, place, and person. A prophet of the tenth century spoke in advance of the desecration of the Bethel altar at the hands of Josiah and the Book of Kings records how it came about three hundred years later (I Kings 13:2; II Kings 23:16 f.). Elijah spoke of a three-year drought (I Kings 17:1; cf. James 5:17, 18). Jeremiah spoke of a seventy-year captivity (Jer. 25:11, 12), and his prophecy was later used by Daniel (Dan. 9:1 ff. cf. II Chron. 36:22; Ezra 1:1). Isaiah told of a captivity to Babylon long before Babylon was a specific menace to Judah (Isa. 39:6-7) and both Jeremiah and Ezekiel spoke of the downfall of Tyre to Nebuchadnezzar (Ezek. 26:1 ff.). Other predictions referred to individuals such as Pashur (Jer. 20), Jehoiakim (Jer. 22:18 ff.), and Cyrus (Isa. 44:28—45:1). These prophecies can only be denied by a radical late dating of the literature in which they are found, which turns them into examples of *vaticinia ex eventu.*

It is not within the intent of this writer to undertake a statistical count of the predictive elements in the Old Testament, as some have done,[8] but to notice some prominent themes. The Greeks conceived of history as moving in cycles, but the prophets, as does all of the Old Testament, presented history in a linear pattern, moving toward a goal. God makes promises concerning the fortunes of Israel and of the nations that come to fulfillment.[9] By the time of the eighth-century prophets and after, the main line of prediction is that Israel is about to fall to Assyria (as she did in 722 B.C.); that Judah is to be exiled by Nebuchadnezzar (which she was in 587 B.C.); that the rise of Persia would make possible a return from exile; and that out of that return a glorious future would arise. Taking his cue from Hosea, B. D. Napier has summarized the Old Testament cycle in terms of: Out of Egypt, into this land, back to Egypt, and out of Egypt again.[10] Hosea (9:3, 6) and other prophets, still using the Exodus motif, point also to Assyria, or Babylon, and return as the program (Jer. 23:7-8; Isa. 40:3-5; 43:16 ff.). The coming Day of the Lord is a prominent part of the motif. While in Amos that day is the day of the downfall to Assyria (5:18-20—Amos used both "exile" and "captivity" (9:4) to describe its outcome), in others the day becomes a symbol of the final day of judgment (Joel 2:30, 31; Zeph. 1:14-16). Zechariah speaks of a day when Jehovah will become king over all the earth. Jehovah will be one and His name one (14:5-9).

Elements of special interest in the prophetic program are the promise of the New Covenant (Jer. 31:31) and the promise of the coming king, a descendant of David (Isa. 9:6, 7; 11:1; etc.). The expectation by the prophets of a special king of the line of David is indisputable. The effort to date the origin of this motif late in Hebrew history does not enjoy the vogue in critical circles it once had. G. Widengren has said: "To blot out from the revelation of the pre-exilic prophets these expectations of a future Messianic state under the rulership of the Anointed of *Yahweh* is a maltreating of the prophets."[11] Although the term *Messiah* occurs in a technical sense in the Old Testament only in Daniel, the messianic expectation can be traced from the promise made to Abraham (Gen. 12:3; Gal. 3:6 ff.), to the promise made to David of one raised to sit upon his throne (II Sam. 7:12 ff.; Ps. 89:3, 4; Acts 2:29 ff.) and to later allusions made back to this promise (Jer. 23:5). G. Von Rad[12] and Zimmerli[13] have called attention to the fact that this and other prophetic promises are encountered not only in the specific prophetic statement, but are also governing factors in the entire presentation of Israelite history in the Old Testament as the "prophetic word" is worked out in specific details of the narrative. But there are also other challenging motifs such as that of the prophet like Moses (Deut. 18:15, 18), of the suffering servant of Jehovah (Isa. 53; Acts 8:31 ff.), and of the one like a son of man (Dan. 7:13, 14; Matt. 26:64).

New Testament Treatment of Prophetic Material

First-century men took prediction seriously and looked for "him who should come." For New Testament writers the prophets were those who saw and spoke in advance (Rom. 1:2; 9:29; II Peter 3:2; cf. Acts 1:16; 2:30, 31; 3:18; 7:52; I Peter 1:10 ff.). They shared with their Jewish readers the belief in the inspiration of the Old Testament and consequently shared the belief in predictive prophecy.[14] While Jews and Christians of this early period differed over the identity of the Messiah and His role, and over the interpretation of some passages alleged to predict His career, they did not differ over the fact that a Messiah was predicted. The successes of the numerous revolutionaries who eventually brought on the war of A.D. 70 and the ready reception given to the claims of Bar Cocheba in A.D. 135 were expressions among the Jews of that expectation.

The appeal to prophecy is a primary appeal in the apostolic preaching, forming a part of what C. H. Dodd called the *kergyma*.[15] It was argued that the prophecies are fulfilled and that the new age is inaugurated by the coming of the Spirit.[16] The salvation offered in the New Testament is that which is described and promised in the Old Testament—not that promised in philosophy or in the other religions of the world.[17] Jesus is "him of whom Moses in the Law and also the prophets wrote" (John 1:45).

This type of interpretation is traced back by the Gospel writers to Jesus who understood Himself to be the fulfillment of the Old Testament expectation (Matt. 5:17; cf. Luke 24:44). When preaching at Nazareth from a text from Isaiah, he affirmed, "Today this scripture has been fulfilled in your hearing" (Luke 4:21). He repeatedly insisted that Scripture must be fulfilled (Matt. 26:54). He reminded His opponents, "You search the scriptures, because you think that in them you have eternal life; and it is they that testify of me" (John 5:39). He assigned to the prophets a place in the kingdom of God (Luke 13:28; cf. Matt. 8:11, 12). He reminded His disciples that prophets desired to see what they saw (Matt. 13:17; Luke 10:24); He rebuked them for being slow of heart to believe all the prophets had spoken (Luke 24:25), but He found it necessary to interpret to them and to open their minds (v. 45) before they understood. He insisted that the predictive power seen in the proph-

ets continued in His own person: "And now I have told you before it
takes place, so that when it does take place, you may believe" (John
14:29). "But, I have said these things to you, that when their hour
comes you may remember that I told you of them" (John 16:4).

The Book of Acts, the Epistles, and the Gospels continue this
same emphasis upon prophecy. For them the sufferings of Christ and
the glory to follow is the major theme—though not the only one—of
prophecy. In a real sense the church was built upon the foundation
of the apostles and prophets (Eph. 2:20). In his early sermons Peter,
when summarizing the career of Jesus, affirmed: "What God foretold
by the mouth of all the prophets, that his Christ must suffer, he thus
fulfilled" (Acts 3:18). "To him all the prophets bear witness, that
every one who believes in him receives remission of sins through his
name" (Acts 10:43). "What God promised to the fathers, this he has
fulfilled to us their children by raising Jesus" (Acts 13:32-33). Paul
insisted that the gospel he preached was promised in the prophets
(Rom. 1:2) and had been preached beforehand to Abraham (Gal.
3:8, 9). The promise to Abraham and its fulfillment realized in Christ
(cf. Gal. 3:6—4:7) occupies a major place in the thought of Paul.
According to the account of the Acts, Paul defended himself before
Agrippa by summarizing his preaching as "Saying nothing but what
the prophets and Moses said would come to pass: that the Christ
must suffer, and that, by being the first to rise from the dead, he
would proclaim light both to the people and to the Gentiles" (26:22,
23; cf vv. 6, 7). He insisted that his preaching concerned the hope of
Israel (29:19-20).

The whole case for the apostolic preaching is quite well summarized in the First Epistle of Peter:

> The prophets who prophesied of the grace that was to be yours
> searched and inquired about this salvation; they inquired what
> person or time was indicated by the Spirit of Christ within them
> when predicting the sufferings of Christ and the subsequent
> glory. It was revealed to them that they were serving not them-
> selves but you, in the things which have now been announced to
> you by those who preached the good news to you through the
> Holy Spirit sent from heaven, things into which angels long to
> look (1:10-12).

But not only is there affirmed by New Testament writers that
there was a general preparation through history for the coming of
Christ but also specific details of Jesus' career such as the work of
His forerunner (Matt. 3:1-3; Isa. 40:3), the Virgin Birth (Matt. 1:22,
23), the birth in Bethlehem (Matt. 2:6), the betrayal by a disciple
(Acts 1:16), and the death and resurrection (Acts 2:25, 26, 34, 35)

are the subjects of prophecy.[18] The claim is not absent from any of the Gospels, but in the Gospel of Matthew a main theme is the thirteen-times-repeated appeal that actions were done "to fulfill that which was spoken by the prophet." As far as the apostolic preaching is concerned, not only the career of Jesus, but also the outpouring of the Spirit on the day of Pentecost, the rejection of the gospel by the Jews, and the Gentile mission are "that which was spoken by the prophet" (Acts 2:16; 13:46, 47; 15:15-18; 28:26-28). In short, the church age is also included in the prophetic vision (Acts 3:24).

Thus from the New Testament vantage point, the Old Testament ends with a sense of incompleteness while looking forward beyond itself to a future event. On the other side, it is the concept of promise and fulfillment which gives meaning to what God has accomplished in the coming, the death, the resurrection of Jesus, the subsequent call of the Gentiles, and in the expectation of the Second Coming. This element is so pervasive in the New Testament that it would not be understandable without it. Any Marcion-like effort to cut the church free from its Old Testament preparation must be vigorously resisted.

The Church and Prophecy

The early church fathers accepted the specific claims of fulfilled prophecy found in Biblical writing but also multiplied these claims in ways that no informed person today would attempt to defend. From the time of Justin Martyr the argument from prophecy became the main line of defense of the Christian message. Before Justin's conversion, the old man he met by the sea had introduced Justin to the prophets as he argued:

> There existed, long before this time, certain men more ancient than all those who are esteemed philosophers, both righteous and beloved by God, who spoke by the Divine Spirit, and foretold events which would take place, and which are now taking place. They are called prophets. . . . .For they did not use demonstration in their treatises, seeing that they were witnesses to the truth above all demonstration, and worthy of belief; and those events which have happened and are happening compel you to assent to the utterances made by them, although, indeed, they were entitled to credit on account of the miracles they performed.[19]

Justin himself later argues with his readers:

> We will now offer proof, not trusting mere assertions but being of necessity persuaded by those who prophesied [of Him] before these things came to pass, for with our own eyes we behold

things that have happened and are happening just as they were predicted; and this will, we think, appear even to you the strongest and truest evidence.[20]

> There were, then, among the Jews certain men who were proph-
> ets of God, through whom the prophetic Spirit published before-
> hand things that were to come to pass, ere ever they hap-
> pened. . . . In these books, then, of the prophets we found Jesus
> our Christ foretold as coming, born of a virgin, growing up to
> man's estate, and healing every disease and every sickness, and
> raising the dead, and being hated, and unrecognized, and cruci-
> fied, and dying, rising again, and ascending into heaven, and
> being called, the Son of God. We find it also predicted that
> certain persons should be sent by Him into every nation to
> publish these things, and that rather among the Gentiles [than
> among the Jews] men should believe on Him. And he was
> predicted before He appeared, first 5000 years before, and again
> 3,000, then 2000, and 1000, and yet again 800; for in the
> succession of generations prophets after prophets arose.[21]

As can be seen from the above-given quotations, Justin not only found Messianic elements in the prophets, but also found current happenings, and he postulated his belief in the future advent upon prophecy:

> Since, then, we prove that all things which have already hap-
> pened had been predicted by the prophets before they came to
> pass, we must necessarily believe also that those things which are
> in like manner predicted, but are yet to come to pass, shall
> certainly happen.[22]

The pattern for the church set by Justin continued. All apologists of the Patristic period repeat to some extent Justin's line of thought. One of its most comprehensive statements is found in Augustine's letter to Volusian.

From the preceding material, which might be multiplied at least a hundred fold, it is obvious that the Old Testament, the New Testament, and the traditional church affirms that the prophet can and does predict the future. This even the most radical scholar would not be inclined to deny. Though exception was taken from time to time by some figures to individual items, and though isolated voices were raised against the whole, the argument held sway until the rise of the modern period. As recently as the so-called Christian Evidence Move-ment[23] nearly every book on apologetics had as one of its mainstays, in its argument for both the inspiration of the Bible and for the Messiahship of Jesus, the argument from fulfilled prophecies.

Prophecy and the Modern Scene

Nevertheless, for the past century and a half the impact of this line of apology has been gradually weakened by different influences until today it must be admitted that ordinarily its impact upon the unbeliever—whether Jew or Gentile—is hardly that of the "strongest and truest evidence" of which Justin Martyr spoke. Concerning the validity of the argument from prophecy modern scholarship is sounding a very uncertain—if not completely negative—sound, and in wide circles it is considered to be a liability in the Christian's arsenal rather than an asset.[24] Even its most ardent advocates feel some need to defend it against attack.

First there is a violent, sustained reaction to the overstatement of the case for prophetic foresight made by earlier apologists which resulted in some elements of absurdity. Such an absurdity is to be seen when Barnabas found in the 318 servants of Abraham a prediction of the cross of Christ (*Epistle of Barnabus* 9:8). In the early church fathers, in some modern fundamentalist treatises, and in a sizeable part of current typology one finds a claim for numerous cases of fulfilled prophecies or types not clearly made in the New Testament. These claims are often joined with claims that alleged "unfulfilled prophecies" must yet be fulfilled in the most literal way.

Second, the interpretation of prophecy has lost face because of repeated disillusionment experienced in both Jewish and Christian circles over the speculations of those who make identifications, set dates, and create hopes—all of which prove in time to be fallacious.

Third, there is a widespread acceptance of a world view which objects to the philosophical presuppositions upon which the concept of predictive prophecy is premised. David Hume, in his famous essay "Of Miracles," included prophecy as also offering the same sort of problems to reason as belief in miracles:

> What we have said of miracles may be applied, without any variation, to prophecies; and indeed all prophecies are real miracles and, as such only, can be admitted as proofs of any revelation. If it did not exceed the capacity of human nature to foretell future events, it would be absurd to employ any prophecy as an argument for a divine mission or authority from heaven. So that, upon the whole, we may conclude that the *Christian Religion* not only was at first attended with miracles, but even at this very day cannot be believed by any reasonable person without one.[25]

For the last century and a half, then, those who have stumbled at miracles have also stumbled at prediction. Both affirm that God has intervened in the process of history. The "Doctrine of Uniformity" leaves no place in the universe for either miracles or prediction. On the other side of the picture, the person who holds to the doctrine of miracles is likely also to find little difficulty with the concept of predictive prophecy.

Fourth, there has been a neglect caused in part from reaction to the excesses of the past and in part from yielding ground to or attempting to come to terms with the critical movement. In most circles (Evangelical circles are an exception), interest has shifted from the study of Messianic prediction to other points of emphasis. Though ethical and social teaching and prediction are not really antithetical to each other in the prophets, in recent study it would appear that those who have stressed the ethical and social values in the prophets have tended to that degree to neglect the predictive elements and those who have centered on the predictive elements have tended to overlook the social and ethical values. The prophets have suffered, as scholars have tended to depict them in the scholar's own image. By some they have been made ethical teachers and by others they are social reformers and creators of monotheism. More recently attention has focused on the prophet's relation to the worship (the cult) situation, on the psychology of prophetic inspiration, on the literary form of the prophetic statement, on the transmission of prophetic literature, and on non-Israelite prophecy. Until the relatively recent rebirth of interest in eschatology in the prophets under the impact of comparative Near Eastern studies, one is surprised at how many books treating the prophets give practically no attention to the question of prediction.

Fifth, the force of the argument from prophecy has been further reduced by the continuous, widespread assertion that there are examples of predictions of the prophets which did not come to pass.

Sixth, the general impact of the critical movement with its stress upon "the historical approach" and with its reaction to the apologetic motive has been to focus attention upon the hermeneutical problems underlying New Testament use of Old Testament prophecy. It is agreed that "proof texting," unrestrained allegorization, and the reading of the New Testament back into the Old Testament are not valid methods of exegesis. First in importance in exegesis is consideration of the intent of the writer and of the context of his statement. Prophetic statements must be interpreted against the background out of which they were uttered. While some church fathers insisted that prophecy had no meaning prior to and apart from its fulfillment, the modern presupposition is that the prophecies conveyed a meaning to their primary hearers which is of primary importance. If one accepts the arguments which many Jews and Christians are making that many of the "Messianic" Psalms described the reigning Hebrew kings;[26] that Isaiah may have spoken of a woman of his own day (Isa. 7:14 ff.);[27] that a collective interpretation of the servant concept in Isaiah (cf. Isa. 53) is possible, one must face the problem of the sense in which these passages can be said to be predictive. Added to the above cases are other passages used in the New Testament where, had one read them in their Old Testament context apart from the New Testament application, he would not have been aware that a prediction was being made.

New attention has been focused by the Qumran discoveries on the question of how unintended meanings can be read into the prophets by the interpreter. It has been observed that the Qumran community read foreign meanings into much of the prophetic literature which it used, as well as applying to its own situation several of the same passages appealed to in the New Testament.[28]

Not less significant has been the impact of form criticism. This very popular type of study, centering on the process of transmission of material, focuses attention on the issues: What is the relation between the "prophetic book" and the prophet, between the prophet and his disciples, between the disciples and the book? Decades or even centuries of fluid, oral transmission are postulated. Repeated reworkings and expansions are envisioned.[29] A late date is assumed for significant passages. To what extent then do we have the *ipsissima verba* of the prophet which the argument from prophecy of necessity assumes? From the opposite end of the problem, the form critic finds himself so uncertain of the New Testament history that he is in no position to judge whether a prophecy has been fulfilled or not. He finds himself unable to determine what is fact and what is to be attributed to interpretation of the early church.

All of the above-mentioned trends have focused attention upon the question of whether we are confronted with valid predictions or whether later interpreters have read into the words that which the prophet did not really envision. In the light of all of these developments, R. Bultmann summarizes the situation for predictive prophecy as he sees it:

> To talk of this kind of prophecy and fulfillment has become impossible in an age in which the Old Testament is conceived of as a historical document and interpreted according to the method of historical science.[30]

The Task Ahead of Us

Modern theology on prophecy, as on many other questions, is involved in a continuous tension between the two poles: "What does the Bible teach?" and "What can I believe?" As we have seen, the teaching of the Bible on the matter of predictive prophecy is crystal clear; hence it is with the second of these poles and in particular in connection with hermeneutics that the chief issues lie.

The traditional stacking up of alleged cases and verses which is seen in the average apologetic treatment of prophecy does not meet the argument which questions the presuppositions on which the whole case rests. While edifying the believer, the multiplying of cases does not prove convincing to the man standing on the outside. It is the need of the present to come to grips with the main issues and to show how prophecy can be convincing to the man who does not have a prior commitment to the inspiration of the Bible and to the New Testament interpretation of Old Testament prophecy. A task of such magnitude cannot be accomplished within the scope of one brief chapter but calls for the combined efforts of many scholars covering many fields. As the issues are complex, so also the dealing with them must be complex. Nevertheless, the following may point to some avenues of approach:

1. Questions arising from absurdities and excesses, whether on the part of ancient or modern practitioners, may be quickly dealt with. Excesses, absurdities, and abuses disgust and blind the unlearned, indiscriminate student, but they do not negate the claim of the Bible that the prophets predicted the future. As with finance, medicine, or any other area of activity, the mistaken, the quacks, and the counterfeits make us cautious; they show the need for restraint; but they do not lessen the value of the genuine article. In particular, it would seem that the continuous record of failure of those exegetes who have claimed to be able to unravel the secrets of the future from prophetic and apocalpytic statements should be a deterrent to such activity. The argument from prophecy, however, should be considered apart from the cloud of these mistaken activities, for no intellectual discipline is free from a history of mistaken practitioners. The scholar who affirms a validity in prediction is not at all obligated to defend every item for which a claim has been made through the centuries.

2. Neglect can only be cured by a reaffirmation of the validity of prophecy on the part of Bible believers which boldly presents the advantages of its case in the face of the less desirable alternatives offered by the modern world. As we have seen, the predictive element in prophecy is indeed a significant one. Books that purport to be summaries of prophetic thought but which concentrate solely on the moral and social aspects of prophecy should be recognized as arbitrary distortions of the prophetic movement. We have been silent too long about the type of Biblical scholarship that instead of expounding the prophets, purges them of distasteful elements, reconstructs them, and, in so doing, distorts them.

3. The allegation that there are prophecies that have failed, if thoroughly dealt with, would require volumes in itself. On the whole, the cases deal with the fates of nations rather than with the Messianic hope upon which we have centered in this study. Every traceable prophet from the eighth to the sixth century has a great deal to say about the nations.[31] Each of the alleged cases of failure in these predictions which have been under discussion for centuries must be evaluated upon its own merits. Chief among them are the prophecies on Tyre. Ezekiel in one of his passages predicts its capture by Nebuchadnezzar (26:7), yet in another he represents Nebuchadnezzar as having labored hard against Tyre but without getting any wages for it, on which account Egypt was to be given to him for a prey (29:17 ff.). Many scholars have repeatedly pointed out that the stress here is in reality not upon the failure of the earlier prediction as some allege, but is upon the lack of recompense to the king of Babylon in taking the city because of the smallness of the treasure he found in it.[32] Evidence in favor of the capture of the city is a cuneiform tablet which includes the king of Tyre among Babylonian officials and also a business document that mentions the Babylonian commissioner of Tyre.[33] A second notable case is that of the prediction of the invasion of Egypt alluded to above (cf. Jer. 46:13, 14). We have very little non-Biblical information bearing on a possible invasion of Egypt by Nebuchadnezzar, but a fragmentary text may imply such an invasion, and, although we are perplexed at the lack of other positive evidence, there is no contrary evidence. We still know the history of the Middle East only "in part."

There are some factors in the nature of Hebrew prophecy which should be thoroughly considered before a charge of failure is accepted. A prophecy is not a decree that must be fulfilled like an edict of fate. Both the promises and the threats of the prophets are conditional. God has reserved to Himself the right to withdraw either promised weal or woe should the behavior of the people merit such a change (Jer. 18:5-10). He did not maintain the house of Eli forever despite His promise to do so (I Sam. 2:30). He did not destroy Nineveh for Nineveh repented at the preaching of Jonah (3:4-10). God relented from threats of locust and fire at the pleading of Amos (7:1-6). He repented of the evil He threatened in the days of Hezekiah at the time when Micah said that Zion would be plowed like a field (3:12; cf. Jer. 26:18-19). Furthermore, the carrying out of a threat may be delayed when in the face of it man repents or prays as was the punishment threatened Ahab (I Kings 21:29) and the imminent approach of Hezekiah's death (Isa. 38:1-6).

In interpreting prophecy, allowance must be made for the use of various figures of speech, of parable, of fable, and of allegory on the part of the prophet; and allowance must be made for spiritualization in interpretation as can be seen in the use of prophecy both in the Old Testament and in the New Testament. The language of poetry (e.g. Isa. 40:4; 35:1 ff.) is not to be literally fulfilled. A. C. Gaebelein's dictum: "The literal fulfillment of prophecies in the past vouches for the literal fulfillment of every prophecy in the Word of God"[34] is not a sound principle for dealing with prophecies and neither he nor any other informed person would consistently insist on a strict literal interpretation of all prophecy. A mass of Biblical uses of prophecy can only be classified as figurative. For example, the expectation of Elijah, fulfilled in John the Baptist (Matt. 11:10-15), cannot be called literal. The bone of contention between different interpreters is merely that of distinguishing between degrees of literalness and of figurativeness. All of these factors should make one slow either to affirm or to accept the charge that a prophecy has failed.

4. The difficulties raised by the Form Critics are more formidable. But even these are less so when the degree of subjectivity and conjecture involved in this type of study is centered upon. It is perfectly legitimate to classify material according to its literary pattern; but to create an imaginary background out of data in a passage and then to conclude that the passage indeed arose out of or was preserved in that background because it fits it, is not very convincing to those who have not previously accepted the presuppositions of this type of procedure. A more fertile imagination may create an alternate but more convincing background. Hence a distinction is to be made between the vogue of this type of study and a demonstration of the validity of certain of its presuppositions and conclusions.

Mowinckel's dictum[35] —that the preservation and editing of prophetic materials by schools of disciples of the prophets is established by the existence of a Second Isaiah—begs the question and convinces only those who had previously accepted the theory of a Second Isaiah. It will take more convincing evidence to really establish the preservation history of the prophetic material which he is expounding.

5. We have already implied that the hermeneutical problem is the major one to be faced. There are those like A. Richardson[36] and B. Anderson[37] who in the face of it are ready to turn their backs upon specific prophecies while attempting to hold on to a general preparation in the Old Testament for the coming of Christ. Jesus' manner of using the Old Testament (and that of the New Testament writers also, for there is no essential difference in method) is attributed either to His having adapted Himself to views held by other men of

the first century or to His having emptied Himself of His divine knowledge so that their views were His (in the case of the New Testament writers, it is assumed that their guidance did not deliver them from the limited views of the day). While both of these positions may contain partial truths—that is, Jesus made *ad hominem* arguments, and He admitted limitations in knowledge on some topics—either of them as they are stated carries with it equally undesirable consequences. The first (often called the Adaptation Hypothesis) leaves Jesus in the position of being a deceiver. He knew He was in error, but nevertheless He went along with the views of the time. The fact is that Jesus proved Himself perfectly capable of upsetting popular ideas like those of the nature of Messiahship, of the following of tradition, and others, when He saw the need to do so (cf. Matt. 5:21 ff.).[38]

The second position (known as the *kenotic* hypothesis) leaves the advocate engulfed in subjectivism when he attempts to decide what is valid in Jesus' teaching. It is clear that Jesus understood every important point of His career in terms of fulfillment of prophecy (John 5:39-47; Matt. 22:43-44). If He was in error in His understanding of the heart of His entire mission on earth, then how is He to be trusted in other matters in the moral and religious realms upon which He spoke? To this point the champions of the *kenotic* view have offered no satisfactory exit from this dilemma, nor can they offer one.[39] The consistent logical alternative to acceptance of Jesus' testimony is a complete rejection of His claims rather than the subjectivism of the contention that there was a vague undefined preparation for His coming through the Old Testament. This *kenotic* position is a last ditch stand to keep from abandoning the case altogether.

A more fruitful approach to the hermeneutic question is to consider the variety of ways in which Old Testament material is used in New Testament writers. We first are confronted with a number of passages that are traditionally Messianic but which are not appealed to in the New Testament at all, such as: the seed of woman as pointing to the Virgin Birth (Gen. 3:15); the vision of peace (Isa. 2:1 ff.); the pierced hands (Zech. 13:6—KJV); and others. Indeed it is striking how many possibilities (even involving details of key sections such as Isaiah 54 and Psalm 16) were passed over by New Testament writers. The modern apologist would also be well advised to avoid the traps into which the church fathers fell which led them to unjustifiable excesses. The more prudent path is to follow the example of restraint set in the New Testament.

But among those passages used by New Testament writers, not all appeals to prophecy consider them as predictive of specific events.

"Fulfilled," "This is that which was spoken," or other formulas have wider connotation than some have been willing to grant:

1. There are some passages from the prophets that describe a situation that could arise many times. An example of such is the warning against unbelief (Acts 13:41; 28:25-27).

2. There is a typology in prophecy as Paul himself declared: "These things happen to them typically (*typikos*) and are written for our admonition upon whom the ends of the ages are come (I Cor. 10:11; cf. John 6:49 ff.).[40] The deliverance from Egypt (Matt. 2:15), the weeping of Rachel (Matt. 2:18), and perhaps even the virgin passage (Matt. 1:23) fall in this category as well as do some episodes in which there is not a direct citation of a passage.

3. There is an allegorical interpretation of an Old Testament episode (Gal. 4:21 ff.); however, this should not be thought to justify an unrestrained allegorical hermeneutic.

4. There is definitely a process of spiritualizing which involves such items as the seed promised to Abraham (Gal. 3:16) and the entire community of the Israel of God (Gal. 6:16).

5. There are some cases in which we are less certain what passage is in mind as in "He shall be called a Nazarene" (Matt. 2:23), "Eye hath not seen..." (I Cor. 2:9), and others. There are passages in which we cannot be dogmatic about the sense in which the Old Testament is being used.

6. There are also those passages, more or less obvious, which both Jews and Christians—though they debate over the specific import—have agreed are Messianic in reference: The messenger who is the forerunner (Mal. 3:1); the birth of the Messiah in Bethlehem (Micah 5:2); the entry into Jerusalem on an ass (Zech. 9:9).[41]

These various uses of the prophets vary in cogency for convincing the unbeliever. It is the more obvious usages of prophetic material rather than the allegorical ones that are the more likely to carry conviction to him.

The New Testament hermeneutic has tensions with that which is most widely called scientific today. The latter demands that the Bible be interpreted as any other book would be interpreted. If prophecy has value, this demand would seem to be a spurious one. Already with the affirmation of any sort of typology we have moved beyond the canons of hermeneutics used in ordinary literature.[42] To deal with the question, some Catholic scholars are postulating a *sensus plenior* (a fuller meaning) in Scripture which is defined as a sense intended by God but not necessarily intended by the speaker.[43] It is the unfinished task of Biblical scholarship to show the inadequacies of the current hermeneutics and to demonstrate to the modern man the values in Scripture usage as first century teachers did for their contemporaries.

In the area of hermeneutics the stumbling block of the cross still remains a major point of division between Jew and Christian, each of whom claims to revere the prophets. The Jew insists, as he always has, that materialistic, nationalistic, and martial motifs in the prophets are normative where the Messiah is concerned,[44] while the Christian modifies these in favor of the picture from Isaiah of the Suffering Servant and the Prince of Peace. He transfers the martial elements from the physical realm to the spiritual. As a justification for the reinterpretation, the Christian claims no lesser authority than that of his Savior who withdrew when they tried by force to make Him a king and who said, "My kingdom is not of this world" (John 18:33-36).

The Claims of Jesus Compared with Others

Under no system of dating can the predictions of the prophets be postdated beyond the end of the Old Testament period. With the Dead Sea Scrolls we have copies or fragments that antedate the rise of Christianity for all the prophetic books. While it is obvious that all of the hermeneutic questions concerning the use of prophecy have not been solved, the force of the general argument is greatest when we ask where the hopes of the prophets are realized. The three alternatives are: (1) Either the hopes have failed, (2) they have already been or are being realized (this alternative does not exclude the possibility that some aspects of the program are being fulfilled and some aspects are yet in the future), or (3) they are yet to be realized. Some champions of each of the alternatives could be found in the modern world.

It is the claim of the Christian movement that it itself is the culmination of these hopes—that it is the Israel of God (Gal. 6:16)—and with H. H. Rowley we must say, "either these hopes were fulfilled in Christ or they have not been fulfilled at all and are not now likely to be."[45] Buddhism has its revered teacher Gautama, but Gautama does not correspond to the hopes of the Hebrew prophets. Not only so, but the life and work of Gautama did not respond to other hopes and promises which long antedated his time in any way comparable to the claims made for Jesus.[45] Mohammedanism claims a background in the Old Testament; but while Mohammed claims to be in the line of prophets, he makes no claims of being him of whom prophets had foretold, and his program of conquest with the sword is quite foreign to the prophetic hope.

First-century Judaism is the matrix out of which Christianity—

whose hope is the Old Testament hope—developed. Modern Judaism subscribes to the ethical and social ideals of the prophets, but is hardly the realization of their future hopes. The prophets would be completely intelligible without post-Biblical Judaism. History has negated the expectations of the Qumran community and of the multitude of Messianic pretenders who have arisen within Judaism from time to time, and the Jewish community itself has turned its back on them. Liberal Judaism, no longer looking for a Messianic figure, leans toward a collective messianic mission of the Jewish people. Many Zionists apply to the Zionist state suggestive phrases from the Messianic passages of the prophets, but many Orthodox Jews reject this identification as lacking the essential elements of the prophetic picture.[47] Orthodox Judaism which projects the Messianic hope into the future[48] is confronted with the insuperable problem of how the Messiah, even if He appeared, could authenticate His claim of descent from David. Judaism has given the world neither another scion of David nor a condition in which every race would worship the God of Israel and would know His law (Isa. 2:1-4; Mic. 4:1-3). Judaism has been unwilling to move into a realization of the dreams which were given the world through the Old Testament.[49]

As Rowley has so well argued, "Jesus was born a Jew because the whole history of Israel was a preparation for him, and because the religion of Judaism alone provided the inheritance he needed." [50] Jesus believed that His death would have the unique power that the death of the servant in Isaiah was expected to have and time has vindicated that belief. The cross has had precisely the anticipated effect which the sufferings of the servant should have.[51] The remnant of Israel resulting therefrom as "a light to the nations" (cf. Isa. 49:6) has spread the knowledge of the one true God by spoken word, by distribution of Scripture, and by printed page in a way that the Jews alone never did.[52] In the motif of anticipation and fulfillment, the Biblical revelation is not to be paralleled in other religions of the world. Here then is to be found a part of the indication that God has been active on the scene of history. Its best defense is to be found in its proclamation that it may become effective in the lives of those yet in darkness.

It should be recognized that the argument from prophecy is not and never has been of such compelling force that its logic could not be denied by unbelievers. The prophets, themselves, despite the succession of their predecessors, were confronted with unbelievers who taunted them to let God do what they threatened before they spoke of it (cf. Isa. 5:19; Ezek. 12:21 ff.). Jesus was confronted with a generation who thought themselves loyal to the prophets, but who did not recognize the correspondence between His career and the expectations of the prophets (cf. John 12:37-41). Even His disciples were unable to grasp some aspects of the Messianic career until Jesus opened their minds to understand the Scriptures and explained their import (Luke 24:44-47). When asked if he understood what he was reading, the Ethiopian could only reply, "How can I unless someone guides me? . . . Does the prophet say this about himself or about someone else?" (Acts 8:31, 34). All of these cases point to the simple fact that to one having learned the gospel and having become a Christian the prophetic preparation for the gospel becomes much clearer than it is to the man who is on the outside. As Paul said about reading Moses, "the veil remains unlifted, because only through Christ is it taken away" (II Cor. 3:14). Consequently, one convinced of the validity of prophecy need not be embarrassed to proclaim its message, though all men have not yet come to an agreement that it has a validity.

1. *Critical and Exegetical Commentary on the Book of Daniel* (Oxford: Oxford University Press, 1929), p. xxvi; cf. T. J. Meek, *Hebrew Origins* (New York: Harper, 1950), pp. 150-151.
2. S. Mowinckel, *He That Cometh*, trans. G. W. Anderson (New York: Abingdon, 1954), 528 pp.; H. Ringgren, *The Messiah in the Old Testament* (Chicago: Allenson, 1956), 71 pp.; A. Bentzen, *King and Messiah* (London: Lutterworth, 1955), 118 pp.; J. Klausner, *The Messianic Idea in Israel From Its Beginning to the Completion of the Mishna*, trans. W. F. Stinespring (New York: Macmillan, 1955), 523 pp.; A. H. Silver, *A History of Messianic Speculation in Israel From the First Through the Seventeenth Centuries* (New York: Macmillan, 1927), 268 pp.; Paul Heinisch, *Christ in Prophecy*, trans. W. G. Heidt (Collegeville, Minn.: Liturgical Press, 1956), 279 pp.
3. "The Interpretation of the Old Testament: III. Promise and Fulfillment," *Interpretation*, XV (1961), 320.
4. *The Servant of the Lord* (London: Lutterworth, 1952), p. 126, n. 2; cf. *The Relevance of the Bible* (New York: Macmillan, 1953), p. 63; and G. von Rad, *Old Testament Theology* (New York: Harper, 1965), II, 45.
5. "Prophecy," *The London Quarterly and Holborn Review*, CLXXXIV (Jan., 1959), 37.
6. It is not the intent of Butler's assertion: "Prophecy is nothing but the history of events before they come to pass" to imply that you could write the history of the world or the story of the career of Jesus from the predictions of the prophets alone as the context of his statement shows, see G. R. Crooks, editor, *Bishop Butler's Analogy of Religion* (New York: Harper and Brothers, 1854), Pt. II, ch. 7, p. 289.
7. Rowley, *The Servant of the Lord*, p. 125.
8. B. Ramm, *Protestant Christian Evidences* (Chicago: Moody, 1953), pp. 81-124; R. D. Culver, "Were the Old Testament Prophecies Really Prophetic?" *Can I Trust My Bible?* (Chicago: Moody, 1963), pp. 91-116.
9. Zimmerli, *op. cit.*, pp. 316 ff.
10. *Prophets in Perspective* (New York: Abingdon, 1962), p. 108.

11. *Literary and Psychological Aspects of the Hebrew Prophets* (Uppsala: Uppsala Universitets Arsskrift, 1948), p. 90.
12. *Studies in Deuteronomy,* D. Stalker tr. (Chicago: Regenery, 1953), pp. 84 ff.
13. *Op. cit.,* p. 317.
14. Cf. Tobit 2:6; G. F. Moore, *Judaism* (Cambridge: Harvard University Press, 1927), II, 323 ff.
15. *The Apostolic Preaching* (London: Hodder & Stoughton, 1944), pp. 15, 17; cf. W. Vischer, *The Witness of the Old Testament to Christ,* trans. A. B. Crabtree (London: Lutterworth, 1949), p. 27.
16. Dodd, *op. cit.,* p. 21 ff.; cf. O. Cullmann, *Christ and Time* (Philadelphia: Westminster, 1950), 253 pp.
17. J. L. McKenzie, "The Significance of the Old Testament for Christian Faith in Roman Catholicism," *The Old Testament and Christian Faith,* ed. B. Anderson (New York: Harper & Row, 1963), p. 110.
18. See the summaries by S. M. Smith, "New Testament Writers Use the Old Testament," *Encounter,* XXVI (1965), 239-250; R. L. Honeycutt, Jr., "The Unity and Witness of Scripture," *Foundations,* VIII (1965), 292-311; and G. Friedrich, "Prophets and Prophecies in the New Testament," *T.W.N.T.,* VI, 833.
19. *Dialogue with Trypho* 7 (*A.N.F.* I, 198).
20. *Apology* i, 30 (*A.N.F.* I, 172-173).
21. Ibid., i, 31 (*A.N.F.* I, 173).
22. Ibid., i, 52 (*A.N.F.* I, 180).
23. J. O. Filbeck, *The Christian Evidence Movement* (Kansas City: Old Paths Book Club, 1946), 216 pp.
24. A thoroughgoing challenge to the argument from prophecy is to be found in K. Fullerton, *Prophecy and Authority* (New York: Macmillan, 1919), 214 pp.
25. *The Harvard Classics,* ed. Charles W. Elliot (New York: Collier & Son, 1910), XXXVII, 414-415.
26. S. Mowinkel, *The Psalms in Israel's Worship* (New York: Abingdon, 1962), I, 48 f.
27. Whether the woman is the mother of Hezekiah as Trypho argued in the second century, or Isaiah's wife as some modern scholars argue, or just any woman of the period is a matter of irrelevance to the case. See Smith, *op. cit.,* pp. 247-248.
28. See the study of F. F. Bruce, *Biblical Exegesis in the Qumran Texts* (The Hague: Uitgeverij van Keulen, 1959), 82 pp.
29. G. von Rad, *Old Testament Theology,* II, 46-48.
30. "Prophecy and Fulfillment," *Essays on Old Testament Hermeneutics,* ed. C. Westermann (Richmond: John Knox Press, 1963), p. 52.
31. E. G. Wright, "The Nations in Hebrew Prophecy," *Encounter,* XXVI (1965), 231.
32. P. Fairbairn, *The Interpretation of Prophecy* (2nd ed., London, 1865; Banner of Truth Trust Reprint, 1964), p. 217; and N. Gottwald, *All the Kingdoms of the Earth* (New York: Harper & Row, 1964), p. 313.
33. E. Unger, "Nebukadnezar II und sein Sandabakku (Oberkommisar) in Tyrus," *ZAW.,* XLIV (1926), 314-317.
34. "Fulfilled Prophecy: A Potent Argument for the Bible," *The Fundamentals for Today,* ed. C. L. Feinberg (Grand Rapids: Kregel, 1958), p. 190.
35. *He That Cometh,* pp. 16, 129
36. *Christian Apologetics* (New York: Harper & Brothers, 1947), p. 179.
37. *Rediscovering the Old Testament* (New York: Association Press, 1951), p. 168.

38. J. D. N. Anderson, "Christ and the Scriptures," in *The Word of God and Fundamentalism* (London: Church Book Room Press, 1961), pp. 54-55.

39. See D. M. Baillie, *God Was in Christ* (New York: Scribner, 1948), pp. 94-97; J. I. Packer, *"Fundamentalism" and the Word of God* (London: Intervarsity Fellowship, 1958), pp. 59-60; R. V. G. Tasker, *The Old Testament in the New Testament* (Grand Rapids: Eerdmans, 1963), p. 37.

40. The translation is from Tasker, *op. cit.*, p. 63.

41. See the studies of J. Brierre-Narbonne, *Les Propheties Messianiques de l'ancien testament dans la littérature Juive* (Paris: Librairie Orientaliste Paul Geuthner, 1933), p. 83, and S. L. Edgar, "New Testament and Rabbinic Messianic Interpretation," *New Testament Studies*, V (1958-59), 47-54.

42. See G. W. H. Lampe and K. J. Woollcombe, *Essays on Typology* (London: SCM, 1957), 80 pp.

43. See R. E. Brown, "The Sensus Plenior in the Past Ten Years," *Catholic Biblical Quarterly*, XXV (1963), 262-285.

44. S. Sandmel, *We Jews and Jesus* (New York: Oxford University Press, 1965), 163 pp.

45. *From Moses to Qumran* (London: Lutterworth Press, 1963), p. 22. Cf. A. G. Hebert, *The Authority of the Old Testament* (London: Farber, 1947), p. 238.

46. Rowley, *From Moses to Qumran*, p. 29.

47. G. A. F. Knight, ed., *Jews and Christians: Preparation for Dialogue* (Philadelphia: Westminster, 1965), p. 65.

48. See J. H. Greenstone, *The Messiah Idea in Jewish History* (Philadelphia: The Jewish Publication Society of America, 1906), 347 pp.

49. See H. H. Rowley, *The Missionary Message of the Old Testament* (London: Carey Kingsgate, 1944), pp. 79-80.

50. *The Relevance of the Bible* (New York: Macmillan, 1953), p. 79.

51. Rowley, *From Moses to Qumran*, pp. 25-26.

52. Ibid., p. 27.

⑨

THE INSPIRATION OF THE SCRIPTURES

Frank Pack

This subject takes us immediately to the heart of the authority of the book we know as the Bible and its uniqueness among all the books of the world. Why can the Bible be called truly The Book? What gives it such a profound place in the history of man, in the experience of the faithful believer, in our own personal lives from day to day? Whatever may be said of its beautiful language, its literary qualities, and its many styles of writing, its uniqueness and power do not lie here. Rather its power as the Living Word that transforms and shapes men's lives lies in the fact that it is a book that claims to have been inspired by God and brings God's Word as its message for each one of us, laying us under its demand and judging our lives. This claim is made simply in the language of Paul in II Timothy 3:16, "All scripture is inspired of God."

The expression "inspired of God" translates a Greek word *theopneustos,* which literally means "God-breathed." Our English word "inspired" and its noun form "inspiration" come from the Latin *inspirare* meaning "to breathe into." Thus when Paul says, "All scripture is inspired of God," he is asserting that all Scripture is an expression of God's Spirit, that God's Spirit is in Scripture as my breath and my spirit are in my words. As my words reveal and communicate to you the thoughts of my mind, so the things of God are made known to men through the words of the God-inspired Scriptures.

What a mighty claim this is! How dramatically it confronts rebellious and sinful man, so often proud in the discovery of his own ways, and so often heedless of the light and direction that come from God.

In studying this theme, we need to have the same honesty and

175

desire for truth that we would in the study of any Biblical theme. We need to lay aside preconceived ideas that may be in our mind and allow the Biblical witness to speak to us fully and completely, approaching this testimony honestly. This is a difficult thing to do, because in this modern age the inspiration of the Bible has been treated so emotionally pro and con. Those who have opposed the traditional position of the Bible's inspiration have spoken derogatorily of the erection of "a paper pope." They have set up a straw man in speaking of "verbal dictation." They declare that this position looks upon God as a boss who dictates His word to the writers as though they were secretaries.

On the other hand, those who have defended the traditional point of view have oftentimes found themselves swept away by a kind of hysteria that has made them claim more for the Scriptures than the Scriptures claim for themselves. There have been times in church history when the pointing of the Hebrew text was claimed to have been divinely inspired, and translations of the Bible had claims of inspiration advanced in their behalf.

It seems to me that the only way believers in the Bible can approach this subject is the same way in which we have endeavored to approach any other subject connected with the Christian faith. First, we must study the claims that the Bible makes for itself. What do the writers claim directly or indirectly about their inspiration? Second, we must study carefully the phenomena of the Scriptures to understand the nature of that guidance from God that is called inspiration.

When we raise the question, "What does the Bible claim for itself?" the cry arises that this is an illegitimate quest. The Scriptures ought not to be appealed to for their own vindication, it is said. Yet in all fairness it seems that a witness should be allowed to give his own testimony, to make his own claims, and set forth his defense. This is recognized as a right in any court of law. We see how this same objection was made during the ministry of our Lord Jesus Christ to the self-testimony He gave. While He introduced other witnesses He Himself recognized the fact, "Even if I bear witness of myself, my testimony is true, for I know whence I have come and whither I am going, but you do not know whence I come or whither I am going" (John 8:14, cf. 5:31). The divine Son of God could not have a higher witness than the testimony that He gave to Himself because of His origin. Likewise the Bible itself makes certain claims that must be heard, and because the Bible claims to be the Word of God, it has the self-authenticating and verifying value that makes it right for us to look at its own testimony.

Some Basic Texts

We can best begin our investigation of the Bible's teaching on inspiration by looking at a group of basic texts on this subject. In beginning the Epistle to the Hebrews the writer states, "In many and various ways God spoke of old to our fathers by the prophets, but in these last days he has spoken to us by a Son, whom he appointed the heir of all things, through whom also he created the world" (Heb. 1:1, 2).[1] This passage of Scripture makes the fundamental declaration that God has spoken to man. He spoke in many and various ways to those of old through His prophets, who were His messengers to bring His unfolding will. He did not give His last and full word to any one of these prophets nor to them collectively. It also tells us that He has climaxed this by speaking unto us today through a Son, the heir of all things in this universe as well as the Son through whom He created all things, by whom He upholds all things, and through whom He redeems a lost and tragically misguided world.

God is depicted upon the pages of the Bible as a God who mightily *acts* to carry out His purposes in the universe and in the affairs of men. But He also *speaks* to man that man may understand His actions and may discern His purposes and yield himself to the purposes of the Almighty. God has acted in events of human history and has told men what these events mean. This passage also tells us that God has spoken through men using them as His messengers and supremely through that man Jesus who is called the Christ and is here called a Son. In Jesus Christ God spoke through His mighty deeds and through His words of teaching given with authority. He also spoke through His death upon the cross and His resurrection from the grave. He spoke through the Spirit-guided apostles who received their commission and their power from the Lord Himself. It was the risen Christ who said, "All authority in heaven and on earth has been given to me" (Matt. 28:18).

The writer of Hebrews further declares that this great salvation was first declared by the Lord Himself and was confirmed or attested to us by those who heard Him. God's witness was added to their testimony through the signs and wonders and mighty miracles that were worked through the Holy Spirit. (Heb. 2:3, 4). Thus in both the Old Covenant and the New Covenant God has spoken, to the fathers through the Old by the words of the prophets, and to us through the New by a Son whose words and deeds have been attested by God through those who heard and who were with Him.

Paul in writing to Timothy declares, "All scripture is inspired by God and profitable for teaching, for reproof, for correction, and for training in righteousness, that the man of God may be complete, equipped for every good work," (II Tim. 3:16, 17). While this passage has primary reference to the Old Testament Scriptures, it expresses a general principle that is applicable to the other Scriptures, including the writings of Paul (see II Peter 3:16). For through the Old Testament comes the testimony pointing to Christ and thus it can instruct one for salvation through faith in Christ. (II Tim. 3:15). These writings are profitable for teaching, for reproof, for correction, and for training that makes the man of God complete because they are inspired by God.

One notices immediately that this passage is speaking of the product or end result, which is the Scripture or the writing. The very nature of the authority of the Bible is bound up with the fact that it is the Word of God. This is why the New Testament can say "the word of God is living and active" (Heb. 4:12). It is God's Spirit that has produced the writing and it is God's authority that is back of the message.

The meaning of inspiration is enlarged to include the human persons who produced the writing in II Peter 1:20, 21. Peter declares, "First of all you must understand this, that no prophecy of scripture is a matter of one's own interpretation, because no prophecy ever came by the impulse of man, but men moved by the Holy Spirit spoke from God." Peter asserts that just as he and the other apostles had not followed "cleverly devised myths" in declaring the great events of the gospel, neither did the prophecies of the Old Testament come out of the private interpretations and guesses of the prophet. He is not writing here concerning the right and responsibility of each individual to read and properly interpret the Bible for himself. Throughout the Scriptures and in the practice of both the Jewish synagogue and the early church this responsibility was taken for granted, as can be abundantly shown.

Peter is discussing the origin of prophecy and refutes the notion that the prophet was giving his own private interpretation when he was foretelling the great events to which the gospel bears witness. No prophecy "ever came by the impulse of man," for it has a higher source than this. "Men moved by the Holy Spirit spoke from God," which emphasizes the fact that these were inspired men. They were borne along by the power of God's Holy Spirit as a sailboat with its sails filled might be borne along by the power of the wind. This is actually the figure Peter is using to illustrate what inspiration meant for these men. They were divinely filled to speak what they spoke "from God." Not only are the writings inspired but the men who spoke God's message and wrote these prophecies were inspired.

To understand how authoritative their message is we recall a statement made by Jesus in a discussion he had with his critics in

John 10:35. His argument turned upon a quotation from the Psalms, saying, "and the scripture cannot be broken." The Scripture's validity cannot be impeached. This principle is not confined to the Old Testament writers, for we hear the testimony of Paul concerning the authority of what he delivered in his preaching. In I Corinthians 2:6-13 he describes a wisdom from above that is greater than the wisdom of the world. It involves things beyond what eye has seen or ear heard or even the heart has imagined, for it is what God "has prepared for those who love Him." In other words, it involves the purposes of God. Paul then tells how we know about these things. "No one comprehends the thoughts of God except the Spirit of God. Now we have received, not the spirit of the world, but the Spirit which is from God, that we might understand the gifts bestowed on us by God. And we impart this in words not taught by human wisdom but taught by the Spirit, interpreting spiritual truths to those who possess the Spirit" (I Cor. 2:12, 13).

This passage shows us that the revelation of God's will to Paul extended all the way to the words that the Spirit taught him to use. The words were the vessels that would convey the spiritual truths God wanted men to have. Verbal inspiration or word inspiration simply means language inspiration, first oral and then written, so that truth from God might be conveyed. These words spoken through men are written by them in real historical situations and form the text through which God speaks to us and makes known to us His mighty acts and the significance of those acts in His plan of redemption.

In the upper room on the night in which He was betrayed Jesus discoursed intimately with His disciples and promised them as another "Counselor," the Spirit of truth would guide and direct them in making known His will (John 14:16, 17). The Holy Spirit would bring to their memories what He had taught them, in addition to revealing the things that they needed to know (John 14:26). He would take the things of God and Christ and make those known to them and show them the things that were to come (John 16:12-15). His activity was not simply to be limited to times of persecution and trial, although He was promised in a special way to take away their fear and terror when they would come to trial and hardship (Matt. 10:20)

Jesus promised further guidance and direction from the Holy Spirit in their teaching concerning His ministry, His glory, and His resurrection, after He was gone. He wanted an authentic and authoritative record of His ministry and teaching to be preserved. Through this word, first given orally and then inscripturated in the New Testament the Christ in all His authority confronts men. "So then faith comes from what is heard, and what is heard comes by the preaching of Christ" (Rom. 10:17).

Some More Specific Claims

Let us now turn our attention from the general to the more specific claims of inspiration. In amount, the evidence is amazing as we look at the Bible's claims in both the Old and New Testaments. Four terms in the Hebrew Old Testament occur very often in one form or another to describe the claim that God is speaking to the prophet, or the king or the priest for His people. These are found in the statements, "the word of the Lord," "thus saith the Lord," "the word of God," and "thus speaks the Lord." The number of times in which these expressions occur is staggering, as the consultation of any concordance or Bible handbook will show. For instance, each one of the twelve prophets beginning with Hosea starts his prophecy with the expression, "The word of the Lord came to . . . ." The Law is filled with the claim of the "Thus saith the Lord."

In addition, the Old Testament is spoken of as "the scriptures" in a number of places in the New Covenant and these writings are considered authoritative. The expression "it is written" occurs again and again to give foundation to action, as in the case when Jesus made use of it as the shield in His temptations (Matt. 4; Luke 4). Our Lord made a sharp distinction between the commandment of God and the traditions of men that broke that commandment in meeting the criticism of the Pharisees about eating with unwashed hands (Matt. 15:9; Mark 7:13). He pointed out the error of the Sadducees in failing to know the Scriptures or the power of God. (Matt. 22:29).

It is very interesting to see how Jesus made use of the scriptures in His controversies. In meeting His critics during the last week of His ministry He asked, "How is it then that David, inspired by the Spirit calls him Lord, saying, 'The Lord said unto my Lord, Sit at my right hand, till I put thy enemies under thy feet'?" (Matt. 22:43, 44; Mark 12:35, 36). To His disciples He gave these words, "These are my words which I spoke to you, while I was still with you, that everything written about me in the law of Moses and the prophets and the Psalms must be fulfilled" (Luke 24:44). This covers the whole extent of the Hebrew scriptures in its three divisions of Law, Prophets, and Writings of which the Psalms is the chief representative. In the expression "from the blood of innocent Abel to the blood of Zechariah the son of Barachiah" we have a reference to Genesis at the beginning and II Chronicles which is the last book of the Hebrew Scriptures, just as we might think of Genesis through

Revelation (Matt. 23:35). Jesus showed the key to the Old Testament in saying, "You search the scriptures because you think that in them you have eternal life; and it is they that bear witness to me; yet you refuse to come to me that you may have life" (John 5:39, 40). At the same time Jesus declared the eternal character of His teaching to His apostles by saying, "Heaven and earth will pass away, but my words will not pass away" (Mark 13:31).

As we turn further in the New Testament we recall that Paul commends the Thessalonians for receiving his teaching "not as the word of men but as what it really is, the word of God, which is at work in you believers" (I Thess. 2:13). He claims for his gospel that it is "not man's gospel," for he did not receive it from man nor was he taught it; it came through revelation of Jesus Christ (Gal. 1:11, 12). He commended the elders at Ephesus to "the word of God that is able to build you up and to give you the inheritance among all those who are sanctified" (Acts 20:32). He claims that what he wrote in I Corinthians was "a command of the Lord" (14:37). He reminds the Thessalonians that in disregarding his letter, they disregard "not man, but God who gives His Holy Spirit to you" (I Thess. 4:8). He describes the resurrection of the righteous "by the word of the Lord" (I Thess. 4:15). He further declares that anyone refusing to obey what he said in the letter should be ostracized from the church's fellowship (II Thess. 3:14). In I Timothy 5:18 he quotes as Scripture a passage from Deuteronomy (25:4) and another found in Luke 10:7 as equally authoritative. It is Peter who places Paul's writing, though difficult at times to understand, on a par with "the other scriptures" in II Peter 3:15, 16. This is only a sample of what may be gleaned as one looks through both the Old and the New Testaments to see the claims that are made in the Scriptures for the authority back of what these men are saying and writing.

The Phenomena in the Bible

The second task that we have set for ourselves is to examine the material we see in the Scriptures in order that we may understand what is meant by saying, "All scripture is inspired by God." As we look at the Scriptures we are amazed by the different types of literature we see. There are so many different literary forms through which God has chosen to express Himself. One senses as he reads the different books that there are varying purposes that control the writing of specific portions of the Bible and that these things were written to specific audiences whose needs were different at different times and the message was designed to meet those needs. One realizes the accuracy of the statement made in Hebrews 1:1 that in many and various ways God has spoken through His servants, here partially and there partially with "line upon line and precept upon precept."

The word has come to men in varying historical circumstances, with different cultural conditioning, since it is in history that God has made Himself known and that God confronts man with His demands. This is the reason why it is so necessary for us to understand the historical circumstances that operate and the backgrounds and cultures that are involved when we come to grasp the meaning of a passage of Scripture in the Bible. This should not startle us since we realize that the Bible is like any other book in this sense, and we should expect it to bear these traits.

We are conscious also of the differences in the abilities and experiences of those whom God has chosen to be His messengers. God's providential ordering of their lives fitted them to do the task that He called them to do. Some messengers have occupied a major place in the transmission of His will while others only a minor role, but a God who promises that He works in all things for good for those who love Him (Rom. 8:28) and who providentially rules and overrules in the affairs of men and nations to accomplish His will is the God who likewise can providentially prepare and develop the kind of messengers through whom He will bring His will to confront man.

Within all the variation the student of the Scriptures beholds also the underlying unity, a unity of God's great unfolding purpose revealed to redeem man from his lost and estranged condition, to enlighten his darkness, and to lead him to life abundant and everlasting. The Word continues to have power to show man his sinfulness and convict him as a sinner of his need for trusting and obeying God's authoritative commands. How the drama unfolds, how God makes use of men and nations to realize His purposes across the great stage of history is a fascinating story, the final chapter of which awaits His own action.

Revelation in History

Because this revelation is given in a historical context there are many ways in which historical data and archaeology have been used to illustrate the accuracy of the basic historical picture given in the Scriptures, and details have been confirmed in remarkable fashion through modern discoveries. One leading archaeologist has spoken of the "remarkable memory of the Bible" through which he was able to identify and unearth remains of civilizations that otherwise were lost to the memory of man.

And yet, one must say in all fairness that there are problems in the materials within the Bible. If we come to the Scriptures with the standards of historiography that have developed within the last one hundred years, we shall find ourselves disappointed in many places because there is neither the preciseness, nor the interest in such clarity of details as the modern historian might be concerned with. For instance, there are minor differences that occur in parallel accounts of events in the gospels.

There are problems that arise which puzzle us as we endeavor to understand and synchronize some of the events described in the Bible with the records that are found elsewhere. What the modern historian finds interesting is not after all what the inspired writer is primarily concerned with, for his purpose is motivated by a different perspective than the mere chronicling of events. The understanding of this purpose will help us to appreciate the nature of the Biblical witness and not to allow ourselves to be entangled with preconceptions that we thrust down upon the material that we find in the Bible.

Many of our problems in the study of the Scriptures may arise from the fact that we still are not able to put ourselves back into the thought world and understand the situations and concepts of the times when certain writings took place. Our own ignorance and inadequacy pose a limitation upon us. But we must at the same time recognize that the Bible itself as it unfolds the message of God must be seen to speak to the various groups of people within the context of their own thought world and to utilize the imagery, the figures of speech, and the methods of teaching that would be helpful and decisive for them. Any humble approach to the Scriptures recognizes that there are many problems within the text of the Bible that still puzzle the honest seeker for truth just as there are problems within the natural world that still puzzle those who study and search to know more of God's nature. These challenge men to further pursuit of the truth.

The Meaning of Inspiration

To make one's own statement of the meaning of inspiration is a very difficult task, and one that should constantly be revised in the light of the Scriptures themselves. We shall endeavor to make such a statement ourselves. Inspiration means that God has powerfully acted through His Holy Spirit in the lives and in the words of His chosen servants, the prophets, and the apostles so that they may declare to men what God wants men to know of His will. Where there were facts and truths that could not be known except through God's revealing action, the Holy Spirit gave these so that the inspired men might properly record God's Word.

Inspiration also covers the guidance of those who were eyewitnesses of events, such as the apostles during the ministry of Jesus, in their selection and recording of the facts. The inclusion of whatever documents, statements, teachings, or other materials that should find a place in the record was under the Spirit's supervision. God is in the fullest sense responsible for His Word, yet the evidence that comes to us in the Bible emphasizes the fact that God respects constantly the human agent through whom He makes known His will. The oral message of the apostles as eyewitnesses empowered by the Holy Spirit came before the written New Testament. Yet that oral message was not different from the New Testament Scriptures, but the writers set down that oral message and the teaching that Christ would have His followers know.

Inspiration does not involve doing violence to the nature of the writers. The distinctiveness of each man's style, the coloring of his personality as evidenced in his vocabulary, the use of the various talents are all a part of the human side of the Scriptures. Inspiration allows for the study, research, and the careful investigation of the writer. Luke in the prologue to his Gospel states,

> "Inasmuch as many have undertaken to compile a narrative of the things which have been accomplished among us, just as they were delivered to us by those who from the beginning were eyewitnesses and ministers of the word, it seemed good to me also, having followed all things closely for some time past, to write an orderly account for you, most excellent Theophilus, that you may know the truth concerning the things of which you have been informed" (Luke 1:1-4).

Luke used his own study and investigation in writing his account, yet was so guided that he taught no error, only what God wanted men to know of the life of Jesus.

The divine and human aspects are blended in the production of the Bible so that it is God's Book for men using human language without doing any violence to their natures. These two aspects, the human and the divine, cannot be placed into neat compartments. Inspiration does not mean that each man will approach his material in the same way. One may follow a chronological arrangement, while another may take a topical or didactic order. One must not understand inspiration as simply an addition of a few words from God to a great many human words from the prophets. God has spoken *through* them. The supervision of the Holy Spirit is complete so that we can say with Paul, "All scripture is inspired of God."

I cannot express the answer to the question "How?" better than in the language used by Lemoine Lewis of the Abilene Christian College faculty several years ago. "Theories of inspiration are legion. The watch words of some are natural inspiration, degrees of inspiration, partial inspiration, inspired concepts, universal Christian inspiration, verbal 'dictation,' verbal inspiration, plenary inspiration, etc. I am skeptical of any solution that cannot be expressed in Bible terms. Here let us be warned by the controversy over the nature of Christ that so distracted the church in the early centuries.

"When God sent His Son into the world He took the form of a man. When He gave His Word it took the form of a book. To reconcile, delimit, define the divine and the human in one is no easier than in the other" ("The Inspiration of the Scriptures," Frank Pack, ed. *Our Bible*, Abilene Christian College, 1953, p. 33.)

As a people who desire to call Bible things by Bible names, and who have been careful to draw away from the involved theological systems that men have built, let us take care to state our faith in terms drawn from the Bible itself.

The central figure of the Bible is Jesus Christ, whom to know is life eternal. (John 17:3). Its whole purpose is to bring men to know God as He is shown in Jesus Christ and help men to find through Him life that is abundant and eternal. It must never become for us a dead letter, a book of mere proof-texts for us to hang arguments upon as we deal with some favorite subject. It is God addressing us and showing us through His Son His salvation. We must listen to what the Bible says, we must heed the message to us, and we must answer its call in humble obedience.

1. Scripture quotations in this chapter are taken from the Revised Standard Version, unless otherwise noted.

PART FOUR

CAN THE BIBLE
INFLUENCE MAN'S CONDUCT?

INTRODUCTION

One of the fundamental premises of psychology is that what one believes—whether in trivial or serious matters—has a profound bearing on his behavior. If, for example, a person believes that lying is necessary to advance in business, then lying becomes a part of his behavior. If one believes that his body is to be kept clean, healthy, and free from drugs (whether the motivation is personal or religious), he will do all he can to keep the body strong and healthy.

Since the Bible has been (at least in past generations) one of the most widely read and revered books in all parts of the Western world, its influence in shaping ideals, purposes, and values is incalculable. Scores of great men and women in various positions of leadership have paid tribute to the positive and wholesome influence of the Scriptures on their lives.

Those who know God's Book will agree heartily with this observation of John Quincy Adams: "The foundations of our society and our government rest so much on the teachings of the Bible that it would be difficult to support them if faith in these teachings should cease to be practically universal in our country."

10

NEVER MAN SO SPAKE

Rex F. Johnston and Morris M. Womack

When the disciples of the Pharisees returned from hearing Jesus speak, they were amazed at His power. Rather than taking Him into custody, they declared to their cohorts, "Never man so spake." The words which these men cried out are still ringing in our ears today, for never has a teacher or leader of mankind had such a mighty impact upon the lives of human beings as has Jesus of Nazareth.

The writers hope to demonstrate two great principles in the following pages: first, Jesus was the Master Teacher, both in method and message; and, second, His influence upon modern educational practices is recognized by leading educators of our day. Jesus was a part of the world into which He was born and was the product of a religious community which believed strongly in education. It is no surprise that He became a master in the art of molding the minds of the masses.

Education in the Hebrew Culture

God has always wanted His children to learn His will. Throughout the history of the Hebrew nation, this was done through educational methods. Some of the admonitions and commandments concerning education are: "Train up a child in the way he should go and when he is old he will not depart from it" (Prov. 22:6). "Apply thine heart unto instruction and thine ears to the words of knowledge. Withhold not correction from the child. . ." (Prov. 23:12-13). "Buy the truth, and sell it not; also wisdom and instruction and understanding" (Prov. 23:23). "My son, give me thine heart, and let thine eyes observe my ways" (Prov. 23:26). These references could be supported with many more which would further substantiate this contention.

From early infancy, Hebrew children were carefully taught. Isaiah says that "them that are weaned from the milk and drawn from the breasts" (Isa. 28:9) would be taught knowledge. That education was begun early is seen from Paul's statement that Timothy was taught from his childhood up (II Tim. 3:15). Fathers were required by the law to bring their children into a relationship with the law. Henri Daniel-Rops states that:

> A father's first duty was to teach his children the commandments: This in any case was the direct order that Yahweh had given, by the voice of Moses, to all the men of Israel; the order that was repeated in the morning and at night in the prayer. "Thou shalt teach thy children my commandments."
>
> In the same way, since the practice of religion and the history of the race both formed part of the Law, fathers told their children of all the wonders that Yahweh had done for His people; they explained the meaning of the great feast to them and showed them how each of the customs that they observed had a holy significance.[1]

In the earliest days, the educational activities, as has already been shown, were conducted by the home. Later on, even though fathers were still admonished to teach their children, schools were established in which students were given a more thorough education. Daniel-Rops gives the following explanation:

> The rabbi Simon ben Shetach, brother of the queen Salome Alexandra and president of the Sanhedrin, opened the first *beth ha-sefer, house of book,* in Jerusalem. His example was followed, and little by little a whole system of public instruction came into existence. Some thirty years after the death of Christ, in about the year 64 A.D., the high priest Joshua ben Gamala promulgated what may be considered as the first educational legislation: there was nothing wanting—the parents were obliged to send their children to school, there were punishments for idle children and those too often absent.[2]

At the age of five, children were sent to the primary school which was connected with the synagogue. The schoolmaster was the "hazzan, the guardian of the sacred books and the minister of the synagogue."[3] Whenever there were more than twenty-five pupils, a special master was appointed. In this stage of their education, the students learned about the Torah, or the holy law of God. The study of the law was used for learning all of the other elements of education (the alphabet, language, history, etc.) rather than the opposite approach.

The second stage of education, for those wishing to continue beyond the primary school, was called the *beth ha-midrash.* This stage of education was usually continued under the famous doctors of the law, and students went to Jerusalem for the study. Gamaliel is believed to have been one of these teachers and Saul of Tarsus went to Jerusalem to study at his feet. Daniel-Rops summarizes,

> The Talmudic tractate *Pirke Aboth,* sayings of the fathers ,... laid down the following stages of a child's development: "At five he must begin the sacred studies; at ten he must set himself to learning the tradition; at thirteen he must know the whole of the Law of Yahweh and practice its requirements; and at fifteen years begin the perfecting of his knowledge."[4]

In brief, it may be said that teaching is one of the most important things that a follower of God could do. From the very beginning God emphasized teaching, and teachers were very important in Israel and were held in high esteem. The Pentateuch emphasized in unmistakable terms the importance of teaching: "And these words, which I command thee this day, shall be in thine heart and thou shalt teach them diligently unto thy children, and shalt talk of them when thou sittest in thine house, and when thou walkest by the way, and when thou liest down, and when thou risest up" (Deut. 6:6-7). This same principle was emphasized by Christ when He gave the commission to His disciples to take His message to all nations (Matt. 28:19-20).

Principles of Effective Teaching

In order for us to properly evaluate the effectiveness of Jesus as a teacher, we must establish some criteria for evaluating teaching. What is effective teaching? What is involved? Is teaching the same as telling? What is the role of the teacher who achieves desired results? When does teaching take place? Teaching takes place when a student learns. We know that learning has occurred when behavior changes, for learning is the modification of behavior by means of experiences.[5] Therefore, teaching is the organization of experiences that result in changed behavior.

What principles should govern the organization of these experiences? In other words, how does a learner's mind work? Psychologists tell us that the mind of a learner must work in the right kind of context if he is to learn effectively. There must be a focus or frame of reference. The right kind of social relationships are important. Since each learner is an individual, he must work in his own individual way. Things learned should be part of a sequence. And, evaluation should take place, for the learner should know how he is progressing.[6]

The effectiveness of teaching, then, depends upon context, focalization, socialization, individualization, sequence, and evaluation. In reality, these are simply inseparable elements of the process of meaningful learning. Learning must be effective, and its effectiveness depends upon its meaningfulness. In the following paragraphs, a brief explanation of each of the above factors of effective teaching will be given.

Context. What are the characteristics of a good context? To refer again to Mursell, there are three characteristics of a good context: First, a good context must be one that develops the excitement and interests of the learner; second, a good context includes concrete experiences with which the learner will be familiar; and, third, a good context demands that these experiences be simple and varied.

Focalization. Focalization, or focus, is closely associated with its contextual setting and arises out of it. The basic question which the teacher should ask concerning focalization is: Will the students be challenged to think because of the situation which I have established? A good focus asks a question which the learners will want to have answered.

Socialization. Socialization includes the voluntary working of members of a group together to achieve certain goals as defined by a particular culture. The vital element in socialization is creative group cooperation. This comes when the teacher and the members of the group being taught learn to know one another.

Individualization. The principle of individualization is well-stated by the following sentence from Mursell: "Meaningful learning must proceed in terms of the learner's own purposes, aptitudes, abilities and experimental procedures."[7]

Sequence. Nothing can be learned unless a person is ready to learn it, and it must be learned according to a valid sequence which is understood by the learner. Certain facts cannot be learned prior to other facts. Furthermore, there are certain developmental tasks which come in proper sequence in the development of the pupil.

Evaluation. Learners, as they learn, must be made aware of their progress in order that they can be motivated to learn more. In other words, their work must be evaluated. This not only allows the teacher to know what he must teach next, but it allows the student to see his own progress-level.

If effective teaching includes context, focalization, socialization, individualization, sequence, and evaluation, what is the role of the teacher? The task of the teacher is to use these principles as guidelines in organizing learning experiences. A teacher is a director of learning experiences.[8]

Jesus, the Master Teacher

It has already been stated that Jesus was the most effective teacher who ever lived. He was a director of learning. As the Master Teacher, He utilized all of the principles of effective teaching.

He used good context. This is evident from the fact that he interested the learners and great multitudes followed Him (Matt. 4:25) and the "common people heard him gladly" (Mark 12:87). A good context not only excites the interest of the learner but also includes concrete experiences with which the learner is familiar. Jesus referred to such experiences. He told the stories of the sower (Matt. 13:3-23), the lost sheep (Luke 15:1-7), the lost coin (Luke 15:8-10), the lilies of the field (Matt. 6:28), the fowls of the air (Matt. 6:26), the rich man and Lazarus (Luke 16:19-31), the prodigal son (Luke 15:11-32), and the Good Samaritan (Luke 10:25-37). The foregoing experiences that Jesus related were also simple and varied. This is additional evidence that Jesus used good context, for simple and varied experiences are characteristic of good context.

Jesus also used good focalization. The key point in focalization is the setting up of a situation that will provoke thought. A good focus also asks a question which the learner wants answered. Jesus did both of these in the story of the good Samaritan (Luke 10:25-39). The story was told in answer to a question, "and who is my neighbor?" (Luke 10:29). At the end of the story, Jesus provoked thought by asking the question, "Which now of these three, thinkest thou, was neighbor unto him that fell among the thieves?" (Luke 10:36). Jesus also provoked though on the part of Peter by asking him three times whether or not Peter loved Him (John 21:15-17).

Jesus achieved socialization by motivating His disciples to work together voluntarily as a group to reach the goals that He had in mind. He called them and they followed (Matt. 4:19-20). "He gave them power against unclean spirits, to cast them out, and to heal all manner of sickness and all manner of disease" (Matt. 10:1). "And as ye go, preach, saying, The kingdom of heaven is at hand" (Matt. 10:7). These references clearly indicate the willingness of the disciples to work together toward the achievement of goals of the group.

Jesus knew the aptitudes of His disciples and therefore used the principle of individualization. He provided extra learning experiences for those who could profit from them. This principle is further illustrated by this very emotional experience in the personal ministry of Jesus: "Then cometh Jesus with them unto a place called Gethsemane, and saith unto the disciples, Sit ye here, while I go and pray yonder. And he took with him Peter and the two sons of Zebedee, and began to be sorrowful and very heavy. Then saith he unto them,

My soul is exceeding sorrowful even unto death, tarry ye here and watch with me" (Matt. 26:36-38).

Jesus was aware of sequence and readiness to learn. He knew that some concepts could not be grasped until other concepts were taught. Therefore, He taught them in proper sequence. Jesus said to His disciples, "I have yet many things to say unto you, but ye cannot bear them now" (John 16:12).

Jesus evaluated the learning of His disciples. When He asked them, "Who do men say that I the Son of man am? And they said, Some say that thou art John the Baptist, some Elias, and others, Jeremias, or one of the prophets. He saith unto them, But whom say ye that I am? And Simon Peter answered and said, Thou art the Christ, the Son of the living God. Jesus answered and said unto them, Blessed art thou, Simon Bar-jona; for flesh and blood hath not revealed it unto thee, but my Father which is in heaven" (Matt. 16:13-17). There were other occasions when Jesus evaluated the learning process of His disciples.

Truly Jesus was a master teacher. He was conscious of and utilized all of the principles of effective teaching: context, focalization, socialization, individualization, sequence, and evaluation.

Educational Philosophies

Jesus also had a valid philosophy which served as a frame of reference within which the principles of effective teaching were implemented. It is true that He wrote no textbook, nor even a scholarly article to an educational journal. However, He did speak words and truths which reflected His own philosophy of education.

The goals of education may be described in terms of relationship concepts, such as self-realization, human relations, both on the basis of an individual's relationship to another and his relationship to people in groups, and the relationship of a person to his environment.[9] Jesus was aware of that need for self-realization. He said, "I am come that they might have life, and that they might have it more abundantly" (John 10:10).

Jesus taught the principle of good human relationship, both on an individual and a group basis. He said, "Love your enemies, bless them that hate you, and pray for them which despitefully use you and persecute you" (Matt. 5:44, 45). Again, He said, "Therefore, all things whatsoever ye would that men should do to you, do ye even so to them: for this is the law and the prophets" (Matt. 7:12). Many of the great thinkers before Jesus had stated some of these principles from a negative point of view, that is, forbidding the misuse of one's fellowman; but, Jesus emphasized the positive qualities of good human relationships.

Jesus was also conscious of the fact that man has to relate effectively to his environment. He taught that a person should seek first the kingdom of God and His righteousness and all the physical things a man needs from his environment would be added to him (Matt. 6:33). When praying the great intercessory prayer (John 17), Jesus emphasized that His desire was for the Father to protect His disciples from the evil one—He did not pray that they be removed from the world, their environment. Christians must learn to compete with and control the elements of the world.

The basic purpose of education might be said to be problem-solving. Hence, the main purpose in all teaching—or, learning situations— is "to help the individual learner open himself up for learning by being able to bring his problems and needs for learning to the surface, and to listen and accept relevant reactions about his problems and behavior."[10] The philosophy of John Dewey also emphasized problem-solving as one of the basic purposes of education. [11] Jesus was aware of the problems of people. One time, it is said that "Jesus, knowing their thoughts said, wherefore think ye evil in your hearts?" (Matt. 9:4). He taught people how to solve their problems by emphasizing the importance of faith. "If ye have faith as a grain of mustard seed, ye shall say unto this mountain, Remove hence to yonder place; and it shall remove; and nothing shall be impossible unto you" (Matt. 17:20).

Jesus encouraged people to ask questions to secure answers to these problems. One person asked Him what he must do to inherit eternal life. This gave Jesus the opportunity to teach the man a great lesson on worldly possessions and their gripping control over us. Jesus told him to sell his goods, give to the poor and follow Him. The young man went away sorrowful, for he had great possessions (Matt. 19:16-22).

Jesus was acutely conscious of the problems of people and their need to solve them. He taught His disciples how to pray (Luke 11:1-4) for the search after a solution; He taught them how to overcome anxiety and fear (Matt. 6:31-34). He was always giving people ideas on how to solve their problems.

The classical philosophy of education concerning ideas is that "ideas present the dimensions of reality. They are pictures, in a sense, of the way things are and the way things ought to be." [12] Indeed, the possession of true ideas is good within itself. The philosophy of John Dewey included the use of ideas in problem-solving, but it also recognized the involvement of feelings, attitudes, interests, and appropriate physical activity.[13] Jesus taught ideas concerning reality, but emphasized activity motivated by the appropriate attitudes and feelings. After He told the story of the good Samaritan, He said, "Go and do thou likewise" (Luke 10:37). The authoritarian philosophy of education is the oldest one and emphasizes the accumulation of facts and de-emphasizes the search for answers.

Other leading philosophies of education are neoromanticism, experimentalism, and realism. Much of what is called Progressive Education is really neoromanticism. In this philosophy, primary attention is given to the growth needs, interests, and desires of the learner.[14] Experimentalism, sometimes called pragmatism, emphasizes human experiences and the need to control them.[15] Realism, on the other hand, points up the fact that there is absolute truth, but that this is the truth of the universe.[16]

Jesus utilized the best tenets of the foregoing philosophies. He was aware of the necessity to recognize the needs, interests, and desires of others. He used the experiences of others and taught persons how to react as they found themselves involved in specific circumstances. Jesus also recognized absolute truth, for He was indeed the truth and the life (John 14:6). He also declared that He was involved in the creation of all things (cf. John 1:3).

Summary

In view of the tremendous influence of Jesus and in view of His truly scientific educational theories, can it be denied that He was the Master Teacher? How could He have known these principles of educational philosophy centuries before they were expounded by the experts in the field?

Not only did Jesus know and use proper context, focalization, socialization, individualization, sequence, and evaluation in His teaching, all of which are principles of effective teaching; but He also was motivated by a valid and ever-modern philosophy of education. He used the best elements of authoritarianism, neoromanticism, experimentalism or pragmatism, and realism. He used educational methods effectively, constantly, and consistently. He believed in person-to-person relationships; He was the master of parabolic teaching; question and answer methods were present in His teaching activities; and object lessons served to illustrate the many truths He expounded to the masses who listened to Him.

When one looks at the history of Christianity and the impact that it has had upon the lives and minds of mankind, truly one can say without equivocation, "Never man so spake."

1. *Daily Life in the Time of Jesus* (New York: Hawthorn, 1962), p. 128.
2. Ibid., p. 129.
3. Ibid., p. 129.
4. Ibid., p. 132.
5. Jeanne L. Rivoire, *1001 Questions Answered about Child Psychology* (New York: Dodd, Mead, 1965), p. 125.
6. James L. Mursell, *Successful Teaching: Its Psychological Principles* (New York: McGraw-Hill, 1946), p. viii, 37.
7. Mursell, *op. cit.*, p. 189.
8. Lawrence Thomas, Lucien B. Kinney et al, *Perspective on Teaching* (Englewood Cliffs, New Jersey: Prentice-Hall, 1961), p. 421.
9. Tom C. Venable, *Patterns in Secondary School Curriculum* (New York: Harper & Brothers, 1957), p. 23.
10. Herman Estrin and Delmer M. Goode, *College and University Teaching* (Dubuque, Ia: William C. Brown, 1964), p. 309.
11. Thomas and Kinney, *op. cit.*, pp. 24-25.
12. Ibid., p. 164.
13. Ibid., p. 179.
14. Venable, *op. cit.*, p. 41.
15. Ibid., p. 44.
16. Ibid., p. 46.

11

PHILOSOPHY AND CHRISTIANITY

James D. Bales

The word *philosophy* originally meant the love of wisdom. It is said that Pythagoras considered himself to be a *lover* of wisdom, because he believed that God only could know wisdom. Philosophy has been defined not only as the love for and the seeking of wisdom, but also the wisdom which is sought and which the philosopher hopes to find.

What Is Philosophy?

Philosophy seeks to understand the principles in the light of which all reality is to be explained. A definition may be determined in part by one's view of the nature and scope of philosophy. In a popular rendition, *philosophy* has been defined as "private wisdom or consolation," but technically it has been defined as "the science of sciences, the criticism and systematization or organization of all knowledge, drawn from empirical science, rational learning, common experience, or wherever."[1]

T. H. Green has "described philosophy as the result of 'a progressive effort toward a fully articulated conception of the world as rational.' "[2] Josiah Royce wrote that philosophy "is not a presumptuous effort to explain the mysteries of the world by means of any superhuman insight or extraordinary cunning, but has its origin and value in an attempt to give a reasonable account of our own personal attitude towards the more serious business of life." W. P. Montague said that it "is an attempt to gain a reasoned conception of the universe and man's place in it." R. W. Sellars thought of it as "a persistent attempt to gain insight into the nature of the world and ourselves by means of systematic reflection."[3]

The word *philosophy* is often associated with a school of thought

201

which is not rooted in the supernatural revelation of God to men. It is a human effort to deal with questions concerning God; the origin of the universe; and the origin, nature, duty, and destiny of man. As such, it is an effort to explain all these without an appeal to divine revelation. Some philosophers have not only rejected revelation, but they have also concluded that there is neither love nor wisdom. In fact, some justify the statement of Cicero that "there is nothing so absurd but that it may be found in the books of the philosophers." Durant put it this way: "Doubtless some philosophers have had all sorts of wisdom except common sense; and many a philosophic flight has been due to the elevating power of thin air."[4]

What Is Christianity?

Christians believe that Christianity is the true wisdom, for Christ has been "made unto us wisdom from God, and righteousness, and sanctification, and redemption" (I Cor. 1:30). In brief, what is Christianity? *First,* Christianity involves revelation. It is not the product of man's search after God and the refinement of man's uninspired spiritual thought (cf. I Cor. 1:21; 2:7-13). God has spoken to us through His Son and those who were sent by Him to reveal and confirm the faith (Heb. 1:1-2; 2:3-4; Jude 3).

Second, Christianity involves redemption. Christianity is not simply a system of moral ideas which set before man the ideal life. Although it embodies the highest moral values known to man, it is more than morality. It presupposes that man has sinned. He is not just ignorant and in need of knowledge, but he is also a sinner in need of salvation. The Old Testament prophesied the death of Jesus Christ for the sins of man (Isa. 53; cf. I Peter 1:10-12). He came "to put away sin by the sacrifice of himself" (Heb. 9:26). Christ came to save His people from their sins, to give His life a ransom for many, and to bring many sons unto glory (Matt. 1:21; 20:28; Heb. 2:9-10).

Third, Christianity involves regeneration. Man not only needs to be reeducated; he also needs to be reborn. The new birth is possible not because man has merited it, but because God has manifested His grace to man. Jesus said that we must be born again in order to enter the kingdom (Titus 3:4-7; John 3:3-5). As a babe in Christ the newborn ones are to grow in grace and knowledge and walk in newness of life (I Peter 2:2; Rom. 6:4; Eph. 4:20-24).

Fourth, Christianity includes the redeemed and reformed life. One who is born into the kingdom is born into a new kind of life. Morality is an essential fruit or part of Christianity. Children of God must not live like children of the devil. The grace of God teaches us and this teaching involves ethical principles (cf. Titus 2:11-14; 3:8).

Christians are called to freedom, but this is not a freedom to live after the flesh but to live after the law of love, for we are under the law to Christ (Gal. 5:13-14; I Cor. 9:21). Instead of following the works of the flesh, we are to bring forth the fruit of the Spirit (Gal. 5:19-21, 20-23).

Fifth, Christianity includes not only a view of this world, but this world viewed in the light of eternity. It is the product of the divine revelation, and just as it is not earthly in its origin, its destiny also in not earthly. It deals with man on earth but it does not leave him earthbound. Man is to set his heart on things above, where Christ is, seated at God's right hand (Col. 3:1-4). He lives in view of eternity, for Christ has abolished death and brought life and immortality to light through the gospel (II Tim. 2:10). Christ's resurrection is the pledge and promise of our resurrection; therefore, Christianity involves the revealed rest (II Thess. 1:7; I Peter 1:3-9).

These things make it clear that Christianity is not simply a system of ideas or a collection of concepts. It involves concepts and ideas but all of these are centered *in the person of Jesus Christ.* Without Christ there can be no Christianity. Revelation flowered forth in its fulness in the person of Christ. Redemption is through Him who is the Lamb of God slain for the sins of the world. Regeneration has been made possible by Him and is wrought through His gospel. The redeemed life finds its perfect example in the life of Christ, and in faith and love for Him are found the highest motivations for this new life. The revealed rest is assured to us because of Christ's death for our sins and His resurrection for our justification. To be without Christ is to be without Christianity. Attacks on Christ are attacks on Christianity. Attacks on Christianity are attacks on Christ, for He is so identified with His Word and people that to reject the Word is to reject Him (cf. John 12:48; Acts 9:4-5). Christianity is Christ-following and Christ-accepting. A Christian is one who has put on Christ and who lives with a realization of this relationship (Gal. 3:26-27).

Christianity is the world view of the Christian. He is not dependent on human philosophy for his positions concerning God, the origin of man, the duty of man, the hope of man, or the destiny of man.

Why Study Philosophy?

Although no Christian can study everything, it is important that some devote considerable time to philosophy, and that all of us have some insights on the subject. A knowledge of philosophy may help us to understand what others are thinking. It also enables us to understand some of the problems which stand between them and faith in God. It will indicate some of the avenues and ideas through which we must approach them. If we do not know how another person thinks, how can we know how to approach him in the most effective way possible? We must start where the person is if we plan to lead him to where he ought to be.

A study of philosophy also enables us to understand what is taking place in the world today. When we realize how basically anti-Biblical some world views are, we do not wonder at the fact that the conduct to which they lead is contrary to Christianity. We should not expect an anti-Christian world view, when lived, to produce the same type of character as the Biblical world view produces. To change the fruit, we must change the seed; to be transformed, men must have their minds transformed through the gospel.

A study of philosophy may help one in clarifying ideas and concepts as well as in endeavoring to deal with problems which are not discussed fully in the Bible. The Bible deals with the fact of knowledge and tells us some things about it; however, it does not enter into a discussion of how it is possible for the human mind to arrive at truth. It does not present us with any hypotheses of epistemology. It does keep us from accepting any hypothesis which would deny any Biblical truth. It keeps us from being agnostics concerning the power of the human mind to arrive at truth. Although it keeps us humble, and thus from assuming that we know it all, it does guard us against relativism with reference to truth or morality. The purpose of the Bible is not to solve every question which the mind of man can raise and explore but rather to reveal God to man and man to himself.

A study of philosophy helps us to understand the nature of many of the attacks made upon Christianity. In this way it helps us to know better how to deal with these attacks.

Philosophy and Unbelief

When a philosophy is based on the assumption that human reason apart from divine revelation can construct the true world view, it is anti-Biblical in its basic assumption. As T. F. Torrance pointed out:

> If Philosophy, by its very nature, where it presupposes a *Weltanschauung,* must also complete itself in a system (and does not the urge towards scientific thought mean the urge towards completing the function of philosophy in a system of some sort?), then it will necessarily be anti-Christian because of the in-turned character of fallen reason. But if philosophy can remain fragmentary and open, and critical at the same time of its underlying point of view, then it might be possible to philosophise in a way that

might not be detrimental to the Christian faith. Such philosophy could never reach a final conclusion, it could only suspend judgment.... Its relative nature would have to be recognized, because Christianity, which operates solely with a reason conformed to the Revelation of God, can only be absolute and intolerant in its claims.[5]

Although the reasons why various individuals have become unbelievers in historic Christianity may be quite varied, usually the justification for their unbelief is based upon a philosophy. In other words, their antagonism to Christianity is ultimately justified on the grounds of its conflict with some particular philosophical view. Christianity is contrary to this philosophy of life; therefore, Christianity must be false. What is the meaning of Christianity, and how did it come into existence? The philosopher wh rejects Christianity seeks to answer these questions by explaining the origin and nature of Christianity in terms of his own philosophical explanation of the universe. Christianity cannot be true; so the only problem is to explain why and how it arose, and why anyone ever thought that it was true. All reality must fit the philosophy, and when it does not seem to do so, so much the worse for reality! It must be trimmed or stretched, as the case may be, and forced into the mold created by the philosophy. The philosophy is the framework in which all reality is to be contained.

When we understand that most of the attacks on Christianity are philosophical in their origin, that they are based on human speculations and not on facts, we shall not be overawed because this or that big name or brilliant intellect is opposed to Christianity. Even the facts which such unbelievers use will have, in many cases, their interpretation determined by their philosophy of life.

A philosopher may be undermining one's Biblical faith, and reshaping one's faith to conform to the philosophy without the person being aware of it. A college student, for example, may not be aware of the fact that the field in which he is majoring is dominated by a philosophy of life based on a non-Biblical or an anti-Biblical world view. In order to major in this field, he must spend much time absorbing the materials which pertain to it. He may not receive any help in detecting, or evaluating, the basic philosophical presuppositions. He may absorb them until they become a part of him and shape his thinking. This will happen unless the individual loves God with all of his being (Matt. 22:37-38). Loving God with his whole self will lead him to evaluate all things from the standpoint of the Biblical world view.

There are some philosophies which omit the fact of sin. In them, everything is the fault of economic and social institutions. If these are changed, the nature of man will be changed. Crime is the fault of society, and nothing much can be done about it until society has been changed so as to conform to this philosophy of life. Without minimizing the influence of others upon us, it is still a fact that the Bible teaches the reality of human responsibility. Furthermore, regardless of the nature of the economic and social order—and we are far from suggesting that one is just as good or as bad as another—the problem of sin and rebellion against God will continue to plague mankind. Christians must be on their guard lest they allow a concept of man which is anti-Biblical to shape their view of man. The following pages contain an examination of some attacks on Christianity which are based on world views which the philosopher assumes, but does not prove, to be true.

Naturalism. Naturalism maintains that everything—past, present, and future—must be explained in terms of present day natural processes. This position is impossible to prove but it is the assumption which underlies some philosophies of life. If everything must be explained naturally, then the origin of our solar system, the earth, life, and man must all be explained in terms of present-day processes. Naturalism, with its doctrine of uniformity, must include some hypothesis of naturalistic evolution. In fact, Charles Darwin and others were first converted to the idea that the past must be explained in terms of present-day laws, and they then came up with various hypotheses of evolution. In the words of Henry Fairfield Osborn: "In truth, from the period of the earliest stages of Greek thought man has been eager to discover some natural cause of evolution, and to abandon the idea of supernatural intervention in the order of nature."[6] Because evolution is an essential part of the naturalistic philosophy of life (although there are theistic evolutionists), Darwin and others accepted evolution even though they, and scientists since their day, recognized that it was not scientifically proved.[7]

One of the inadequacies of naturalism, and of evolution, is their inability to explain the reality of morality from a naturalistic standpoint. Their explanation, in one way or another, explains away the reality of the moral realm.[8]

Hegel (1770-1831). In the author's judgment, Hegel has been one of, if not the, most influential philosophers in the Western World, at least, in the past two centuries. We shall endeavor to present briefly one aspect of his philosophy.

Although many philosophers used the dialectical approach to reality long before Hegel, he thought that all before him had imperfectly understood it and imperfectly applied it. He maintained that they did not understand the real nature of negation.[9] Perhaps Hegel's earliest predecessor was Heraclitus, who viewed everything as being in a state of change. This was due to the conflict between extremes or opposing positions, and out of this conflict a harmony or balance developed.[10] According to Richard Kroner, Plato coined the word *dialectic*.[11] The word meant "discourse" or "debate." In debate there is the clash of opposing positions, and out of this clash there can come a better understanding based on the combination on a higher level of certain elements of the opposing positions.

The "Socratic dialectic" endeavored to expose the error in the beliefs of the nonreflective by bringing out, often through the use of questions, the contradictions in their positions. One could then endeavor to arrive at a harmony and thus a better insight into reality.[12] The conflict may be between two individuals who hold to opposing extremes. These positions are in conflict. Through the clash of the contradictory positions each individual may learn something, and from the discussion there may emerge a better understanding which embodies some of the elements in each of the contradictory positions. The first position or extreme we call the *thesis;* the opposing extreme, which is the reaction to the first extreme, we call the *antithesis;* and the harmony which arises out of the conflict we call the *synthesis.*

Hegel thought that this is the pattern according to which all nature and history moves, and in the light of which all must be understood. Every position starts out as a unity or a whole, but it carries within itself potential differentiations which finally come to the front. These constitute the anti-thesis which brings about the negation of the thesis. But, the negation is not total, for out of the creative tension or conflict emerges on a higher level the synthesis which catches up within itself certain aspects of the contradictions (the thesis and the antithesis). Thus, there is again the emergence of unity but on a higher level.

All thought and all reality pass through these stages. As Mackintosh pointed out:

> Thesis, antithesis, synthesis—these, Hegel argues, are the stages by which thought and being alike take their way onward or upward by a spiral progress, by the alternate production and removal of contradictions. The secret of the world is in the relations of Yes to No, and then of both to Nevertheless. At each point reality makes headway by evoking antagonism to its own imperfection, then capturing this antagonism for a richer combination inclusive of, and completing, both terms in the former contrast. Each stage of the evolution, that is to say, is accomplished in three succes-

sive movements which are nothing but the three necessary opera-
tions of the thinking mind; the triple formula just indicated
constitutes the structure not of thought only, but of all life and
history. In this sense the famous aphorism holds true: "The
rational is the real, and the real is the rational."[13]

The dialectical interpretation of reality means not only that everything changes but also that it changes through creative tension or
contradictions. The dialectic is "therefore, a dislocating power," but
it does more than dislocate. It "builds up a new unity with higher
organization."[14] Hegel thought that others before him had misun-
derstood the process of negation which results from the conflict
between the thesis and the antithesis.[15] Thus, the antithesis does not
just cancel out; it also preserves. Hegel used the term *aufheben* (to
annul, or to preserve) "to mean both together. The thesis is cancelled
as such by the antithesis, but preserved with the antithesis in the
synthesis."[16] In this sense not only was the thesis negated by the
antithesis, but the antithesis (the negation) was also negated by the
synthesis.

If the dialectic is true, periods of happiness are the blank pages in
the history of the world, according to Hegel, since "they are periods
of harmony—periods when the antithesis is in abeyance."[17] Even
these periods, however are not actually periods of total inactivity, for
forces are at work which will create the antithesis with its ensuing
conflict.

The history of the world is the history of the unfolding in
progressive development of the Absolute, the Original Source, or the
Original Reality. It is how Reason or the Absolute Spirit not only
unfolds but also comes to consciousness of itself. The Absolute first
exists *in itself* as a unified whole, but within this unity there are
contradictions, and the second stage of the Absolute is the antithesis
of the first. It is the stage when the Absolute is *out of itself;* wherein
it is self-differentiated. The third stage is the union of the two
previous stages; the first stage being that of pure universality and the
second stage of pure difference.[18] When the Spirit has developed to
the place that it is conscious of itself as spirit, there is absolute
knowledge, for the Spirit now knows itself as spirit. Spirit passed
through many triadic stages (thesis-antithesis-synthesis) before it
reached the final synthesis. In the final synthesis all contradictions
have been removed and there is perfect harmony. And this must be a
final synthesis, for unless there is a final synthesis toward which
history is moving, one could not say that there has been any progress
at all. Without a goal and a direction it is impossible to say that one
is making progress.[19] How this dialectical approach shaped Hegel's
attitude toward God is pointed out by Thomas N. Munson.

His division of Absolute Religion into the kingdom of the Father (God in his eternal idea in-and-for-self), of the Son (the eternal Idea of God in the element of consciousness and ordinary thought, or difference), and of the Spirit (the Idea in the element of the church or spiritual community) is almost a philosophical commonplace. It is typically a dialectical reflection: Hegel's universal utensil of intellectual ingestion. God, for example, is defined dialectically in the early lines of Absolute Religion. "We define God when we say that He distinguished Himself from Himself, and is an object for Himself, but that in this distinction He is purely identical with Himself, is in fact Spirit."[20]

There are those who maintain that Hegel was actually an atheist, while others claim that he was a pantheist who thought that God came to consciousness only in man. In this chapter, we are concerned only with the dialectic of Hegel, since it has provided the framework in the light of which some philosophers have reconstructed Christianity. Two such reconstructions will now follow as illustrations.

F. C. Baur (1826-1860). F. C. Baur founded the Tubingen School of theology which explained Christianity in the dialectical framework set forth in the philosophy of Hegel. The history of Christianity, therefore, must be explained on the basis that an original movement called forth its opposite, and out of this clash of opposites a compromise arose which was a synthesis on a higher level of certain elements in both previous movements. As summarized by Morton Scott Enslin, Baur believed that in

> its earliest stage Christianity was a form of Judaism: Jesus was the Messiah of the Jews, not the founder of a world religion. Such was the view of the Jewish Christian wing under the leadership of Peter and James. In contradistinction to this view *(thesis)* Paul maintained that Jesus was the Messiah of the whole world, and Christianity was wholly distinct from Judaism and thus unrestricted by the Mosaic law *(antithesis)*. Out of this clash, which convulsed the church throughout the first century, arose the later reconcilement and more or less colorless "union Christianity" of the second century *(synthesis)*. Upon this Procrustein bed all the writings of early Christianity were forced to lie. Only those writings which revealed the intensity of this struggle were apostolic.[21]

The Book of Acts was viewed as a second-century document which was designed to smooth over, as it were, the early history of Christianity. It was, in other words, a rewriting of history.

A recent book on the origin of Christianity by Hugh I. Schonfield applied this same approach. In his review of the book, Robert C. Campbell wrote that Schonfield has simply revived the argument of the Tubingen school in its extreme form of a Pauline-Petrine dissension.

Besides Jesus, the heroes are Peter, James, and the Jerusalem church. They never saw Jesus as a founder of a religion or church, or as a revealer of God, or as deity. He was simply a man convinced he was the Messiah.

Paul and John are the villains. Their Christology and doctrine of redemption through the cross relate to heathen mystery religions, not to Jesus and the apostles. Moreover, they drew heavily on Jewish occultism rather than the Scriptures.[22]

Thomas J. J. Altizer. Thomas J. J. Altizer furnished another illustration of a theologian who took the dialectical approach to reality and then reconstructed Christianity. In order to understand what he meant by the assertion that "God is dead," it is necessary to understand the following aspects of his philosophy of life. (See the writer's book entitled *The God-Killer.*)

First, Dr. Altizer is a naturalist in that he believes that all the past can be explained in terms of natural processes. He repudiates the very concept of a miraculous, supernatural revelation. He may not use the term *naturalist* to describe himself philosophically, but his position involves it since he believes that scientific advancement has made it impossible for us today to accept the Bible as supernatural revelation.

Second, however, Dr. Altizer does not take the position that things have moved according to what we ordinarily think of as scientific laws. He is not only a naturalist; he is also dialectical. The dialectical approach to reality maintains that the process which we call reality expresses itself in both nature and history. This process unfolds itself in a pattern of movement, countermovement, clash and the emergence of a higher movement. This synthesis negates or brings to an end the two previous movements. But this synthesis is not the final unfoldment, or consummation, of the process which is at work in nature and in history. Therefore, it becomes a thesis which calls forth its antithesis. And out of the clash between these two, another synthesis emerges. This continues indefinitely, according to some, or until a final synthesis is reached, according to others.

This position maintains that the original source of everything, or every movement once existed in a state of unity. However, it contained within itself contradictory elements which, as they developed, were in opposition to and destroyed the first movement. This antithesis itself was negated or destroyed as a result of the conflict. A transformed state emerges. In other words, the dialectical philosophy maintains that in everything there are contradictory elements which develop into open antagonism and that progress emerges out of the conflict of contradictions. This framework is the universal framework in which all nature and history moves. Progress is seen through the clash of contradictions and it is ever upward and onward. It is not a return to the past, but a forward thrust into history in which the original reality unfolds itself on ever ascending levels.

Dr. Altizer does not specify the nature of the original source, but he cannot be consistent and view it as a divine, personal, conscious, living Being. This would mean that the eternal God exists; and if the eternal God exists, the living, eternal God could not actually die. Dr. Altizer views the whole movement of nature and history as a divine process. Since he believes that the final synthesis of this divine process is one in which there is a full manifestation of the process in human flesh, he cannot be consistent and believe that the final synthesis is lower than the beginning thesis. If the beginning thesis was a divine, eternal Being, the final synthesis could not be lower. Yet it would be lower than this if the final synthesis was just a "glorified" but mortal humanity. If he is consistent in his dialectical approach, he must maintain that the ultimate reality was not of the nature of a self-conscious, personal, living Spirit. The original thesis must have been without personality, life, and consciousness; for these qualities are found late in the history of the process. It would be without any of the attributes of Deity. In other words, this is but another way of maintaining that the original reality is matter itself. As far as the author knows, Dr. Altizer never says this; nor does he really attempt to give any definition of the original source, except to call the whole thing a divine process.

In the light of this dialectical process, what does Dr. Altizer mean by the death of God? Does he mean that the divine process evolved a living personal God who later died? He makes statements at times which indicate that a living, personal God once existed; but he does not mean this in the way it sounds, unless he is grossly inconsistent. To be consistent he must maintain that through this process there developed in the human consciousness a belief that there was a God who was wholly other than man and set over against man. This God was spirit who was in opposition to man in the flesh. This concept of God began to be emptied of the spirit by being manifested in the flesh of Jesus. But Jesus became, In Dr. Altizer's dictionary, a name for the continuing process of the increasing identification of the divine with the human, of "spirit" with flesh. Finally, the idea of God is completely emptied and thus God ceases to exist. He died, in other words, in that He was completely emptied into Jesus. Jesus thus became the name for the "Great Humanity Divine" which has dialectically evolved.

This is the final synthesis, or the third age of the Spirit, in which

Christ is completely identified with every human hand and face. Placed in a dialectical framework, this means that at once there was a thesis or movement called God and an antithesis which was man in the flesh. Out of the clash between spirit and flesh there was a progressive development in which there was an emptying into man of the concept of God as spirit. Thus the spirit becomes flesh. God dies by being completely sacrificed in the creation of the new humanity. In some sense not only does the spirit become flesh, but flesh becomes spirit so that the final synthesis is the "Great Humanity Divine," the one Man. In other words, the Christ, which now is, is a concept or notion which is wholly incarnate in our flesh. This is the dialectical explanation of the death of God.

Another position held by Dr. Altizer is that all religion is but a creation of man. It is the result of the "product of human grasping and will to power." All religion is idolatry, since man is worshiping what he himself has created. Dr. Altizer obviously exempts his system from the charge that it, too, is but a reflection of his human strivings, impulses, graspings, and will to power. His is a "religious-less" Christianity. Therefore, all of us are idol worshipers except Dr. Altizer and the selected few who have refused to bow the knee to "Baal." Dr. Altizer views his attacks on the Bible as attacks on an idol.

If this analysis of all religion is correct, one could not maintain that God once actually existed as a Personal Being who later died. Instead, the very idea of God was the creation of man's grasping and will to power; and as man's desires and will to power changed their direction, the concept of God died. The modern man, according to Dr. Altizer, wills to be autonomous. He wills to be free from all restraint from God and His sovereign will. Therefore, as man once willed the existence of God as he sought help outside of himself, man now wills the death of God as man regards himself as totally self-sufficient.

Another very important concept to which Dr. Altizer holds is that all of man's values—including religion, morality, beauty, truth, and so forth—are but the reflection in man's consciousness of the particular historical moment in which he lives. Our particular historical circumstances shape our consciousness, our thoughts, and our feelings. The only reality reflected in our consciousness is the particular historical situation in which we happen to be living. And since everything is in a state of dialectical change, the historical situation is constantly changing through the centuries. Therefore, there is constant change in the consciousness, the feelings, the morals, the ideals, the thought, and the religions of man. This means that although at one time the historical circumstances reflected in man's conscious faith in God, since the historical circumstances have changed, the death of God is now being reflected in man's consciousness. In other words, God never existed as a Personal Being, but only as an idea in the consciousness of man, as man for some reason was forced to reflect such a concept by something in his historical moment. The historical situation has changed, and the consciousness of modern man—modern man as defined by Dr. Altizer—no longer reflects faith in God. God died in history as historical changes caused a change in man's consciousness.

Dr. Altizer is also a moral relativist. He believes that all moral law is but the reflection of a given period of time, and that with dialectical progression moral law changes. There is no eternal moral law in the light of which man's conduct should be evaluated.

Dr. Altizer is not only a moral relativist, he is also in favor of the reversal of the moral law of the Bible and the churches. He thinks that it is a system of satanic repression which creates a sense of guilt and resentment in man. Man should be a completely free individual who is not bound by the law of another; at least if that other is God. The simplest way to visualize the reversal of the moral law of the Bible is to take the "not" out of the moral laws which have "nots" and put them in the moral laws which do not have any "nots."

Dr. Altizer also repudiates Western logic and thinking according to a reasonable process. He substitutes for it some sort of "vision" which men such as Hegel, Nietzsche, and William Blake have had as they interpreted life dialectically. To this irrationalism we shall turn later.

It will be observed throughout the writing of Dr. Altizer that there is no real effort to provide us with any criteria whereby we can have any assurance that his drastic, and supposedly final, revision of Christianity is right. Although Dr. Altizer is against the idea that some past state of human history can contain a message and standard for our day, he seems to think that history is rushing toward a final synthesis which is even now in the process of being reflected in the consciousness of a few who are willing to negate the past and to open themselves to the future.

The World's Wisdom Knew Not God

The Scriptures teach that through human reason man can discern the fact of God's existence (Rom. 1:19-21). Human reason is also vitally involved in the evaluation of the credentials of Christ, the study of His teaching, and the application of His precepts and principles. We are to love God with all of our minds as well as the rest of our being (Matt. 27:37-38). However, the Bible is very clear that through human wisdom alone man cannot attain to a sufficient understanding of God's will. He cannot fathom the divine scheme of redemption. The Greeks prided themselves on their philosophies, but Paul told them that their effort to understand God and life by human reason without any recourse to divine revelation was foolishness (cf. I Cor. 1:18-31).

The world through its wisdom knew not God (I Cor. 1:21). We may go further and say that the world through its wisdom did not even have an adequate understanding of man. Although Christians need to be as considerate and thoughtful as possible in approaching others, the Christian must take his stand on the Biblical revelation and challenge the efforts made by certain philosophers and philosophies to understand the Biblical world view. As Dietrich von Hildebrand pointed out, the Christian must reject any philosophy which denies the "existence of objective truth, the spiritual reality of the person, the difference between soul and body, the objectivity of moral good and evil, the freedom of the will, the immortality of the soul," and the existence of God. "The very nature of the Judaeo-Christian revelation makes for an absolute incompatibility with any epistemological, metaphysical, or moral relativism, with any materialism, immanentism, subjectivism, or determinism, to say nothing of atheism."[23]

They Became Fools

When the Gentile world denied the true God, they finally went into idolatry and immorality. This does not mean that the first deniers of God must of necessity fall immediately into gross immorality. They may be held back by the influence of a faith which they now deny. While affirming atheism, they may consistently cling to the moral principles which are rooted in theism. However, sooner or later the fruits of atheism will manifest themselves in a society. Those who are brought up on unbelief will bear the fruits of unbelief since they are not held back by an early training which included a nurturing in theistic faith. The psalmist spoke of the fool who hath said in his heart there is no God (Ps. 14:1-4), and Paul said that when people turned from God they "became vain in their reasonings, and their senseless heart was darkened. Professing themselves to be wise, they became fools" (Rom. 1:21-22). He then catalogs some of the immoralities into which they fell (Rom. 1:24-32). In our own society we see people not only doing these things, but justifying them.

The Biblical teaching, that when men turn from God they become fools, has been confirmed in those human philosophies which have endeavored to build a world view without God (cf. I Cor. 1:19-20). What is this wisdom of the world of which Paul writes? Does it have reference to man's study of science, farming, etc? No. A study of the context shows that Paul refers to the philosophies of men which set themselves against God and/or the revelation of His will. The wisdom of the world is man's effort to learn the truth about God, man, man's duty, and man's destiny, and to learn it not only apart from divine revelation but also in repudiation of divine revelation.

God has so constructed reality that, when man denies God, sooner or later man affirms a wisdom of the world which is self-defeating. His own wisdom is self-destructive and sooner or later reveals its own foolishness. Let us give some examples. First, there are those who deny God and affirm that man is but matter in motion. They then glorify the mind of man and regard themselves as rational beings too intellectual to believe in God. But, if atheism is true, what can they mean by rationality? If man is but matter in motion, all of his thoughts are but matter in motion which have been put in motion by other motions of matter. As one atheist put it, thought is but a vibration in the brain which has been produced by material mechanisms. To say, "I think," is to describe a physical sensation, just as when one says, "I itch." Since this physical vibration is not the result of the forces of nature thinking their way through to conclusions based on evidence and sound reasoning, it follows that the thoughts cannot be rational insights into reality. They are simple physical sensations physically produced. After glorifying the mind and denying God, the atheist, when consistent, ends up denying his own rationality.

There are others whose wisdom of the world leads them to deny God and to affirm that man ought to search for truth. Furthermore, they may say that belief in God keeps one from searching for truth. Yet, some of these same individuals will affirm that all is relative, that there is no truth. If there is no truth, their philosophy cannot be true, but is a system of errors and an affirmation of foolishness. Why should one be so foolish as to search for truth if there is no truth?

Some affirm that man must be intellectually honest, and that his faith in God keeps him from so being. Some of these will then say that there is no moral law—and all of them should say it, for if there is no Moral Judge of the Universe, there is no moral law—and all morality is in a state of flux. If this is the case, "honesty" is a vain and misleading word and there is no moral law which says that one *ought* to be honest or that one has an obligation to do anything or to desist from anything.

Still others say that there is no God, but that man ought to serve humanity. This is to invoke moral law, which they must repudiate if they are consistent. Furthermore, who is this humanity which one ought to serve? Their philosophy of life maintains that man is but matter in motion and at best he is just a short-lived animal. If this evaluation of man is correct, why should anyone serve man? What is man that anyone should be mindful of him?

Charles Darwin

Charles Darwin furnishes us with an excellent example of a man who retreated into irrationalism rather than face the reality of God, whose existence he felt compelled to admit. The following quotations make it clear that when he had to choose between God and irrationality, he chose irrationality. Such a choice, it should be observed, was not the product of rational reflection! Note the following quotations:

> Another source of conviction in the existence of God, connected with the reason, and not with the feeling, impresses me as having much more weight. This follows from the extreme difficulty or rather impossibility of conceiving this immense and wonderful universe, including man with his capacity for looking far backwards and far into futurity, as the result of blind chance or necessity. When thus reflecting I feel compelled to look to a First Cause having an intelligent mind in some degree analogous to that of man; and I deserve to be called a Theist. This conclusion was strong in my mind about the time, as far as I can remember, when I wrote the "Origin of Species," and it is since that time that it has very gradually, with many fluctuations, become weaker. But then arises the doubt, can the mind of man, which has, as I fully believe, been developed from a mind as low as that possessed by the lowest animals, be trusted when it draws such grand conclusions?[24]

> Nevertheless you have expressed my inward conviction, though far more vividly and clearly than I could have done, that the Universe is not the result of chance. But then with me the horrid doubt always arises whether the convictions of man's mind, which has been developed from the mind of the lower animals, are of any value or at all trustworthy. Would any one trust in the convictions of a monkey's mind, if there are any convictions in such a mind?[25]

> On the other hand, if we consider the whole universe, the mind refuses to look at it as the outcome of chance—that is, without design or purpose. The whole question seems to me insoluble, for I cannot put much or any faith in the so-called intuitions of the human mind, which have been developed, as I cannot doubt, from such a mind as animals possess; and what would their convictions or intuitions be worth?[26]

If Darwin had been consistent in his loss of faith in rational reflections he would have doubted the hypothesis of evolution. This hypothesis was an explanation, drawn up by the human mind, of life and its manifold forms. If the mind cannot be trusted, why trust it when it draws such tremendous conclusions as are embraced in the various hypotheses of evolution? If Darwin had included this doubt in the introduction to his *Origin of Species,* it would have notified the readers that they were not to take the book seriously: for it was a product of mind, and the convictions of man's mind cannot be trusted. However, as far as we know, Darwin never used this type of argument against the "truth" of evolution; even though he admitted that evolution had not been proved.[27] These things reveal that there was a powerful bias against God in the mind of Darwin; otherwise, he would not have invoked irrationalism when faced with the reasonableness of faith in God. In effect, Darwin became a self-confessed fool in his flight from God, for a man labels himself a fool when he discredits man's mind; for this includes his own mind.

Altizer's Atheism

Note another illustration that some philosophers end up in foolishness, and without any rational basis on which to distinguish even one brand of foolishness from another. Dr. Altizer said that by embracing "madness" and suspending common sense, Norman Brown came up with a "truly prophetic vision" of a new man.[28] By embracing the dialectical interpretation of reality, and giving it his own special content, Altizer came up with the "vision" of the gospel of "Christian atheism." No matter how rational Altizer may be in some of his thinking, he holds to positions which embrace the doctrine of irrationalism. On what do we base this accusation?

First, he maintains that we must break away from Western logic and not be bound by "the logical laws of identity and contradiction."[29] What are these laws? By the law of contradiction, we mean, as Henry Calderwood pointed out in his *Vocabularly of Philosophy,* that "a thing cannot be and not be at the same time, or the same attribute cannot at the same time be affirmed and denied of the same subject" in the same sense and at the same time. The law of identity maintains that a thing is itself and not something else. For example, Bales is Bales and not Altizer.

Altizer is saying that unless we break away from these laws, we cannot understand the forward moving word which transforms itself. In other words, if we do not think dialectically, we cannot understand Dr. Altizer's position and the true word. If we demand any rational evidence or any logical thinking in this matter, we are foreclosing the possibility of receiving the word. One must throw away rationality in order to comprehend and to accept Altizer's vision. As a matter of fact, we understand it without throwing away rationality; but certainly to accept it we must turn to the irrational.

Nietzche, however, thought that to maintain that evolution had so proceeded that "human reason must be true is downright simple-minded."[30] In other words, it was false to assume that the process of the world would so develop that the human mind could arrive at truth. What is important is not truth, but that which one thinks will sustain life; the particular kind of life in which the individual happens to be interested.[31] Why should one assume that the dialectic has anything to do with rationality? Even if it be true that things proceed dialectically, this would not mean that any rhyme or reason is involved in the whole scheme; or in any phase of the process. Unless Dr. Altizer assumes that a rational being is the cause of man, he has no grounds for saying that rationality can be found in man now. If there is no rationality in the beginning of the process, what reason does he have to assume that rationality developed in the course of the process? The process is one that inevitably moves according to its own inner laws of motion (thesis, antithesis, and synthesis). How is it possible for these laws to have any rationality about them, unless they had some rationality in the beginning? But does Dr. Altizer maintain that the ultimate reality involves a Being with reason? As far as we can determine, he does not so believe.

It would also be irrational to believe in the reality of morality. For unless the original source is a moral being, then what right has one to assume that the process can evolve real morality? One might call it moral, but what reasonable and moral grounds could one occupy to affirm, for example, that repression is bad and that freedom is good? How could one morally assume that the man subjected to the will of another is in a state of bondage and the man who is under his own will only is in a state of freedom; and that the state of freedom is better than the state of bondage? Unless there is moral meaning in the beginning, why does one assume that there is moral meaning in some other part of the process? Dr. Altizer does not believe that the original source is a moral being.

If neither reason nor morality is involved in the source or in the process, on what grounds can Dr. Altizer maintain that his position is reasonable and that ours is unreasonable? How can he affirm that his system is moral and ours is immoral? How can he regard his system as one of freedom while ours is one of satanic repression? Since Nietzche used reason, even though he assumed that the world had not so proceeded as to make human reason valid, how could he believe that his reasons involved in his description of the world actually described the world? If there is no possibility of rationality, how can his rational productions, as Gordon H. Clark pointed out, "correctly describe the irrational world? Or conversely, if the world is such an evolutionary irrationalism, what hope is there of saying anything reasonable about it? If Nietzsche's theory is true, it must be false."[32] We can say the same of Dr. Altizer. He evidently thinks that he presents a reasonable case for his position. And yet, Dr. Altizer repudiates Christian theology since it so "binds itself to the abstract and static categories of our dominant Western logic," that it is not open to the dialectical dynamic movement of the world.[33] With Nietzsche he rejected the "logical laws of identity and contradiction."[34]

How, then, can he appeal to identity and contradiction in his presentation of his position? When he identified his position as the third age of the Spirit and as the true apprehending of the word, he is distinguishing it from our system. He is appealing to its identity. When, on the other hand, he appeals to the law of the opposite, or the conflict of contradictions, he is appealing to the law of contradictions. And although, supposedly, the dialectic ultimately brings these into a unity on a higher level, he does view them as in contradiction on the lower level. Thus, Dr. Altizer thinks that to affirm that God is dead is to contradict the affirmation that God is alive. He believes that the third age of the Spirit is in contradiction to, and certainly not identical with, the Christianity of the Bible. How, then, can he discredit both the logical laws of identity and the law of contradiction? If his rejection of these laws is right, even the dialectic is wrong. He must assume these laws in order to present his own position.[35]

Second, irrationality is inherent in atheism. As an atheist, Altizer should believe that the eternal reality is matter instead of the personal Spirit. There is no choice between the eternal reality being a conscious, living Spirit or being the opposite of spirit. We know in this life consciousness, life, the moral, and the rational. We know also matter and its relationships. If the ultimate reality is not of the nature of a rational Being there is but one other possibility: the ultimate reality is of the nature of matter. In this respect, Dr. Altizer cannot be an agnostic. An agnostic is one who states, concerning the existence of God, that the nature of the problem is such and the nature of the mind of man is such that we cannot make a decision rational between the two. Thus, we must suspend judgment. It is saying in effect that there are fifty good reasons for faith in God and fifty against faith in God. The situation is so delicately balanced that one cannot make a rational decision. However, this is not a rational conclusion. If there are fifty good arguments for God, certainly the rational thing is to take the way of greatest hope, which brings the most meaning into life, and the way that is most positive. However, after saying that we cannot know, the agnostic lives as if he did know that God does not exist. Furthermore, when he is arguing against theism, he sometimes indicates that he is very positive, or at least quite sure, that God does not exist.

Logically speaking, Dr. Altizer would also find it difficult to be an agnostic because of his faith in the dialectic as the key to reality. If the dialectic is true, the concept that God is alive gives rise to the concept of its opposite; the belief that God is dead. The synthesis must be higher than the first position and the second position. This would mean that there must be a Supreme Being, a super-human being of some sort. The synthesis could not be less than God, the original thesis. To say it again: Dr. Altizer has said that the affirmation that God is alive is negated by the affirmation that man is alive and supreme. This leads to a synthesis in which there is a being greater than the original concept of God and greater than man. Thus we would again come to a faith in God and not to agnosticism. Perhaps it will be replied that agnosticism is the synthesis. Faith in God gives rise to the atheism which denies the existence of God. Agnosticism is the synthesis which maintains that it is 50-50. But, the synthesis itself becomes a thesis; and the uncertainty that God exists leads to an antithesis which denies the uncertainty. This emerges in a synthesis which is a full conviction of the existence of God. Or one might put it this way: the 100 percent faith in the existence of God gives rise to the opposite, agnosticism, the 50-50 position. The synthesis is 100 percent faith on a higher level. Dr. Altizer cannot object to this and be consistent, since he believes the dialectic is the key to reality. Furthermore, he has no standard by which to say that a particular antithesis or synthesis is wrong; thus, it must be left to each individual to decide which is which. There is no censor who stands above the dialectical processes and evaluates the position taken by different individuals and decides which one is right. There is no supreme dialectician who can pass upon the dialectical analysis of any situation made by anybody.

However, Dr. Altizer has announced that he is an atheist. Materialism ends up in irrationalism. For materialism maintains that all there was to begin with was matter in motion, and matter is all there is now. This would mean that our very thinking is the product of the action and reaction of matter upon matter. We think as we think because of internal and external physical pressures. These pressures are not in a position to say that the thoughts which they cause are an insight into reality. Instead, thinking is but a physical twitch which has been caused by other physical twitches. Altizer thinks as he thinks because the forces of matter force him to think in this way. If thinking is but a vibration in the human body, mechanically and materially produced, there is no reason to maintain that thought can be rational. In such thinking one does not advance an hypothesis or possible explanation; evaluate and test this hypothesis by experiment and logical analysis; he does not gather facts to see whether or not the explanation can account for them; and then draw conclusions which he may retest from time to time. Instead he is forced to a particular conclusion, not upon the basis of any logical analysis or gathering of the facts, but on the basis of brute pressure. Therefore, Dr. Altizer's own thoughts that the dialectic is the key to reality, his own rejection of God, his affirmation concerning the future synthesis, are all just how Dr. Altizer happened to vibrate due to his internal and external physical pressures. This may be all very interesting to those who are concerned how a particular arrangement of matter, labeled Altizer, vibrates, but it has no relationship to reality or to truth. Certainly no position can be the truth about life if, in effect, it denies rationality and the possibility of arriving at truth. We do not say that Dr. Altizer understands this, but it is the logical conclusion of his atheism whether he realizes it or not.

Third, Dr. Altizer is a partaker of irrationalism when he maintains that all thought, all feeling, and all values are the product of one's particular historical epoch or situation; and that the human consciousness is simply the reflection of this historical situation. He here shares a basic position of Karl Marx.[36]

If this be true, Altizer cannot logically think his way through to a reasonable position. Instead, he simply reflects in his consciousness and in his thoughts a particular class, or perhaps other aspects of the historical setting in which he is involved. His consciousness and his thoughts are not a decisive force in life, but rather are the reflection of the decisive historical situation in which he finds himself. Is this historical situation itself rational? Dr. Altizer would say that in the past it has not been; and that the reflections in our minds concerning God and the Bible are but reflections of a past historical setting which has now been outdated. They are irrational reflections. What right, then, does he have to claim that today's reflections in his mind are rational reflections? They are just as much the product of his particular historical setting as are ours. And by what standard could he say that he reflects a rational setting while we reflect an irrational setting? Even if he so claims, it would not mean it was true. He would have no way of proving it, for the simple reason that even this claim is just a reflection in his mind of whatever situation he finds himself in. He could never know whether or not it was an insight into reality.

Could it be that irrationalism is involved in Dr. Altizer's attraction to the doctrine of the death of God, which was proclaimed by madmen in Dostoevsky's *The Possessed,* and in Nietzsche, who himself was insane for a considerable portion of his life?[37] Nietzsche seemed confused even as to who he was; at least he signed some of his notes "Dionysius" and some of them "the Crucified."[38]

Dr. Altizer has been a student of Oriental mysticism, and for a time practiced mysticism. Could it be that the Buddhist effort to achieve the "Void" has had an influence on Dr. Altizer? Involved in at least certain schools of Buddhism is the idea that "conceptual thought can establish no point of contact with reality."[39] Their dialectic is nihilistic, for it tries to show that "all intellectual expressions are 'void' of reality."[40] The goal is the destruction of words and concepts underlying them.[41] When one realizes that all is Void, he has arrived at the understanding of Nirvana.[42] One endeavors to get away from all intellectual concepts, including the concept of causality.[43] In such a case, the dialectical philosopher could not view the dialectic as the cause of all changes. Buddhism seems to be striving for a goal for which there are no words or concepts, for all concepts partake of error. Anything they say about it is false! They seem to be striving for the happy goal that an occasional student of the author seems to have achieved for at least a brief period of time—the goal of the Absolute Void, the Absolute Blank. Could it be possible that Dr. Altizer, in mystical efforts to achieve the Void, may have lost contact with the rational to such an extent that his religion and philosophy reflect the irrational? Regardless of the explanation, we do not have to know all the influences which have contributed to his irrationalism in order to detect the irrationalism itself.

All Is Rational?

With Hegel, Altizer might, on the other hand, conclude that all is rational. Since the world of experience is the embodiment of the ultimate idea, and since he regarded this as the embodiment of reason, Hegel concluded that a thing is rational not because it meets the standard which a reasoning mind has said it must reach to be rational, but because it is embodied in experience.

> In other words, instead of reason being an external criterion, it exists only as embodied in the phenomena of experience itself. We are not to set up a standard of our own by which to judge things; we have only to watch experience unfold, and detect, if we can, the laws involved in this unfolding. Reason is objective in things, not subjective in ourselves. Reality exists, and that reality reveals itself in history.[44]

All reality is the progressive development of the Rational, and therefore all reality is rational. But, if all is rational, then our beliefs are rational since they are a part of the all; and the ultimate reality is progressively working in us as well as in Dr. Altizer. Hence, our belief in God is rational. Atheism would also be rational; but now more so than theism!

It is the author's conviction that God has so made reality that when man denies God, he ends up with positions which deny the rationality of man. Although we shall not explore the idea here, we are convinced that it also ends up with the destruction of the dignity and value of man. For man without God is simply an evolved animal whom nature has ground out of nonconscious matter and will grind back into nonconscious matter.

We caution the Christian that, when he is dealing with an unbeliever, he must not assume that the unbeliever accepts the Biblical world view. Therefore, one would not label the individual a fool or the philosophy as foolishness and then proceed from there. Instead, he should start where the individual is and show him that a particular philosophy leads to irrationalism, and thus to foolishness, and in contrast with this give reasons for accepting the Biblical world view. We must not just assert that some philosophies make fools out of men; we must first prove it. We cannot prove it to them from the Bible before they have been led to faith in the Bible. Instead, we must start by proving from certain philosophies that reason is undermined and all men made into fools, including the philosopher who formulated this particular world view or who holds to it although it was first formulated by others.

Philosophy Cannot Destroy Christianity

It is possible for an attack, which has its source in philosophy, to destroy the faith of some believers. However, in its very nature a philosophical attack cannot destroy Christianity's foundations, even if Christianity were false. Christianity claims to be based on certain historical facts. God's revelation to man was made through and in connection with these historical facts, and gives us the meaning of these facts. If Christianity were false, it could be shown to be false only by showing that the alleged facts were not facts or that they have been misinterpreted. If it is a fact that Jesus Christ was predicted by the Old Testament and was raised from the dead, we are justified in accepting Christ's interpretation of these facts as well as His teaching on other matters. These facts did take place, and they have been rightly interpreted by our Lord (although we do not have the space here to prove our claim), and no philosophy can destroy these facts and their meaning. Human speculations cannot destroy facts of history, and therefore they cannot destroy God's revelation which was made in history and in connection with definite historical persons and places. Speculations are no more able to destroy these things than forceps are able to pick up ideas.

Human philosophy is based on human speculations concerning origins, the nature and reality of man, and the destiny of man. Such speculations cannot determine whether or not certain things happened in the past, or whether they will happen in the future. There are philosophies which deny the reality of matter, but this does not do away with matter, and the philosophers who hold to this position "stub their toes" on a lump of matter just as definitely as do the rest of us. There are philosophies which deny the reality of rational thought, and yet it is still possible to think rationally. When a philosophy does not accept the fact of God and of His revelation, it does not mean that atheism is true but that the philosophy is false. A philosophy which leaves no room for the moral realm does not eliminate the moral realm but pronounces itself untrue to reality.

Philosophy did not create Christianity, nor can philosophy destroy Christianity. But philosophies have been used to destroy the faith of some, and to furnish the basis for the "reconstruction" and thus the destruction of faith in Christianity. Such people are robbed of their true past, their hopeful present and their meaningful future.

All Things Are Yours

What should be the Christian's attitude toward philosophy? Philosophy, in the sense of the love of wisdom, is in harmony with Christianity, for the true wisdom is found in God's revelation of Himself in Jesus Christ. Although it is foolishness to the Greeks and a stumbling block to Jews, "unto them that are called, both Jews and Greeks, Christ the power of God, and the wisdom of God. Because the foolishness of God is wiser than men; and the weakness of God is stronger than men" (I Cor. 1:24-25). Christ has been "Made unto us wisdom from God" (I Cor. 1:30). On the other hand, when philosophy is viewed as man's attempt to formulate a world view without divine revelation, Christianity must say that such an attempt is not only untrue to reality but that it is anti-Christ in its basic assumption that reality can be adequately explained without God and His revelation.

However, a Christian should avail himself of any truth which may have been arrived at by any thinker. He should recognize that man was created in God's image and that the mind of man can arrive at truth. Without the divine revelation, man can learn from the reality which surrounds him, and of which he is an important part, that God exists (Rom. 1:20-21). Furthermore, there are some problems presented by life and thought to the mind of man with which the Bible does not deal or does not deal directly. A philosopher, even though he is an atheist, may have thought deeply on such problems and may have insights which are true. Truth should be accepted by Christians regardless of who arrived at it or who first called it to their attention. With the Word of God as our standard to protect against concepts and ideas which would destroy Christianity, Christians should be receptive to all truth (cf. I Cor. 3:21-23).

The humility taught in Scripture should keep the Christian from concluding that he automatically knows, and knows with precision, the answer to every problem which is raised by philosophy. As Arthur F. Holmes pointed out: "One cannot infer from Christian premises conclusive answers to every philosophical problem." For example, what is the exact relationship of mind and matter in a human being?[45] The Christian, of course, cannot accept a position which denies the reality of either mind or matter, but Christianity does not tell the Christian the answer to all the problems which can be raised concerning this relationship. Obviously here, as in science, one should accept facts even though he is unable to answer all questions which can be raised with reference to the facts.

When possible, the Christian should utilize philosophical insights in order to communicate more effectively with people, to build on any truth which the philosophy may have acknowledged, to understand better how to implement any moral and spiritual principle in a given situation, and to better understand people and their problems. All truth belongs to him as a child of God, and he should utilize truth regardless of who first stated it or called it to his attention. Although he realizes that he himself does not see all of the truth at any one time, nor has he completely understood all the applications of truths which he does basically grasp, he recognizes that it is both his duty and his privilege to be always receptive to truth. And in many other cases the Christian may be able to point out that Christianity furnishes the only secure foundation for some truth which a philosopher has discerned.

1. Dagobert D. Runes, ed., *Dictionary of Philosophy* (New York: Philosophical Library, 1960), p. 235.
2. Samuel Harris, *The Self-Revelation of God* (New York: Scribner, 1887), p. 251.
3. As quoted by Neal W. Klausner and Paul G. Kuntz, *Philosophy: The Study of Alternative Beliefs*, (New York: Macmillan, 1961), p. 2.

4. Will Durant, *The Story of Philosophy* (New York: Simon and Schuster, 1926), p. 2.

5. *The Modern Theological Debate* (London: Inter-Varsity Fellowship, 1941), p. 31.

6. *The Origin and Evolution of Life* (New York: Scribner, 1918), pp. ix-x. This attitude has been documented from the writings of Darwin, T. H. Huxley, Herbert Spencer, and others in Dr. Robert T. Clark and James D. Bales, *Why Scientists Accept Evolution* (Grand Rapids, Mich.: Baker 1966).

7. Frances Darwin, ed., *The Life and Letters of Charles Darwin* (New York: Appleton, 1898), II, 210; G. A. Kerkut, *Implications of Evolution* (New York: Pergamon, 1960. See additional quotations in *Why Scientists Accept Evolution*. The Creation Research Society published material which deals with the fact that evolution has not been scientifically established. Write 2717 Cranbrook Rd., Ann Arbor, Mich. 48104.

8. See William F. Quillian, Jr., *The Moral Theory of Evolutionary Naturalism* (New Haven: Yale University Press, 1945) and James D. Bales, *Communism and the Reality of Moral Law* (Nutley, N. J.: Craig, 1969).

9. James Hastings, ed., *Encyclopedia of Religion and Ethics* (New York: Scribner, 1924), VI, 580.

10. Vergilius Ferm, ed., *An Encyclopedia of Religion* (New York: Philosophical Library, 1945), p. 226.

11. Ibid., p. 226.

12. *Encyclopedia Britannica* (New York: Encyclopedia Britannica Co., 1910), VIII, p. 156.

13. Hugh Ross Mackintosh, *Types of Modern Theology* (London: Nisbet, 1949), pp. 103-104.

14. *Encyclopedia Britannica*, II, 552, Werner's edition.

15. Hastings, *Encyclopedia of Religion and Ethics*, p. 580.

16. G. R. Mure, *An Introduction to Hegel* (Oxford: Clarendon, 1940), p. 135.

17. *Philosophy of History*, tr., J. Sibree, (New York: Collier, 1905), p. 73.

18. Hastings, *Encyclopedia of Religion and Ethics*, p. 573.

19. Compare Hastings, *Encyclopedia of Religion and Ethics*, p. 580.

20. "Hegel As a Philosopher of Religion," *Journal of Religion*, January, 1966, p. 17.

21. Ferm. *op. cit.*, p. 797.

22. *Christianity Today*, Sept. 13, 1968, p. 1209. See also Schonfield's volume, *Those Incredible Christians*.

23. *Trojan Horse in the City of God* (Chicago: Franciscan Herald, 1967), pp. 49-50.

24. Francis Darwin, ed., *Life and Letters of Charles Darwin* (New York: Appleton, 1898), I, 282.

25. Ibid., p. 285.

26. Francis Darwin, ed., *More Letters of Charles Darwin* (New York: Appleton), I, 395.

27. *Life and Letters*, II, 210.

28. Thomas J. J. Altizer, *Mircea Eliade and the Dialectic of the Sacred* (Philadelphia: Westminster, 1963), 169.

29. *The Gospel of Christian Atheism* (Philadelphia: Westminster, 1966), p. 79.

30. Gordon H. Clark, *Thales to Dewey, A History of Philosophy* (Boston: Houghton Mifflin, 1957), p. 496.

31. Ibid., pp. 496-497.

32. *Op. cit.*, p. 498.

33. *The Gospel of Christian Atheism*, p. 79.

34. *Ibid.*; cf. Clark, *op. cit.*, 496-498 and Mack B. Stokes, "Reflections on the 'Death of God'," *Christian Advocate, January 27, 1966, p. 11.*
35. Clark, *op. cit.*, p. 498.
36. *Oriental Mysticism and Biblical Eschatology* (Philadelphia: 1961), pp. 155-156.
37. Altizer, *Mircea Eliade*, pp. 107-115, 176-200.
38. Ibid., pp. 191-192.
39. Marx, *op. cit.*, p. 135.
40. Ibid., p. 137.
41. Ibid., p. 151.
42. Ibid., p. 141.
43. Ibid., p. 136.
44. A. K. Rogers, *A Student's History of Philosophy* (New York: Macmillan, 1925), p. 447.
45. *Christianity and Philosophy* (Chicago: Inter-Varsity Press, 1960), p. 34.

12

THE RELATION
OF FAITH AND PSYCHOLOGY

Donald Sime

Some years ago a Hindu psychologist visiting this country noticed many empty church buildings. At the same time, on his visits to mental hospitals he noticed the crowded conditions and heard of the long waiting lists. He made the comment that if the church buildings were full during the week maybe the hospitals would not be so full. Here is one psychologist who saw some value in religion. It is true that many psychologists are active Christians and are able to relate to both their professional work and their Lord at the same time. There have been others in psychology who have, to some degree or another, been antireligious.

An important point to understand is that psychology is not a final and fixed body of knowledge. Even the very concrete discipline of physics has had some radical changes in outlook in the last thirty years. Psychology has been a more unstable field than physics since it deals with a higher order of reality which is much harder to observe and evaluate. One might say that psychology is in its adolescence. We are certainly past the beginnings of studies and theories in the field of psychology; on the other hand, there are still problems within the field and numerous viewpoints which do not always correlate well. There are, for example, schools of thought which stress mechanical or mathematical models for the primary essence of the mind, and there are those who stress the ego or the consciousness as very important. There are also several schools of thought that range between these two and sometimes beyond them.

Perhaps one cause for a lack of a comprehensive system of thought in psychology is the fact that so many psychologists in the past have denied the value of philosophical studies or have denied that psychology has anything to do with value systems. It is becoming more and more evident that psychology has very much to do with such matters; and it seems obvious that psychologists who disclaim this have their own philosophy and value systems influencing their work and research. As philosophical points of view and value systems are taken seriously in psychology, it is likely that more comprehensive systems will develop. There may never be only one major psychological viewpoint since even in philosophy there have been at least two opposing schools of thought from the earliest philosophers to this day. There have been realists and nominalists, or existentialists and idealists throughout philosophical history. Most schools of philosophy have been related to one or the other philosophy or some combination of them. Perhaps something like this will develop in psychology—perhaps it is already happening today.

What do we mean by psychology? Basically is is the systematic study and accumulation of knowledge about the human psyche. *Psyche* is a word for the mind; it includes thought, the subconscious mind, emotions, feelings, motives, desires, and so forth. With this in mind we can look at both the problems that have been raised for Christians by psychology and also the contributions made by psychology to Christian thought.

One of the foremost problems raised by psychology has been expressed in various ways but in general has to do with the concept of wish-fulfillment. This concept is that the human mind is capable of projecting or imagining something to be true because of a strong desire or need. There are various interpretations of this, such as Freud's discussion of the tribal theory in his work on monotheism. Others deal with it in terms of a basic human function. When one examines the theory it is quite evident that there is some truth in it, and that is that people do, because of strong needs or desires, believe things that are not verified in objective reality. This happens often in mental illness or in mob psychology and sometimes in hippie-type groups in which there is a basic instability underlying the entire culture. It should be observed, however, that in all of these cases we are dealing with abnormal psychology. There are instability, trauma, strong emotions that precede and work toward the development of these wish-fulfillments. One would be hard pressed to demonstrate any instance in history when these mechanisms have worked for a large segment of the population for a long period of time, especially under careful scrutiny of scholars as has been the case with the Christian belief in God. It is certainly possible for the population to believe in superstitions when they have been so taught, but this is not wish-fulfillment; it is another process. The fact that something is taught does not make it true or untrue. Christianity claims to have a verification in the life-style created by the Spirit and so is not dependent only upon teaching, even though teaching is a major factor in the propagation of the gospel.

Another thought concerning wish-fulfillment is that it does not seem likely that man would through such a process believe in the God who is described in the Bible. It would be more reasonable to assume that man would project some of the kinds of gods or idols that are seen in the so-callled primitive religions. These gods are there for tribal protection, they are fairly easily placated through group rituals which are satisfying to the persons involved. The God we read about in the Old and New Testaments is a righteous God who makes claims upon our lives, and One in whom we find a growing and an ennobling spirit as we follow Him. There are Pollyannas who rather strongly believe everything is working out. Their belief is usually unrealistic because it is not based upon any work or demand upon themselves. It is just a blind trust in things working out for good. In primitive religions we see gods who will protect the tribe and who are easily placated through ritualistic observance. In Christianity we do not see the same kind of material promises nor do we find God placated by simple ritual—nor anything less than complete commitment upon the part of the participant (Matt. 6:33).

Carl Jung made an interesting comment in regard to this kind of thinking. He said that a psychologist who noted that everyone he talked to had a belief in God or a need to believe in God could only say that this was the universal trait or belief on the part of people. He could not say whether or not there was a God. That question is not resolved by the fact that many people believe or disbelieve. Suppose, for example, that a boy were lost and a psychologist found him and asked him what he wanted. The boy would no doubt answer, "My mother." Suppose further that the psychologist asked him whether he really needed a mother. The answer would probably be, "Yes, I need a mother to take care of me and to make me feel safe." It would be rather foolish, then, for the psychologist to tell the boy that he doesn't really have a mother because he needs one and that he has just projected the idea of a mother. In fact, it might be more consistent with what we learn in physics about the over-all harmony of this universe to say that where there is a universal need there must be some reality answering to that need. Just as children need mothers and mothers give birth to children, just so it might well be argued that man cannot find satisfaction in anything less than God and therefore, there must be a God. This is one form of the ontological argument and it is at least as logical as the opposite.

Another problem that has been seen by some in the field of psychology is that psychotherapy becomes a substitute for religion. The psychiatrist becomes a substitute for a savior. This view affirms that we have problems and have needs to be worked out and that therapists can satisfactorily achieve this goal. Therefore we really do not need any supernatural and supranatural power existing beyond the physical realm. When one looks at the modern developments in psychotherapy, it is evident that therapy as a process is not a substitute for religion. The process merely helps in adjustment; the real questions of life and of meaning are still there. A person can be well-adjusted to himself and to the social context but there is a further adjustment to ultimate reality that is not possible merely through therapy, as long as therapy is only a process. In actuality many therapies have become more than a process, affirming value systems or a larger reality to which the person can relate. Logotherapy was one of the earlier therapies of this type but many existential psychologies have arisen, especially on the Continent, in the last three decades. The more psychotherapists deal with these basic questions which philosophers would call ontological questions, the more we see psychotherapy taking on the nature of a religion itself. It affirms some of the same values and meanings that are affirmed in Christianity. One very concrete example of this is the organization Alcoholics Anonymous. Their process states many of the things that are found in the gospel; that there is an ultimate power, and that they must be open to this power and trust this power to do things they cannot do themselves. So it is with many of the modern psychologies—they must deal with these ultimate issues.

Therapy alone does not become a means of salvation. What happens in therapy is that when the atmosphere is conducive, the inhibitions to the unconscious mind and feelings are relaxed and people can then express some of their negative feelings which have been troubling them. This is a step in the right direction but, ending there, therapy is unsuccessful. Good therapy is not merely a ventilation of negative feelings. What must then happen is that positive feelings must be built towards oneself, towards one's social situation, and even beyond. In other words, as the negative feelings are dealt with, positive feelings emerge and these positive feelings are related to the same value system that Christianity has been talking about for a long, long time. That is, one must gain a positive attitude toward oneself, toward his fellowman, and toward the future and beyond. So psychotherapy as a process merely helps one adjust in his reach toward a more adequate value system. It turns out that the requirements for successful mental health begin to approach the same view of reality and the value system that Christianity has believed in throughout the centuries.

Another area of problems might be summed up as the brain-versus-mind discussion within psychology. Many psychologists in various ways have held to the theory that the brain, that is, the gray matter, with the nerve cells, is the sum total of the psyche. Others believe that there is a mind which uses the brain but is not identical with it. Maltz in his book *Psychocybernetics* says that when he studied psychology he found these two views within psychology. His particular conclusion was that we have a mind which uses the computer-like brain, but not that the brain is all there is to the psyche. Those who hold that the brain is all that there is generally work on the assumption that if something can be explained by physical reality that there is nothing more to it and have proceeded to try to explain all of human life in physical terms. They really have not succeeded in this, but even if they were to succeed it would not prove that there is not another dimension to the psyche even though we could account for the various functions of the psyche in mechanical, or physical terms. The reason for the basic assumption goes back to the history of Western science in which the idea of parsimony has been more and more adhered to. That is, that the simplest explanation is the true one, and that the less outside, complicated matters are taken into account, the better it is. We are very much in a situation that Conger, in his book *New Ways in Evolution,* has put the evolutionary case. He says that we can explain the world in either evolutionary terms or creationist terms. Both are logical within themselves, but as a scientist he prefers to choose one that does not bring in outside factors. This is what has happened many times in psychology. As you can see, we are beginning with an assumption one way or the other. There is no attempt to prove it, and there is no means devised yet to prove an assumption like this.

To put it in illustrative terms, a historian told of a judge in one of the eastern states who, while listening to the plea of a man found guilty of murder, heard the man say that he was a product of his heredity and environment and could not help himself. The judge's answer was a classic. He said, "Well, if you are right, then I also am a product of my environment and heredity and I sentence you to life imprisonment." If it is true that we are merely great learning computers, then some of us have learned to trust in God, and others have not, and we certainly should not argue with the one who believes in God or the one who believes in mind, for that matter, because the brain produced that person's belief just as it produced our belief.

The real issue is in terms of the consequences of life. For example, if someone were headed toward a cliff, we know from our observation that if he falls a great distance he will die. No matter what our brain-mind situation is, most of us will feel compelled consciously to teach him or correct him so that he will not make the error of falling over the cliff. And so, no matter what our basic assumption is, we still have the same basic problems in terms of the consequences and meaning of life. There may, in fact, be some truth in the idea that we are products of these nonconscious factors, heredity, environment, the subconscious mind, and so forth. For example, quite often we are conditioned to think certain ways and we have a hard time breaking this conditioning. Or in a more positive way, we may be communicating the same thing as far as words go but something quite different depending upon the emotional situation. It is well known, for example, in personal evangelism that the rapport or love that is present in a situation is of great importance, no matter what words are used in the discussion. In other words, there are things in both our past history and our present which are nonconscious which have an influence upon us. Our psyche must be thought of as broad enough to include these items. At the same time we must never limit the psyche to the brain because it not only cannot be proved but it implies a nonreal situation in terms of conscious activity and responsibility.

Psychology as a science is not only responsible for raising problems, some of which we have discussed, but it also has brought many contributions to Christian thought. One of these is the understanding of the total mind, including emotions. For example, the word *attitude* as understood in psychology deals with total responses, including feeling, to a particular item or concept. This view greatly enriches our understanding of the word *faith* in the New Testament. Many times faith is spoken of in terms of openness, in terms of trust, dependence, and not in terms merely of knowledge or belief in the usual English sense of the word. When one does a thorough study of the Old and New Testament uses of the word for faith, he finds that the understanding of attitudes held in modern psychology greatly enriches the understanding of the Biblical terms. Another area in which psychology helps is in our basic understanding of the Scriptures. For example, Paul's discussion of sin dwelling within the mind is very close to what modern psychology has come to believe about the subconscious versus the conscious mind, that within us we have the desire and impulses which, if followed exclusively, lead to ruin. We talk about following the id impulses or looking to some higher order, but often we are talking about the "flesh and the spirit." To be sure, Christianity transcends much of psychology. For example, those who have realized that we must not merely live by basic impulses do not always recognize that we cannot live by the conscious mind nor by the superego alone. To put our trust in ourselves at any point, whether in pride, feeling, or will, is destructive. All of these, as Paul would put it, are living by the flesh. All of these must be subjugated then to the spirit, to our relationship, our trust in God, who will then work in us. Certainly this concept is much easier to understand, once one understands modern psychology.

We also find in many ways that psychology has a tendency to verify the New Testament understanding of man. For example, Paul says in Ephesians, "Be angry, and sin not and do not let the sun go down upon your wrath" (Eph. 4:26). This is an excellent summary of much of modern psychiatry. We are to be angry, that is to recognize and be aware of our feelings and emotions and sin not; that is, not lead destructive lives and not let the sun go down on our anger. We must work out some method of resolving these emotions and not let them go on eating away inside. Another example where there is a great harmony between modern thought and the Biblical message is seen when Jesus said, "Seek and ye shall find" (Matt. 7:7; Luke 11:9). Many times in the New Testament we are told we must earnestly and eagerly seek and then things will fall into place. We are beginning to realize more and more in modern psychology that really deep motivation guides and brings into being our future. It is not always what we consciously desire but what is really deep within us that we seek. There is a harmony both in the fact that these things do happen when we really desire them and also that they must happen at a very deep level. If, for example, a student says he desires a college degree but deep down for some reason or another he does not really desire it, he will not put in the time, he will not make the sacrifices, to complete his program successfully.

Another area in which psychology has contributed greatly to our understanding of the New Testament is in the area of group dynamics. There is an increasing awareness today of the power of the small, intimate group in our lives. The group has the power to change us, to help us develop, to help us grow inwardly; and it is the same kind of group that we read about in the New Testament. The early church had this intimate kind of fellowship that we are now realizing has so much importance in modern life. Many of the elements of the group experience are mentioned in the New Testament in terms of sharing, confessing, and the like. So here again we find a convergence of modern psychology and Christian thought.

A final area of contribution that we will mention is that of learning psychology. Christianity is a teaching religion (cf. John 6:44-45). There is much that we can learn about how people learn from modern psychology which can be incorporated in a very practical way into our Bible school programs. So here again is a practical area in which psychology contributes to our Christian work and understanding.

In conclusion it can be said that the discipline of psychology has both created problems for, and added insight into, Christianity. Since psychology deals with the closest thing to the spirit, the human mind, it can prove to be a great foe or a great ally to those who call themselves Christians.

13

OUR MORAL CRISIS

J. P. Sanders

In the last decade tremendous changes have taken place that deeply affect every facet of our way of life. One does not need to be an astute scholar to be aware of the fact that, along with the tremendous technological changes, a revolution has occurred in the area of the social and moral habits of the American people. This revolution is often referred to as the moral crisis of our generation. We are aware, too, that a great deal more is involved here than the mere fact that more people seem to be breaking previously established cultural and moral codes. Will Herberg has described it by saying, "The moral crisis of our time consists primarily, not in the widespread violation of accepted moral standard—again I ask, when has any age been free of that?—but in the repudiation of those very moral standards themselves."[1]

Every generation has always had a large number of people who violated its moral code. Generally, however, they regarded themselves as violators and looked upon the code as an ideal to which they ought to measure up even though they did not. Some students have cheated in every generation of college students as far back as one can remember, but even those who engaged in it regarded it as wrong and a failure to measure up to a standard regarded as proper and right. The difference between the present situation and the past is that the student who cheats today simply shrugs his shoulders and says, "Who's to say it's wrong? I like it and it gets me a good grade, and why isn't what I like just as good as what someone else likes?" In other words, there are no absolutes, no standards that are recognized as being obligatory upon all men, whether they recognize them as such or not. This type of relativism has taken control of a very large segment of the American mind. But while this is characteristic of a much larger section of our society than at any time before, it is not absolutely new. In "The Song of the Jolly Beggars" Robert Burns has this to say,

> A fig for those by law protected;
> Liberty's a glorious feast.
> Courts for cowards were erected;
> Churches built to please the priests.

James Douglas comments on Burn's poem in these words,

> The Jolly Beggars is the most immoral poem in all literature. It does not merely defy morality; it treats morality as a fantastic fable. . . . It is not easy to create a world where the soul and the flesh are completely insulated against the forebodings of conscience and the presage of moral responsibility, yet Burns does it without an effort. It is well that men are not as logical as Burns, for if they were, society would be split into fragments within a week.[2]

But, new or old, the problem is a very real one today and is having a tremendous impact not only upon our thinking but also on our way of life.

It may seem paradoxical in the light of what has just been said, but there is an increased interest in the subject of ethics today. Ethics has to do with our thinking about right and wrong, the way we live, how we solve our problems. People are interested in these issues and they talk about them. Television panelists frequently discuss moral issues. Even though previously accepted standards are being rejected, and many reject the possibility of finding any standard that is satisfactory, they nevertheless recognize the force of these issues with their inescapable consequences in our lives.

Is there any standard that all men ought to follow? It is our conviction that the Christian faith provides an answer to this question. Before we become involved with the Christian standard, let us notice some of the other standards that men have followed at different periods in history and which still underlie much of the thinking of our generation.

Pleasure

It was about a century ago that a distinguished historian, Jacob Burckhardt, observed, "When men lose their sense of established standards, they invariably fall victim to the urge for pleasure and power."[3]

Pleasure is one of the oldest standards used to distinguish between right and wrong. The doctrine by which pleasure or happiness is regarded as a standard is known as "hedonism." The hedonist holds that the goodness of any act is to be determined by the quantity of pleasure that it yields. The *psychological* hedonist, who regards man as a creature who seeks to avoid pain and gain pleasure, holds that whether one wills it or not, he unconsciously seeks those things that provide him the greatest pleasure. Consequently, there is a basic selfishness which lies behind all that he does, even in those acts that appear to be self-sacrificing and altruistic. The *ethical* hedonist holds to the point of view that men have a moral obligation to pursue pleasure. Pleasure is the ultimate good that ought to be sought and to which all activity should be directed. Aristippus, an ancient Greek philosopher, founded a school in the town of Cyrene in which he advocated this doctrine. Happiness as the one and only good was the basic principle of his school of thought. Epicurus, another famous name in Greek philosophy and early Greek teaching, sought to rid the cyreniac doctrine of its more objectionable features, but basically accepted the hedonistic point of view. He regarded the standard of goodness as the greatest quantity of pleasure throughout the whole period of one's life. In this way, he sought to eliminate certain forms of intemperance and dishonesty because they ultimately resulted in more pain than pleasure. The "absence of pain in the body and trouble in the soul" was Epicurus' way of defining pleasure. Among the more modern representatives of this point of view are John Locke, Jeremy Bentham, and John Stuart Mill. The names of Bentham and Mill have become famous for their doctrine of utilitarianism. This standard of goodness regards the pleasure of the greatest number, rather than one's own individual happiness, as the standard of goodness.

Among the difficulties involved in hedonism is what is known as the hedonistic paradox. It is generally understood that a person who makes pleasure or happiness the goal of his pursuit is not likely to find it. The happiest people in the world are not those who are seeking happiness, but those who are unselfishly giving themselves to some other goal, and who discover happiness in the pursuit.

The modern counterpart of the earlier hedonistic philosophy is the modern Playboy point of view. This view of life is wholly self-seeking and irresponsible. It rejects whatever restrains the individual (laws, conventions, or conscience) and pursues its own satisfactions. It talks of liberty, which is really license, and glorifies all forms of sexual indulgence as the way to health, sophistication, and freedom. It is both anti-Christian and pagan in outlook.

The editor of a leading magazine says, "We cannot understand people today, unless you are aware that there are many people who seriously hold that philosophy." There is no doubt that this point of view has been prevalent throughout history. One who is

acquainted with the literature of the Greco-Roman world of the first
century is aware that this philosophy dominated the lives, no doubt,
of the majority of the people. It is evident from the reading of the
Book of Romans that Paul was fully aware of the excesses to which
human beings had gone as they, consciously and unconsciously,
demonstrated the effects of this point of view in their lives.

But Christianity introduced a new point of view which did much
to change the nature of human society, in the Western world particularly. This became the basis or resulted in the development of a new
ethical code which has influenced our Western civilization particularly.

Christian morality became the norm by which all standards of
conduct were to be judged and did provide a goal toward which men
ought to strive. When men have violated this standard, they have
recognized that they were wrong and looked forward to being able to
rid themselves of the wrong that they might do the right. The
modern Playboy philosophy is a conscious rejection of this ethical
code that has pervaded Western civilization. Its impact on our times
has resulted in the new permissiveness. This new permissiveness
becomes evident particularly in the rejection of traditional Christian
behavior in reference to sexual morality. The result is that the
Christian faces, to a certain extent, the same problem he faced in the
first century. That is, he must reject conventional standards so that
he does not conform, either in attitudes or in conduct, to the world
around him; but he seeks transformation by the renewing of his mind
into the kind of person that God wills him to be, which is shown to
us so clearly in the person of Jesus Christ.

It is very evident from the study of Paul's correspondence to the
Corinthian church that he was facing opponents who were making a
specious plea for sexual laxity[4] (I Cor. 6:12 ff.). They were twisting
Paul's teaching on the freedom of the Christian person to provide a
basis for their sexual freedom. "All things are lawful, meats for the
belly and the belly for the meats," but Paul quickly denies that the
two appetites are on the same level. The body is not for fornication,
he says, but for the Lord. Paul's argument is a distinctly religious
argument. It is more than a human and rational argument. It can
only be understood in the light of man's relationship to God and
God's purpose for man. Paul insists that fornication is a violation of
the sacred tie that ought to exist between the Christian and Christ.
The body belongs to Christ and should be used for His glory.
Consequently it is a violation of the sacred covenant that one has
with Christ to take his body and make it a member of a harlot.
Immorality is, in a peculiar way, a sin against the body and also
against Christ. The body has been purchased by Christ; and conse-

quently becomes the fitting temple for God's Spirit. Paul recognizes the fact that the sex act produces a united life with its object of cohabitation so that the two form a kind of single self. Paul uses the very same language that God used in the beginning in reference to Adam and Eve (Gen. 2:24). It was God's purpose that in meaningful marriage this union should take place in the building of a harmonious and permanent relationship. To take one's body and join it to a harlot, one has to withdraw it from Christ and thus violate the covenant established when one becomes a Christian.

No doubt many people in Paul's day held to the Greek idea, that the soul was something imprisoned in the body. They held that matter was evil and that the body made of matter was necessarily and in itself an evil thing. Others held that one was able to live irrespective of his body, and they used this notion to justify all kinds of sexual indulgence. These various gnostic tendencies, even in their incipient stages, must have been felt in the early church. Against them we find not only Paul but also John bringing vehement denials and rejections. It is clear that Paul recognized that the whole self, both soul and body, was the Lord's, belonged to Him, was a member of His body, and was to be dedicated to His service. Within the permanent relationship of Christian marriage both soul and body were to find partnership under Christ (in harmony with His will) that was to result in the highest physical and social well-being for both partners.

Hedonism rejects the very ground in which the Christian concept of man is rooted. In contrast to the Biblical view, which represents man as God's creation and bearing God's image, naturalistic hedonism regards him merely as a part of nature. There is no place for the supernatural. Man is a chance product of physical activity, an organization of atoms, which, on having reached a certain level of organization, expresses itself in terms of human consciousness and human activity. Since there is no God, there is no soul. Neither is there any absolute standard to guide conduct. Relativism is the result.

The Christian's concept of how man ought to behave is intimately related to one's basic understanding of what human nature is. We cannot very well determine how even a machine should function until we know what it is. Even David Hume said long ago that "the science of man is the only solid foundation for the other sciences."[5] If a man is a piece of matter which in the course of time and chance somehow arrived at a condition of consciousness, then the approved standards of his behavior will be quite different from those standards acceptable to one who regards himself as having been created by an infinite Intelligence who is the source of goodness and who works all things according to the counsel of His will. At least until fairly recently within our Western civilization the assumptions underlying man's essential nature had their roots in Christian teaching. Man possessed a moral consciousness because of having been created in God's image. This was the distinguishing mark of his nature. Since man had been created in the image of God, he had a responsibility to his Creator and he would be judged by his Creator as to the faithfulness with which he discharged this responsibility. Those who reject belief in God naturally reject this account of man's origin, and since there is no creator, one could not possibly have any obligation to him. It is not difficult to see, therefore, that the ethical standards of these two points of view will vary greatly. Geddes MacGregor says that the humanist in his repudiation of God becomes involved in self-deception:

> Although he may talk of man's dignity, he can only do so by borrowing from a point of view that he has theoretically rejected. "Where there is no God, there is no man," writes Berdyaev, meaning that the values traditionally associated with man are lost when he is taken out of relation with God, as surely as the 100 watt lamp burning in my room will go out as soon as somebody touching a fuse breaks the electric circuit. Instead of pretending to all sorts of rights and glories and dignities as a human being, it would be more realistic for me to face the fact that apart from my relationship to God I am only a mass of protoplasm interacting in various ways with other protoplasmic masses and exhibiting a variety of needs. According to one writer, that "is what a person is."[6]

The Christian does not contend that there is anything wrong with pleasure as such, that is, that anything is wrong because it is pleasurable. What he does reject is the idea that pleasure is the chief good to be sought and the standard by which conduct is to be judged. Closely associated with this, too, it rejects the idea that pleasure makes an act good. Because there may be a certain element of pleasantness discoverable in all good acts, this does not mean that the pleasantness is what makes the actions good. C. S. Lewis has pointed out the fact that it is God who " . . . made all the pleasures. All our research has not enabled us to produce one. All we can do is to encourage humans to take the pleasures which God has produced, at times, or in ways, or in degrees which He has not forbidden."

The Playboy philosophy emphasizes freedom and regards it as the liberty to do as one pleases and the right to follow one's own inclinations. The Christian emphasis is upon freedom that one might seek the goals and the good that God has set before him. Freedom is a means and not an end. This involves freedom from sin with its accompanying slavery to bad habits and also freedom from harsh legalism (Gal. 5:1) Peter said "As free, and not using your liberty for a cloak of maliciousness but as the servants of God" (I Peter 3:16). The Playboy emphasis upon free love is a violation of all of these Biblical concepts of the true nature of freedom. True love is willingly to risk involvement and to commit itself, to accept the consequences of its acts. It is willing to bind itself "for richer, for poorer, for better or worse, in sickness or in health, until death us do part." Any attitude involving less than this hardly deserves to be called "love." The new freedom claimed by many who have adopted this philosophy does not appear to be increasing mankind's happiness, even apart from its evil results.

It has been pointed out by David A. Hubbard that the chief weakness of the Playboy philosophy is not that it puts too much emphasis on sex but that it does not put enough and that the Playboy view of sex is below the level of that of Biblical morality. Since God created man, male and female, the image of God is expressed in terms of maleness and femaleness in the relation of each to the other. It is pointed out further here that sex is primarily a covenantal relationship, and it is thus to be reserved for marriage where the two partners, within the firm commitment of the marriage bond, demonstrate in their commitment to one another the eternal relationship which God has with humanity, the human family.[7] This gives meaning to Paul's use of marriage to illustrate the relationship that exists between Christ and the church (Eph. 5).

The same author suggests that the Biblical view of sex provides also the answer to the problem of homosexuality. Homosexual practices break the basic male and female relationship of life rooted in the order of creation.

> In a scriptural sense sex is not what you do but what you are. What you do in a sex act is just the fullest, most complete expression of a relationship which is already binding, which is already covenantal in its significance because it is taken by two people who vowed before God, in their own time-bound circumstances, to try to demonstrate and live out the basic relatedness of all life. Christ calls his people to enjoy to the fullest the meaning of our sexuality, but he calls us to do this within the unconditional commitment of its covenantal character.[8]

Christian Ethics

The Christian standard of goodness is to be found in the Word of God. Its source lies beyond the sphere of human activity and is made known to us by revelation. "No one has seen God at any time; the only beloved Son who is in the bosom of the Father, he hath declared him" (John 1:18). This standard is not derived from any element within human nature; neither man's rational nature, as the Greeks held, nor through the scientific study of human experience, whether it be that of the individual or of the community. "No one knoweth . . . the Father but the Son, and he to whom the Son willeth to reveal him" (Matt. 11:27). The Christian point of view rejects the idea that "what ought to be" can be derived from "what is."

Lindsay in his *A History of the Reformation* calls our attention to the fact that history knows no reformation in the realm of morals without a religious impulse. Morality is grounded in the nature of God, who is, Himself, the ground of all ultimate values. The good is good because it is in harmony with the nature of God's character. We ought to behave in a godly way because God Himself is the author of our being. As David H. C. Read points out, the imperative corresponds with the indicative. "We ought to behave like this, for ultimately this is how the universe is governed."[9] Thus, there is a basic connection between our belief in God and our moral obligation. All obligations are in some way related to the nature of God and thus all His commandments are the result of His wisdom for man's good. It is the character of God Himself that determines the moral demands that are made of men. "Ye shall be holy: for I the Lord your God am holy" (Lev. 19:2). "Ye therefore shall be perfect even as your heavenly father is perfect" (Matt. 5:48). The New English version provides this translation, "You must therefore be all goodness just as your heavenly father is good." Jesus revealed the goodness of God in His own conduct, which was the embodiment of His teaching. Jesus appealed to men to follow Him, to take up His way of life, to think as He thought, to feel as He felt, and to relate themselves to others as He related Himself to His fellowmen. Peter said, "He left us an example that we should follow in his steps." He did not become involved in theological discussion concerning the nature of truth or of life. He simplified it by personifying the truth in His own life. "I am the way, the truth, and the life," He said; "He that hath seen me hath seen the Father" (John 14:6, 9).

Any position that denies the supernatural must obviously seek ground of ethical conduct somewhere else. Naturalists base their arguments for their conduct on many things. Some, like John Dewey, think of moral standards as more or less hypotheses arrived at through a study of human interests and human needs as these are discovered in society. And, of course, conduct which has become obligatory because society assumes it to be essential to its welfare may later be abolished, if society reaches the conclusion that such conduct is no longer expedient. If society has a valid code and if it is grounded only in community need, then, of course, society has the right to change it. Nearly always there will be some persons in any social group who regard themselves as more enlightened than their fellows. They are likely to feel free to reject the standards whenever their interests dictate.

Then why does society find certain codes of conduct essential to its well-being and, at least in some instances, why have these changes been in the direction of improving? Why is it better to be brave than cowardly, honest than dishonest? Most persons will agree that these qualities are good for a community. Why is it that we are discovering at the present time that good will, understanding, forbearance, and forgiveness promote good community relations and that pride, self-assertion, and selfishness are threatening the breakdown of communities and civilizations? It would seem that there is good reason to believe that these better virtues are imposed upon us, not by the will of the community—even though they may have been learned in the community—but because they belong to the very structure of reality. Problems that we are facing today in our interpersonal relationships, international relationships and in race relationships are revealing the need for these basic qualities. The virtues which were commended by Jesus find their roots in the nature of God Himself. James Reid points out that one of the reasons we cannot accept the theory that the standards of life have been produced by society is the fact that in nearly every situation where an unusually great teacher has appeared, society has rejected him, at least at first. His message was a criticism of accepted mores and he demanded a kind of conduct not regarded as expedient by the leading members of the society.[10]

If the moral laws have their roots in society, why was Jesus Christ, the greatest of all moral teachers, rejected and put to death by the community to which He came? Why has society so often put to death the best people of any group? Is it not because these claims on their loyalty and obedience have a deeper source than our own sense of what is good for society and for our own interests?[11]

> The sense of moral obligation has deeper roots than our own social advantage. It secures this in the long run, for it is on moral foundations that society must be built if it is to be stable and healthy. This has been proved in countless cases. But the argument from advantage is not what gives goodness authority over us. In point of fact, it is only when we are ready to listen to the voice of conscience, whatever may happen, that the best things we hope for come to us; material prosperity of all kinds is a by-product of goodness; it is found when we seek goodness first.[12]

In Galsworthy's *Maid in Waiting* the girl says, "I am decent because decency is the decent thing," but her mother goes on to ask the further question, "Why is decency the decent thing if there is no God?"

The moral demands that are placed upon us and that we recognize in life, consequently, we believe are based on the nature of God Himself. When we talk about ethics being grounded in religion, we are following the Biblical teaching that lies behind both Judaism and Christianity. It is not difficult for the Christian to see "that the universe itself is on the side of the goodness, the justice, the love, the integrity that we experience as moral demands on us."[13]

The profound ethical insights that Jesus revealed in His teaching cannot be explained satisfactorily except on the basis of His claims which are revealed in the New Testament. He was the Word that became flesh and dwelt among us. "God having of old times spoken to the fathers through the prophets hath in these last days spoken unto us through his Son." If you regard Him simply as "a good man," Himself the product of blind chance who accidentally appeared on our earthly stage, then there is no adequate basis for the marvelous ethical insights revealed in His teaching. Our generation needs Christ and His teaching.

> Christ is the world's greatest possession, and the world should know more of it and get more of its value out of it. Christ is not a mere example to whom we can refer the question: "What would Jesus do?" He is a spiritual power in which we can dip and find strength, with whom we can commune, on whom we can draw. There is no distinction between the historical Jesus and the living Christ. The latter is simply the former realized, entered into, enjoyed, used.[14]

Jesus recognized the priority of love. When asked what is the greatest commandment of the law, He replied, "Thou shalt love God with all thy mind and heart, soul, and strength. This is the first and great commandment. The second is like unto it; thou shalt love thy neighbor as thyself" (Mark 12:30). God's love expressed itself to the people of the old covenant in doing for them, not what they deserved, but what they needed in order to achieve their highest possible well-being. He sought their salvation, and to this end even the disciplinary action of His providence was evident. God's love for Israel was not based on their merit; it was not given as a reward for service. He sought to do all things for them that were possible to make them the kind of people He wanted them to be. Consequently, an attitude of mercy and loving-kindness is seen throughout all His relationship with the people of the Old Testament. The supreme example of God's love for man is found in His revelation through Christ. He was the Word made flesh. God became incarnate in human form that we might be able to know Him and to comprehend the meaning of His love. Christ and His teaching constitute the final and complete revelation of God's love and God's will to mankind. Consequently, His life and His teaching become the norm on which the Christian's judgments are to be based. Just as God's love for Israel shows itself in His concern for their needs, so the brotherly love the Christian manifests in his conduct expresses itself in working for the interest and well-being of one's neighbors. The Christian standard is that one should do good to others, not for his own sake, but for their sakes. Even parental love expresses itself in terms of the child's needs, rather than the parent's pleasure. Paul said, "Let no man seek his own, but each his neighbor's good" (I Cor. 10:24). When Jesus was asked, "Who is my neighbor?" He responded by telling the story of the Good Samaritan in which He shows not merely who one's neighbor is, but what is meant by neighborly love. The Samaritan was neighbor to the man who had been robbed and expressed his neighborliness by rendering a service to him in terms of his need and without thought of personal reward. "If you do good to those who do good to you, what do you more than others?" Jesus asked. The superiority of the Christian ethic is demonstrated when it reaches beyond the thought of personal reward and seeks the real good of the person loved. Not only did the teaching of Christ show itself in this way to be superior to the religion of the scribes and the Pharisees, but also in this very same way, it stands in contrast to the ethical systems of hedonism and naturalism. Nietzsche regarded Christianity as meaningful only for weaklings. It was impossible for him to understand how a person could deny his own self-interests. Consequently, he interpreted Christianity as an attempt of the weak to gain their satisfaction in life by rejecting as unworthy the things that they actually wanted, but couldn't achieve. Nietzsche was unable to understand the meaning of Christian love, which provides its adherents with the power to renounce the things the naturalists want as the source of successful living.

Wisdom and Love

The chief virtue among the Greeks was wisdom. The highest activity to which one could give himself, according to Aristotle, was thinking, an activity of reason. And wisdom provides one with the highest possible satisfaction. In contrast, the chief virtue of Christianity is love. It is love that is the fulfilling of the law. And Christian love does not seek its own satisfaction, but the highest good of the person loved. The ethics of Aristotle never required that one should neglect his own interest in promoting the needs and the welfare of others. Christian love is willing to go to extreme lengths, even to lay down its life for others, "I lay down my life for the sheep," Jesus said. "I am willing to spend and be spent for your souls," Paul said. This is not the Greek doctrine of moderation, but the Christian doctrine of the extreme.[15] It is exemplified in Christ on the cross and in Stephen praying for those who were stoning him to death and in Paul wearing himself out that he might minister to the needs of the Christian people (II Cor. 5). It is only as men respond to the demand for the renunciation of inordinate self-love, which is the source and spring of the greed and selfishness which permeate the interpersonal relations of mankind, that there is any hope of a bright social future. It is only as men love God that they will rise to the heights of self-renunciation.

Christian Law and Situational Ethics

The term, "New Morality," was perhaps first used in a Papal Encyclical that was issued in about 1966. This encyclical was concerned with certain statements that were found in Bishop Robertson's *Honest to God* and perhaps Paul Tillich's *Morality and Beyond.* The term "situational ethics" itself was popularized by Fletcher's book that bears the title *Situational Ethics.* These men seek to clarify their position by distinguishing it from the hedonism of the Playboy philosophy. The point of view of Fletcher is not a relativistic point of view altogether since he holds that there are some universal principles that should be regarded as right by all people; but he reduced all these principles to one—the obligation to love. Fletcher holds that we face the alternatives of accepting a rigid legalism, an antinomianism, or accepting situational ethics.

In setting forth these alternatives an unnecessary bifurcation between law and love is made. Throughout the entire Bible law and love are woven together. To illustrate, we go back to the giving of the Ten Commandments. Before God gave these commandments to the people of Israel, He wrought a series of magnificient miracles by which He demonstrated His superiority over all the gods of Egypt. Each plague was an attack on one of the Egyptian deities by which Jehovah showed His supremacy over that pagan god. Following this series of miracles, God delivered the people of Israel from Egypt, redeeming them from slavery, making them free. Then, in a very brief time after the Exodus, He gave them law. Their redemption was an expression of His love; their freedom was the gift of His grace. Then came law, by which their love was to be channeled as they related themselves both to Him and to one another. "I am the Lord thy God who brought thee up out of the land of Egypt," and then occurs the first commandment, "Thou shalt have no other gods before me." Whatever reality there may have been for other gods, they did nothing for Israel. Since Jehovah redeemed Israel, He wanted them to have no other gods before Him.

Jehovah wanted to be known among His people as He revealed Himself through His prophets, rather than as their artists imagined Him. Consequently, we have the second commandment, "Thou shalt not make unto thee any graven images."

God's name stands for God Himself. Hence, His name is holy. Jehovah wanted His people to hold His name in reverence. Hence, He said to them, "Thou shalt not take the name of the Lord thy God in vain."

To save them from the oppression of masters, and even the oppression some individuals might apply to themselves, He gave them the fourth commandment, "Remember the sabbath day and keep it holy."

As the young grow up, they need the guidance that comes from experience. Lacking experience themselves, they need help to avoid life's pitfalls and to point them to life's true values. So Jehovah gave the commandment, "Honor thy father and thy mother that it may be well with thee."

God wanted Israel to understand that human life is sacred. It can come from no other source than God Himself. Consequently, He said to them, "Thou shalt not kill."

The family is a sacred institution, the matrix into which new human life is born, and it serves to introduce the growing individual to the world at large. Here the individual finds his first learning experiences. Here he is first told about God. To preserve the integrity of the family, that it may serve its divine purposes, God said, "Thou shalt not commit adultery."

Property, too, possesses a certain sacredness. As human life develops, it needs to develop the sense of responsibility for the proper use of possessions. And because of this need, God said, "Thou shalt not steal."

A man's good name is a helpful prop in living a good life and his honor and reputation are precious. Consequently, we should learn to respect, not only our own good name, but our neighbor's as well. Hence the commandment, "Thou shalt not bear false witness."

It is not right for man to desire that which his neighbor possesses to the extent that this desire throws his neighbors' possessions in jeopardy. Consequently, we have the tenth commandment, "Thou shalt not covet anything that is thy neighbor's."

It is hard to regard these commandments as either meaningless or arbitrary. They are not a set of rules imposed for the purpose of making life difficult. These laws were the gifts of God's love to provide the norm for conduct that the lives of the people might be useful and profitable. The highest well-being of the people could be achieved only through proper respect for these laws. Hence, any dichotomy between love and the laws of God is unnecessary.

Situation ethics overlooks man's tendency to rationalize. Where each man is left to determine the meaning of love for himself in his own situation, his rationalization often results in his doing what he likes rather than what he should. Logic to many people is merely a thing of emotion and enthusiasm, and if left to test the meaning of love in their own situations, they are likely to be led by their impulses. It is very easy to convince ourselves that we ought to do what we want to do. Consequently, in God's wisdom He saw fit to give man law to provide the boundaries for love, and in this way he introduced content and meaning into the context of love. The law constitutes the concrete forms in which the principle was to express itself.

All through the Bible in both the Old and New Testaments we have teachings to observe and commandments to follow. These are not contrary to the law of love. They are God's way of showing us how to apply the meaning of love in the various situations of life that we face. In other words, God not only tells us to love, but he tells us how. We cannot always trust our own impulses. We cannot wait until we find ourselves in a difficult situation and then have the objectivity to apply the principle of love and expect to come out with the right kind of answer. If a person hasn't decided what is to be done before he gets into some situations, there is not much likelihood that he will do the right thing. Consequently, the need for our being taught the law so that prior to critical situations we will know what should or should not be done and thus have that much advantage in doing the right.

Situation ethics fails to provide us the full meaning of love. The God who is love gave us the commandment to love, and no other commandment that He has given us could possibly be out of harmony with the essential character of His own nature nor with the expression of this principle in our own lives. That these other commandments necessarily result in a legalism is an assumption that simply cannot be sustained in the setting of the Scriptures. One may take a legalistic attitude toward anything, even toward the commandment to love. But just because it is possible does not mean that it necessarily follows. It is possible for us to possess the principle, for us to know its content as this content is found in the specific laws of life, without becoming legalists. Certainly Paul was no legalist. He emphasized his love in each of his epistles and it was he who provided the wonderful psalm of love in the letter to the Corinthians. He says that love is the fulfillment of the law, yet in each of his epistles he provides many commandments through which love was to find concrete expression. He wanted to provide guidelines so that his readers would love intelligently.

Situation ethics is unusually concerned with problems of sexual morality. The unusual situations so often discussed are those involving sex. Here again the Scriptures provide us with the information that we need for man to be the kind of creature God intended him to be. The Scriptures provide us with the information needed to give sex its proper and meaningful place in life. God created man, male and female. Dr. Hubbard aptly expresses it in these words,

> The image of God is expressed partially in terms of our maleness and femaleness and our capacity to relate one to another. The book of Genesis suggests what is developed in other parts of Scriptures that sex is primarily a covenantal relationship. It is the way within the confines of marriage, that we demonstrate on our own level the eternal relationship which God has for the human family. It is for this reason Hosea can use marriage as an analogy of the relationship between God and Israel. It is for this reason that the Apostle Paul in Ephesians 5 can use marriage as an illustration of the relationship between Christ and His church.[16]

Hubbard goes on to point out that in this same context

> We also have an answer to the question of premarital and extramarital 'testing.' Are we working out the meaning of a lifelong covenant? Is there an eternal . . . quality to the relationship? Is this an adequate expression of the total relationship between man and woman? Are we fully responsible for each other? These are questions that can only be answered affirmatively in marriage.[17]

Since God created man male and female, it is only by respecting God's unique creation and using it in terms of the fulfillment of His will that we find the covenantal meaning that we should and the joy and satisfaction that remains permanently. It is only in this way that love can express itself and meet the approval of God and provide for our own well-being.

Jesus did not draw any distinction between love and law. He said, "If you love me, you will keep my commandments." Certainly He could be regarded as no legalist. He vehemently denounced the bigotry of the legalism of Pharisaical self-righteousness. Yet He realized the need of law. He gave commandments to His disciples and told them that if they loved Him they would keep these commandments. They were necessary in order that the disciples might use their freedom properly and that their lives might be guided into the full expression of duty that Jesus had imposed upon them. Many experienced and highly informed people find it difficult to apply the principle of love in the particular situations with which they are faced in life. The recent convert and the immature are in need, not only of a principle, but also of the special guidelines that law provides. God's love for His people is selfless, understanding, and forgiving, and every command that He has ever given is the result of His wisdom for our good. When we learn that it is through His teaching that we discover our own highest good, and when we seek both our good and the good of others, we will find that the observance of Christ's teaching provides us the most adequate expression of love that it is possible for us to know.

Conclusion

The answer to our moral crisis and the way out of our ethical dilemma lies in the acceptance of Christ and in the revelation of the nature of God that He has shown us. His standard of goodness, finding its source in God rather than in man, provides the only adequate standard to guide us through our problems. We must recognize the need of a source of goodness which lies beyond the human realm. Centuries before Christ, the weeping prophet of Jerusalem reminded his generation, "It is not in man that walketh to direct his steps." The late C. S. Lewis reminds us, "The human mind has no more power of inventing a new value than of planting a new sun in the sky or a new primary color in the spectrum."[18] Man must possess the humility to recognize that this is true. It is nothing short of pride that causes man to reject what God offers and to seek for the solution to his problems within himself. Perhaps this is the reason that Jesus in describing the ideal citizen of the kingdom began with the beatitude, "Blessed are the poor in spirit, for theirs is the kingdom of heaven" (literally translated, "Blessed are the beggars in spirit). It is only when we come to recognize our own spiritual poverty that we beg for help. This first beatitude is fundamental to all the others and provides the attitudinal foundation on which all Christian virtues are built. "Following God's will results in the maximum happiness and satisfaction for the doer because what God wills is actually the greatest good for man, although it may not appear so in advance."[19] Long ago the psalmist reminded us of a similar point of view when he said, "The fear of the Lord is the beginning of wisdom." God's will provides the solution to man's plight, if he only has the humility to recognize it.

But the implementation of this is not easy. The basic conflict in our human nature must be recognized. Paul recognized it, and in describing his own situation, he describes what every sensitive conscience discovers within itself. "Not what I would, that do I practice, but what I hate, that I do. . . . . For the good which I would I do not: but the evil which I would not, that I practice" (Rom. 7:15, 19). MacGregor, in his *Introduction to Religious Philosophy,* quotes a stanza that is applicable:

> Within my earthly temple there's a crowd:
> There's one of us who's humble, one who's proud;
> There's one who's broken-hearted for his sins,
> And one who, unrepentant, sits and grins;
> There's one who loves his neighbour as himself,
> And one who cares for naught but fame and pelf.
> From much corroding care I should be free,
> If once I could determine which is me.[20]

The solution to this conflict between the higher and lower self, the spirit and the flesh, Paul found in Christ, "Wretched man that I am, who shall deliver me out of the body of this death? I thank God through Jesus Christ our Lord" (Rom. 7:24-25).

> Trust in the Lord with all thine heart; and lean not unto thine own understanding. In all thy ways acknowledge Him, and He shall direct thy paths.—Proverbs 3:5-6

Let the redeemed of the Lord say so.—Psalm 107:2

1. "What Is the Moral Crisis of Our Time?", *The Intercollegiate Review,* Vol. 4, Nos. 2-3 (Jan.-March 1968), p. 63.
2. Quotes from James Rein, *Why Be Good?* (Nashville: Cokesbury, 1939), p. 25.
3. Quoted by Herberg, *op. cit.,* p. 67.
4. William Barclay, *Letters to the Corinthians,* 2nd ed. (Philadelphia: Westminster, 1956), pp. 61 ff.
5. *Treatise of Human Nature* (New York: Oxford University Press, 1941), Introduction.
6. *Introduction to Religious Philosophy* (Boston: Houghton Mifflin, 1959), pp. 135, 136.
7. "The Covenant Companion," *Fuller Bulletin,* March 24, 1967.
8. Ibid.
9. *Christian Ethics* (Philadelphia, New York: Lippincott, 1969), p. 26.
10. Op. cit., p. 60.
11. Ibid.
12. Ibid., p. 61.
13. Read, op. cit., p. 26.
14. A. C. McGiffert, *Christianity as History and Faith* (p. 143), quoted by L. H.

Marshall, *The Challenge of New Testament Ethics* (New York: St. Martins, 1947), p. 353.
15. Charles H. Patterson, *Moral Standards,* 2nd ed. (New York: Ronald, 1957), p. 315.
16. Op. cit.
17. Ibid.
18. *Christian Reflections* (London: Bles, 1967), p. 75.
19. Millard Erickson, *The New Evangelical Theology* (Westwood: N. J.: Revell, 1968), p. 167.
20. P. 339.

14

TRADITION AND TRUTH

Herman O. Wilson

So then, brethren, stand fast, and hold the traditions which ye were taught, whether by word, or by epistle of ours.
Paul, II Thessalonians 2:15

The causes of superstition are: pleasing and sensual rites and ceremonies; excess of outward and pharisaical holiness; overgreat reverence of traditions, which cannot but load the church, the stratagem of prelates for their own ambition and lucre. . . .
Francis Bacon, "Of Superstition"

Tradition as a force in shaping man's thought and conduct is exceedingly old. No one can say how old it is, since oral tradition undoubtedly antedates written words by many centuries. Scholars speculate that even before the dawn of history, man passed on to his descendants such arts and skills as he possessed, as well as his views of natural phenomena, the care and management of property, and stories of ancestors, chieftains, and heroes.

H. G. Wells, for example, traces the power of tradition to prehistoric times:

> Primitive man added to his powers of transmitting experience, representative art and speech. Pictorial and sculptured record and verbal tradition began. Verbal tradition was developed to its highest possibility by the bards (early poets, who composed and sang songs of great deeds). They did much to make language what it is today.

> With the invention of writing, which devleoped out of pictorial record, human tradition was able to become fuller and much more exact. Verbal tradition, which had hitherto changed from age to age, began to be fixed.[1]

Every reader of history, religion, science, or philosophy is aware of the power of tradition for good or evil, and of its hold on individuals and institutions. Basically, tradition is something handed down or transmitted from one age to another.

A modern dictionary defines *tradition* as follows:

> 1. The handing down of statements, beliefs, legends, customs, etc., from generation to generation, especially by word of mouth or practice. 2. That which is so handed down. 3. Theol. (a) (Among Jews) an unwritten body of laws and doctrines, or any one of them, held to have been received from Moses and handed down orally from generation to generation. (b) (Among Christians) a body of teachings, or any one of them, held to have been delivered by Christ and His Apostles but not committed to writing.[2]

According to Jewish writers, *tradition* means the "doctrines and sayings transmitted by word of mouth from father to son and thus preserved among the people." These traditions make up a large part of the oral teachings (oral law) of the Jews; and much of the Halakic teaching (the body of Jewish law supplementing the Scriptural law) goes back to Moses and Mount Sinai.[2] A modern Jewish authority says this of ancient tradition:

> . . . Judaism has consciously stressed the importance of tradition. Rabbinic Judaism operates with the concept of a double Torah, that which is written down in the Five Books of Moses, and that which was given by God to Moses by word of mouth, and which was handed down orally through the generations. The oral Torah interprets and explains, and also supplements the written law . . . . Even after the oral Torah was itself reduced to writing in the Talmudic literature, the element of living tradition was not eliminated.[4]

The same source goes on to stress the value of long-standing tradition, "holding that the oldest materials of the Bible were preserved orally for a long time before they were written down."[5] Indeed, many archaeological finds have substantiated such traditions. The article adds:

> Jewish law distinguishes clearly between ceremonies commanded by the Torah and those which have only the force of custom (*minhag*). The authorities have held that customs which are generally observed, and which are not in themselves objectionable, should be followed with the same fidelity which is accorded the prescriptions of the Torah.[6]

In Deuteronomy, God impressed upon His people Israel the necessity of preserving His word without change and of observing all its commands and ordinances: "Ye shall not add unto the word which I have commanded you, neither shall ye diminish from it, that ye may keep the commandments of Jehovah your God which I command you" (4:2).

The Israelites are then warned to remember all "the things which thine eyes saw" when God delivered them from bondage, and then He adds: "but make them known unto thy children and thy children's children; the day that thou stoodest before Jehovah thy God in Horeb, when Jehovah said unto me, Assemble me the people, and I will make them hear my words, that they may learn to fear me all the days that they live upon the earth, and that they may teach their children" (4:9-10).

In the same passage, Moses declares: "And Jehovah commanded me at that time to teach you statutes and ordinances [Heb. *mishpatim* or traditions] that you might do them in the land whither ye go over to possess it" (4:9-14).

It becomes quite clear from such sources that tradition became a vital influence upon the thinking and practice of the Jewish people, influencing mores, customs, ceremonies, and worship. Certain parties laid more stress on tradition than others. "The case of the Pharisees and Sadducees is unique—for the Pharisees were in many ways the party of progress and innovation, yet they upheld claims of the traditional Oral Law against the Sadducees, who denied its binding character."[7] The Israelites used the terms *Shem'uah* or *Shema'tha* (to hear) for their legal traditional customs. "Cabbala (that which is received) is a term used in the *Talmud* for citations from the prophets and *Hagiographa*."[8]

Thus it becomes apparent that tradition is first oral, a retelling of an event, of a command or ordinance, which may be handed down orally for an indefinite period of time before it is committed to writing. The etymology of the word *tradition,* from the Latin *tradition, traditio,* action of handing over, implies: (1) a deposit or fund of doctrine, (2) depositaries, or persons charged to receive and transmit the deposit to their successors. Most religions possess or claim to possess some basic truth going back to an ultimate source of authority, and these truths or traditions are preserved and passed on to succeeding generations.

The record of Israel's exodus from Egypt, of their wilderness wanderings, and of God's words spoken to Moses in Mt. Sinai shows the process: "And Moses went up unto God, and Jehovah called unto him out of the mountain, saying, Thus shalt thou say to the house of Jacob, and tell the children of Israel: Ye have seen what I did unto the Egyptians, and how I bore you on eagles' wings and brought you unto myself. . . . These are the words which thou shalt speak unto the children of Israel" (Exod. 19:3-6). The Ten Commandments, heart of the Jewish law, are introduced with the sentence: "And God *spake* all these words, saying . . . " (Exod. 20:1). Repeatedly' God speaks to Moses, who is to carry the words or ordinances of God to the people (Exod. 20:22; 21:1; 24:1; and elsewhere). Note the double responsibility laid on Moses: "And Jehovah said unto Moses, come up to me on the mount, and be there: and I will give thee the tables of stone, and the law and the commandments, which I have written, that thou mayest teach them" (Exod. 24:12). This passage illustrates quite well both the deposit (law and commands) and the depositary (Moses). It also makes Moses responsible for teaching these laws to the people. Later passages (Exod. 34:32); 35:1) show that Moses faithfully obeyed God's command.

The manner by which an oral tradition was preserved and passed on may be seen in the explicit directions given by God for the annual observance of the Passover (Exod. 12) and the obligations of the fathers, at a later time, to teach their children both the origin and the significance of the Passover meal (Exod. 12:24-28).

Eventually, perhaps generations later, these words, commandments and ordinances of God were written down and became the *Torah,* or written law of the Jews. When they were put in written form they became Scripture (from the Latin *scribere,* to write, *scriptura,* the product of writing). The details of this process—the writing of the sacred traditions and their eventual inclusion in the "received" or canonical Scriptures—is not within the province of this study. It is the process itself, the message of God given directly to a person appointed to receive it and man's faithful transmission of this message (deposit) to God's people that concerns us here.

At a later time priests and prophets, chosen as God's spokesmen, would likewise receive messages from God and give them to Israel. A formula found again and again in the Old Testament record is "And Jehovah said unto. . ." (for examples: Judg. 7:4; I Sam. 2:27; 3:10, 11) or the familiar expression "Thus saith Jehovah," used so often by the prophets.

It was no doubt inevitable that as time passed teachers and priests would feel called upon to define, limit, or interpret the laws handed down from the past. Under the heading "Tradition" a standard Bible encyclopedia defines the term:

> (a) some oral laws of Moses (as they supposed) given by the great lawgiver in addition to the written laws; (b) decisions of various judges which became precedents in judicial matters; (c) interpretations of the great teachers (rabbis) which came to be prized with the same reverence as were the Old Testament scriptures.[9]

Thus tradition came to have two distinct meanings: first, the will of God communicated directly to His messengers, Moses, Joshua, David, the prophets, for example; and transmitted at first orally but later made a part of the Holy Scripture; secondly, the opinions, interpretations, and decisions of judges, rabbis, and other teachers. The latter kind of tradition is often at variance with revealed truth and is likely to show the bias or prejudice of human judgment. It became known as the traditions of men or "tradition of the elders" (Matt. 15:2; cf. Gal. 1:6-7, 12, 14). Christ found a clear conflict between "the commandment of God" and the "tradition" of *corban* (Matt. 15:3-6) by which some of the Jews escaped the responsibility of caring for aged parents, and He said, "And ye have made void the word of God because of your tradition" (v. 6) and added, "But in vain do they worship me, teaching as their doctrines the precepts of men" (v. 9).

A close study of the Sermon on the Mount will show that Christ revered the law and the teachings of the Old Testament but rejected the sayings or traditions of men (Matt. 5:17, 18). This He did by repeatedly saying, "Ye have heard" but adding, with authority, "But I say unto you." His purpose seems to have been to clear away the long accumulation of judgments and interpretations which not only obscured but often contradicted God's expressed will.

After saying that no part of the law shall pass away until "all things be accomplished," Christ warns that the standard of righteousness must "exceed the righteousness of the scribes and Pharisees" if a man is to enter into God's Kingdom. The Jewish view of righteousness had become rigid, self-centered, and without compassion. Thus in the Jewish community a strict legalism had banished love or compassion and had made the law a yoke, as Peter says, "which neither our fathers nor we were able to bear" (Acts 15:11).

In the Savior's discussion of legalism and human tradition, He pointed out that sacrifice, in itself, cannot please God when the worshiper is not living peaceably with his brother (Matt. 5:23-26). He also corrected the view that the marriage bond can be broken for personal reasons and cited infidelity of the marriage partner as the only justifiable cause for divorce. He reproved the making of oaths and showed that a man's word—his simply yea or nay— should be sufficient evidence of truth. By rejecting the idea of "an eye for an eye and a tooth for a tooth," Christ introduced two revolutionary concepts: *nonresistance* ("Resist not him that is evil") and *grace*, the distinguishing mark of the new and spiritual interpretation of law: "And whosoever shall compel thee to go one mile, go with him two" (Matt. 5:38-41).

One of the crowning examples of Christ's reinterpretation of

God's will is found in His statement: "Ye have heard that it was said, Thou shalt love thy neighbor, and hate thine enemy: but I say unto you, Love your enemies and pray for them that persecute you; that ye may be the sons of your Father who is in heaven. . ." (Matt. 5:43-45). The command to "love thy neighbor as thyself" is of course found in the law (Lev. 19:18), but the corollary ("hate thine enemy") is not a part of the law but a typically human tradition. In fact, the same context in Leviticus which calls upon the Israelites to show love to neighbors also commands fair treatment and compassion for strangers: "And if a stranger sojourn with thee in your land, ye shall not do him wrong. The stranger that sojourneth with you shall be unto you as the home-born among you, and *thou shalt love him as thyself* [emphasis added]; for ye were sojourners in the land of Egypt: I am Jehovah your God" (Lev. 19:33-34).

Obviously, if the Jewish nations had followed this injunction, the saying "thou shalt hate thine enemy" could never have been accepted or tolerated. This addition—a contradiction—surely underscores the weakness of human nature and, at the same time, the unquestioned acceptance of an evil tradition.

In many other matters the basic conflict between man's narrow and literalistic view of the law and God's will or *intention* for man can be pointed out. Here are three examples:

(1) The charge that the disciples of Christ violated the Sabbath (Matt. 12:1-8).

(2) The condemnation of Christ for healing a man with a withered hand on the Sabbath. Note Christ's reference to their own practice of lifting a sheep from a pit on the Sabbath day lest the animal suffer or die, and his emphasis on human compassion: "How much then is a man of more value than a sheep!" (Matt. 12:9-12).

(3) The offense to the Pharisees when the disciples did not wash their hands before eating.

In summary, we may say that Christ did not reject the moral principles or laws of the Jewish Torah; instead, He conserved and reaffirmed these principles. What He cast aside as worthless or harmful was the narrowing, restricting concepts of rabbis and teachers who so overlaid the teachings of the law with their hundreds of precepts, judgments, and interpretations that the real purpose of God's will had been either lost or radically distorted. Christ gave a *spiritual* import to what had become a slavish obedience to technicalities which stifled all freedom of expression and joy in serving God. He put the emphasis, not upon rituals, sacrifices, and man's clever interpretation of terms, but upon justice, mercy, faith, and compassion. These were the intended fruits of a godly life; but, unfortunately, these desirable qualities had been generally neglected and despised in man's zeal to keep the letter, not the spirit, of the Law.

Tradition and the Early Church

The New Testament has its own traditions, just as the Old dispensation had. Some of the passages refer to an oral tradition—often based upon the teaching of Christ or one of the apostles. The first evidence of an ordinance or tradition handed down by a body of Christians concerns the decisions of the Jerusalem conference—a meeting of "apostles and elders"—to decide what requirements of the Jewish law should be laid upon Gentile converts. The new converts were being troubled by certain men "who went out from us and have troubled you with words, subverting your souls; to whom we gave no commandment; it seemed good to us, having come to one accord, to choose out men and send them to you with our beloved Barnabas and Paul. . ." (Acts 15:23-26). Two important facts in this narrative deserve emphasis: one, certain unauthorized teachers had gone about teaching that Gentiles must be circumcised and must keep the Mosaic law (Acts 15:5); two, that the decisions regarding those commandments which must be observed by Gentiles were arrived at by a thorough discussion and then a coming "to one accord."

Then the whole process of the forming and transmitting of tradition is given: trusted men are to be sent out "who themselves also shall tell you the same things by word of mouth"; secondly, the decisions handed down by the conference in Jerusalem were divinely directed: "For it seemed good to the Holy Spirit and to us to lay upon you no greater burden than these necessary things: that ye abstain from things sacrificed to idols, and from blood, and from things strangled, and from fornication; from which if ye keep yourselves, it shall be well with you. Fare ye well" (Acts 15:28-29). It is interesting that these restrictions based upon Old Testament teaching are negative and that they prohibit practices which were very common in pagan religions. Notable, too, is the fact that nothing is said about the supposed need of circumcision—or the keeping of the Sabbath.

When these precepts were delivered, the record shows that the converts received them joyfully, and two of the ablest leaders, Paul and Barnabas, remained in Antioch "teaching and preaching the word of the Lord," and so did other brethren (Acts 15:32-35). At this time, about seventeen years after the beginning of the church in Jerusalem, no books which now make up the New Testament had been written. All the teaching—except for the decrees issued at Jerusalem—was based upon the remembered words of Christ or the guidance of the Holy Spirit (see John 14:15-18; 15:26-17; 16:8-15).

The apostle Paul, who was specially chosen to preach the gospel to Gentile nations, refers a number of times to traditions which he personally delivered to Gentile churches. Concerning his teaching that man is head of woman as Christ is the head of the church, Paul states: "Now I praise you that ye remember me in all things and *hold fast the traditions, even as I delivered them to you*" (I Cor. 11:2 emphasis added). To the same church Paul wrote to answer questions about marriage and celibacy, and he makes this significant statement regarding his teaching. "But unto the married *I give charge, yea not I, but the Lord,* That the wife depart not from her husband. . . . *But to the rest say I, not the Lord:* If any brother hath an unbelieving wife, and she is content to dwell with him, let him not leave her" (I Cor. 7:10-12 emphasis added). Later in this same context the writer again gives definite teaching but with a clear limitation: "Now concerning virgins I have no commandment of the Lord: But I give my judgment as one that hath obtained mercy of the Lord to be trustworthy. I think therefore. . ." (I Cor. 7:25-26).

To the Church of Thessalonica, Paul wrote: "So then, brethren, stand fast, and hold the traditions which ye were taught, whether by word, or by epistle of ours" (II Thess. 2:15). In the same letter he warns against those who "walk disorderly" and "not after the tradition which they received of us" (II Thess. 3:6). The binding quality of this letter (typical of many letters which the apostle wrote to churches or individuals and which later became a part of the New Testament canon) is seen in this statement: "And if any man obeyeth not *our word* by this epistle, note that man, that ye have no company with him. . ." (II Thess. 3:14). Two vehicles of tradition are made evident here—oral tradition, or preaching, and written letters.

Paul made a sharp distinction between man's teaching and the revelation of Christ. To his converts in Galatia he wrote: "For I make known to you, brethren, as touching the gospel which was preached by me, that it is not after man. For neither did I receive it from man, nor was I taught it, but it came to me through revelation of Jesus Christ" (Gal. 1:11-12). "Take heed lest there shall be anyone that maketh spoil of you through his philosophy and vain deceit, *after the tradition of men, after the rudiments of the world, and not after Christ*" (Col. 2:8, emphasis added). Finally, Paul's deep concern for the purity of the gospel is emphasized in his statement about the resurrection of Christ: "For I delivered unto you first of all that which I also received: that Christ died for our sins according to the

scriptures. . ." (I Cor. 15:3). This passage makes clear the difference
between true or trustworthy tradition (the deposit of faith which is
then treasured and passed on carefully to others in the faith) and the
vain traditions of men (false doctrines, unauthorized commandments) "after the rudiments of the world, and not after [the teaching
of] Christ."

A quotation from a religious encyclopedia states:

> Just as in Israel the great Exodus and saving events were told in
> memory of Yahweh's gracious intervention for His people, then
> later committed to writing, so in the early Church an oral
> tradition preceded the written tradition collected together into
> Sacred Scripture. The Bible is a document of tradition, the New
> Testament an embodiment of the kerygma, or preaching, of
> Jesus and His followers, of His life and that of the early Christian
> community.

> Oscar Cullman, a Protestant scholar, agrees that the oral tradition
> prior to the first writings was certainly quantitatively richer than
> the written tradition.[10]

The opening of Luke's record of the Lord's life and teachings
shows the care with which he "traced the course of all things
accurately from the first" and how he received his information from
"eyewitnesses and ministers of the word." As historian, Luke refers
to "many [who] have taken in hand to draw up a narrative" of
Christ's life and works (cf. Luke 1:1-4).

Luke's account shows more clearly than the other synoptic Gospels the manner of gathering, assessing, and recording the facts of the
gospel story. Clearly, this is a prime example of tradition in the best
sense of that term: the truth or record of the events (the deposit of
faith) is transmitted by reliable observers (eyewitnesses) to Luke,
who then sets in order the many events in the earthly life of the Son
of man and hands over to others, in this case, Theophilus, possibly an
influential Greek convert, the record now called "The Gospel according to Luke."

Later, in the dedication of the Book of Acts to the same recipient,
Theophilus, Luke continues his account of the events following the
resurrection and ascension of Christ. In the same way as in the earlier
record, Luke gathered information from various men, especially from
the Twelve, and from his own personal experience with Paul and
others on missionary journeys. In both records he shows the qualities
of a true historian—a scrupulous effort to get the truth, to record the
facts fairly and fully, and to let the characters in the story—Christ,
the Jewish rulers, Peter, Paul, and many more—reveal themselves by
their own words and actions. He avoids any special pleading, he

records what he or others actually saw and heard, and his words are clear, unimpassioned, and remarkably objective. Thus his two records, like the other New Testament books, have the "ring of truth." There is no evidence to indicate that any of the writers of the New Testament ever tried to "doctor" the records or twist prophecy or events to serve a preconceived purpose. These were simple and honest men, not motivated by personal ambition or any self-interest, who sought to give a reliable account of remarkable events connected with the life, the works, the death and resurrection of the man who had lived among them and had changed not only their lives, but human history as well.

One of the major problems in the early church concerned the gathering, preserving, and eventually deciding what stories, materials, and letters were genuine and worthy of being placed in the New Testament canon. Whatever had been received and believed, whether transmitted orally or in writing, was regarded as sacred tradition (i.e., something to be handed on). As late as the third century, the churches made no distinction between oral and written tradition.

> The church settled the New Testament canon by means of tradition; and, being regarded as apostolic, tradition came to be the test of apostolicity, and this easily led to an overestimation of it. It became a source of Christian truth by the side of the Scriptures and was appealed to in support of propositions which are not found in the Bible or are found there only doubtfully. Chrysostom regarded the "unwritten deliverances" of the apostles as much a matter of faith as their letters. . . .[11]

Although the problem of determining what "gospels," what letters, what traditions to accept and which to reject was one of the crucial matters in determining not only the canon, but the course of Christian doctrine through the ages, the examination of this subject is outside the province of this study. It is enough here, we trust, to say that much of what is accepted as orthodox teaching in both Catholic and Protestant circles depends ultimately upon received tradition. As one writer affirms, "Throughout the Middle Ages it was orthodox doctrine that divine revelation flows in two streams—Bible and tradition."[12] Yet, as we have noted, tradition played a very important part in the decisions which determined which books were to be received as genuine.

In the Catholic Church, tradition has always had a prominent place, and according to James Moffatt, the Council of Augsburg, in 1530, pronounced the church to be not only the custodian but the interpreter of the Bible and tradition—the two sources of doctrine. [13] Truth, therefore, it declared, is summed up "in the written scriptures and the unwritten traditions." Furthermore, the church (the medieval church) determined what Christ meant by certain expressions and it asserted its right to make changes.[14] Tradition, says Moffatt, continued to be used to define, clarify, or enrich the faith and to defend the truth.[15] These actions were carried out through ecumenical councils and later by the Roman Pope as head of the church and avowed successor of Peter. (A good summary of the Catholic view of tradition is found on pp. 96-97 in Moffatt.)

Irenaeus, one of the early "Christian Fathers," writing about the year 180, laid great emphasis on tradition. He is quoted as saying: "And what if not even the apostles themselves had left us any Scriptures? Ought we not to follow the course of that tradition which they delivered to those whom they entrusted with the churches?"[16]

In the next section we shall see the breaking away from oral tradition, saints' legends, and unauthenticated stories of the post-apostolic era.

The Protestant Revolt

As indicated earlier, the medieval church resorted to councils, nine in all, to regulate the faith, to settle officially what doctrines should constitute the orthodox position, and to defend the church and its doctrines against heresy and heretics. Out of the various councils came carefully formulated creeds which set forth the official or "correct" view and condemned all other views. Since the church and government were allied in the Middle Ages, the will of the church was enforced by excommunication, the terrors of the Inquisition, or by interdict—a papal decree denying the sacred rites of the church to a whole community or country if the king refused to bow to the will of the pope. Moyer says, "Pope Innocent developed the interdict to the extent that it became a dreaded moral, economic and political weapon in his hands" and Innocent and other popes used this means repeatedly to enforce their demands.

A kind of unity was maintained, therefore, by the determinations of the councils, the promulgation of the creeds, and the strict enforcement of compliance with the hierarchical decrees. Any deviation from the orthodox teaching was ruthlessly punished. (For details on this period see readings listed at the end of this chapter.)

Long before the rise of Luther and the historical beginnings of the Protestant Reformation, various priests, teachers, and intellectual leaders in the church had called for reforms and a more enlightened attitude toward doctrine. Among these were Abelard, who wanted to elevate reason above dogma; Erasmus, who derided many of the priestly abuses and pled for more tolerance; Peter Waldo, founder of the Bible-centered Waldensians; Savonarola, a priest in Florence who openly attacked the pride, greed, and luxury of the popes; John Wycliffe in England, and John Huss in Bohemia. These men, and many other less famous leaders were revolted by the arrogance, corruption, and ignorance of the hierarchy and honestly sought to reform, not to destroy, the church. But all such leaders were subjected to the threats or vengeance of the powerful church. Yet their lives and works—and in several instances their martyrdom—foretold the coming revolt against the oppressive church.

Out of the Protestant movement came three significant principles, namely:

(1) That faith, not works, is the basis of man's salvation.

(2) That all believers are priests in the Kingdom of God, and that every man has access to God through Jesus Christ.

(3) That Scripture rather than oral tradition is the expression of God's will for the Christian.

"The Roman Church held strict views of the inspiration and infallibility of Scripture, but it held also that the tradition of the church was its infallible interpreter."[17] When Protestants challenged a Catholic dogma and used Scripture to support a position, the church declared their views of no account because only the established church had the right to interpret the Scriptures. One outcome of the Reformation was the insistence on the right of private interpretation.

"The emphasis upon Scripture versus ecclesiastical tradition freed Protestantism from this Roman yoke and gave it a foundation upon which to build a reconstruction of Christian faith and practice."[18] Many of the reformers, including Luther, believed strongly that any educated person (i.e., one understanding the rules of grammar and syntax) could correctly interpret any passage of Scripture. Unfortunately, these two principles (the right of private interpretation and the view that all Scripture is immediately clear in its meaning) became the cause of endless disputation and division among Protestants.

The wrangling and dividing which marked (or marred) the history of the Protestant movements fulfilled the warnings and dire prophecies of the Catholic theologians, who had insisted on the authority and validity of one universal church. We have seen, however, the repressive means used to maintain this facade of a unified and unchallenged hierarchy. When the two chief pillars of the Catholic edifice were overturned—the sacredness of ecclesiastical tradition and the right of the Roman clergy to be the sole interpreter of Scripture and tradition—the power and influence of the once dominant church was greatly diminished.

Tradition—Good or Bad?

There can be no denying that tradition exerts a powerful influence in almost every phase of life. In American government the traditional limit of two terms for the president was established when Washington refused a third term on the grounds that such a long term in the highest office might lead to the very abuses of power against which the colonies had revolted. This tradition went unchallenged until Franklin Roosevelt campaigned for and won a third term as president. Another tradition, held almost as a sacred rite, is the use of a Bible in the ceremony by which our presidents are sworn into office. Other traditions, such as an annual Thanksgiving proclaimed by the president as a national holiday, go far back into our history.

Colleges and schools have generally set great store by cherished tradition. Our marriage ceremonies, especially those which have a religious setting, are filled with tradition, e.g., the father "giving" the daughter to the groom, the exchange of vows and rings, the bridal veil, and many other details which "solemnize" the happy event. Dress, speech, letters, forms of public address and ceremonies are largely regulated by tradition. So also are introductions, the conduct of public meetings, manners at home and in society. Moffatt, in *The Thrill of Tradition,* shows that tradition represents a movement in history. Basically, he says, it means a "transaction between human beings as they lived and moved in the same group at the same time." In this way one generation is linked to another and there is "a continuity of experience," which helps to stabilize society. We feel, he says, "the throb of being in contact with some living truth or force which is older and larger than ourselves."[19]

Culture itself is an expression of those experiences, attitudes, achievements, and values which serve to unite and distinguish an age or a people. In ancient Greece, for example, the works of Homer, Hesiod, and Pindar, not only expressed the national *ethos,* but the characters and situations in their literature gave the Greeks a sense of identity, pride, and unity. Homer's epics are often referred to as the "Bible" of the Greeks, for the heroes served as models for young men to imitate, and the good kings and queens also set a standard for later rulers. A living tradition can and does unify, guide, and elevate a people or an institution.

There is another side of the coin. Tradition has often outlived its purpose or usefulness and, when this occurs, it becomes not only meaningless but positively harmful. Bagehot remarks:

The whole history of civilization is strewn with creeds and institutions which were invaluable at first, and deadly afterwards.

Progress would not have been the rarity it is if the early food had not been the later poison.[20]

As long as tradition serves man's needs, it is of great value; when it is followed for no good reason except for its venerable antiquity, it is then senseless and useless. Moffatt quotes Miguel de Unamuno, the Spanish philosopher, on the power of tradition:

> I do not know what is to be hoped from people who have been materialized by a long indoctrination of implicit Catholic faith. where beliefs are a matter of routine—people in whom the inner spring appears to be exhausted, that inward disquietude which distinguishes the essential Protestant spirit.[21]

As we have shown, tradition served many good purposes and in ancient Israel (the father's explanation of the meaning of the annual Passover meal) is an excellent example of a meaningful and unifying tradition—see Exodus 12. On the other hand, literally hundreds of rabbinical rules or traditions had grown up around each law (1521 regulations applied to the keeping of the Sabbath alone),[22] making their religion, as Peter said, "a yoke which neither we nor our fathers were able to bear" (Acts 15:10).

The leaders of the Reformation, almost to a man, saw the harmful effects of traditions which had outlived their usefulness and which often hindered change and progress. These men generally agreed that the reforming of religion could best be accomplished by returning to the Bible and to a plain "thus saith the Lord." So they called upon their followers to put aside all unscriptural practices, all creeds (which they saw as divisive rather than unifying), and to reestablish the forms of worship and government which were characteristics of the apostolic church. Their aims and hopes were high as they made a direct appeal to the sacred Scriptures. Yet denominational differences in doctrine, worship, titles, forms of church government, preaching, and terms of admission soon became manifest. Thoughtful and serious churchmen deplored the unchristian divisions and rivalry, but found no answer to these problems.

The right to interpret the Scripture for oneself, a privilege so hard to win, became the chief cause of division. Every strong leader emphasized particular doctrines or practices which seemed to him to characterize the church in its ancient purity. The old issues, Arianism versus Athanasianism, Trinitarianism versus Unitarianism, and many other problems, still troubled the church and caused separations. Each new sect or party struggled to maintain a degree of unity and to avoid further divisions—but the efforts were unavailing. Scores of new churches or parties sprang up in all parts of Western Europe and became vigorous in spreading their own version of the gospel, and proselytizing.

Regrettably, the leaders of the new movements resorted to the old, discredited devices of creeds, confessions, traditions, and disfellowshiping in their efforts to solidify their gains and to preserve the peculiar distinctions. Luther, for example, wrote many books, tracts, and even two catechisms, to indoctrinate and unify his followers. Others acted in similar fashion. So new traditions supplanted the old, and new rituals and creeds gave a degree of unity to the new parties. (Any good church history will give the reader ample information about the multiplying of sects, creeds, and controversies during the centuries following the break with Rome and the rise of Protestant churches.)

How Do Traditions Begin?

It may be useful to ask how traditions in the churches get their start. One means is the taking of a Scriptural or Biblical example of how something was done and making that *the* way of performing an action. Acts 2:42 tells of early disciples continuing "steadfastly in the apostles' teaching and fellowship, in the breaking of bread and the prayers." Some leaders noted here four activities of the church—teaching or preaching, the communion or supper, the fellowship (often construed to mean contribution), and prayers. In simple faith some groups, especially in earlier generations, took this as a pattern for their services and even followed the exact order of the four elements mentioned here. A second example is the practice in some fundamentalist groups of having a collection only on Sunday morning, basing this practice upon the directions Paul gave to the Corinthian church (I Cor. 16:1-2), even though this was a "laying by in store" for benevolent aid to the poor in Judea. This basis for establishing a tradition may be called a *precedent*.

In his essays on *English Traits*, R. W. Emerson comments on the slowness of the British to change their ways:

> Every English man is an embryonic chancellor: his instinct is to search for a precedent. The favorite phrase of their law is, "a custom whereof the memory of man runneth not back to the contrary". . . . They hate innovation. ("Manners")

Many others besides the English feel very comfortable when they are able to cite a precedent.

A second source of many traditions (closely related to the first) is *literalism*. This can be illustrated in the practice of footwashing, based upon the incident when Christ was teaching a lesson in humility and rose from the table to wash the feet of the disciples (John 13:1-16). Obviously, this was not intended as an ordinance in the church, for it took place at the Passover feast which Christ ate with the little company just before His betrayal, and His purpose is expressed clearly: "Know ye what I have done to you? Ye call me Teacher and Lord: and ye say well; for so I am. If I then, the Lord and the Teacher, have washed your feet, ye also ought to wash one another's feet. For I have given you an example, that ye should also do as I have done unto you" (John 13:12-15).

Another illustration of Biblical literalness is calling on the elders to anoint the sick in the congregation with oil (James 5:14). One other limited interpretation of a Biblical passage has to do with the manner of serving the wine or fruit of the vine. Because Matthew reports, "And he took a cup and gave thanks, and gave to them, saying, Drink ye all of it; for this is my blood of the covenant. . ." many earnest believers have contended for a single cup—fixing their eyes on a literal point rather than on the purpose of the memorial. Such literalness, of course, overlooks the fact that "cup" as used here is a figure of speech (metonymy) meaning the contents of the cup.

A third way in which tradition may be established is through the *teaching* or *practice* of a strong or respected leader. A good man plants his feet solidly on some idea or practice and by the power of influence sways a great many men. Emerson undoubtedly had this in mind when he said, "An institution is the lengthened shadow of one man." Thus a Fox becomes the founder of Quakerism, a Luther of Lutheranism, and a Mary Baker Eddy of Christian Science. In such cases the views and practices of the great personality are passed on to his followers, who seldom go beyond the limits established by the leader. The followers of St. Francis still take vows of celibacy and poverty, and go out to preach to the poor. Because Alexander Campbell was a fairly well-to-do man and refused to take any pay for his preaching, many preachers who followed him had to live in poverty—though not by choice! This type of tradition may be called the cult of *personality*.

A fourth type of tradition is based upon *inference*. Since the New Testament has much to say about the importance of teaching as a means of building or strengthening Christians, most Protestant churches give a great deal of time and energy to classes for instruction. The great majority of these churches spend large sums on "Sunday schools," or among some groups, "Sabbath schools," though there is no clear teaching in Scripture to authorize the practice. Most church leaders are probably unaware that the Sunday school is a fairly recent addition to church programs, having arisen, according to most authorities, in England in the early days of the

Methodist revival. Robert Raikes is usually credited with originating the Sunday school in England in 1780 to teach children of the poor to read and spell in order to read the Bible for themselves.

Another example of inference is the practice of religious groups in building and maintaining church buildings. Nothing is said about church-owned property in the New Testament. Often the churches met in private homes, or sometimes in a synagogue, or even in the open. A more recent example is the providing in modern church buildings of baptistries (though their introduction sometimes met with outcries and strong opposition), nurseries, fellowship halls, and adequate facilities for conducting classes. Nearly all such additions have been opposed by literalists who say, "Where can you find these things in the Bible?"

A final source of tradition, and perhaps the most troublesome of all, is the *pattern* theory. Though this resembles the precedent, it goes far beyond it and builds on a much flimsier foundation. Briefly stated, this theory holds that in the New Testament, Christians are given a precise pattern for worship, church organization, church discipline, and all essential activities done in the name or under the supervision of a congregation. The basis cited for this theory is usually Hebrews 8:5: "who serve that which is a copy and shadow of the heavenly things, even as Moses is warned of God when he is about to build the tabernacle: for *See, saith he, that thou make all things according to the pattern* that was showed thee in the mount" [emphasis added]. The argument runs about as follows: If God gave Moses a blue-print or complete pattern for building the tabernacle, and every piece of furniture in it, and every part of the service was strictly ordained, then we have in our guide, the New Testament, a similar pattern which must be followed. This view, to most scholars, is completely unfounded.

By contrast with the Old, the New Testament has almost no specific commandments—the details of the Lord's Supper or Communion being one of the exceptions. It gives, as a rule, general *principles* and leaves the means of carrying these out to the good judgment of men. Thus we find such commands in the Great Commission (Matt. 28:19-20) as "go," "make disciples," "baptize," and "teach." Various means through the ages have been used to make disciples; in our time, in addition to the old means, we have used the printed page, gospel meetings, cottage meetings, radio, television, and motion pictures.

Does the New Testament give a pattern for worship, or for the selection of church officers? Much is said about worship; it is directed toward God and to His Son, our Savior; it should be sincere, i.e., "from the heart"; "in spirit and in truth" (John 4:24), and in harmony with God's will. Yet we have no pattern or arrangement of what some have called "elements of worship"—songs, prayer, preaching, exhorting, communion, testimonial, and giving. Apparently there was great latitude in the conduct of the worship service in the early church. From Acts and the letters we get many glimpses of worship, but there appears to be no liturgy or formal pattern. In the First Letter to the Corinthians, Paul lays down several general principles to guide their meetings and make them profitable, to wit: (1) "Let all things be done unto edifying," (2) let the participants "prophesy [or teach] one by one that all may learn," (3) pray and sing "with the spirit and the understanding also," (4) and finally, "let all things be done decently and in order" (I Cor. 14:15, 26, 40). The freedom in the church had led some of the enthusiastic members to try to speak or to pray and to give "ecstatic" messages (NEB) all at one time. Thus Paul warned them to take their turn and to observe decorum, "for God is not a God of confusion, but of peace."

In broad terms we can say that the Christian worship was spirited and spiritual, often spontaneous and varied, but united in its purpose. Certainly it was not dull, half-hearted, or planned for show, nor does it seem to have been dominated by any individual. The term *worship* in the Scriptures almost invariably refers to action or activity (praising God, bowing before or petitioning God, reading His Word), and not to what we call a "service."

Tradition, then, regulates most of the details of Christian worship and the carrying out of the functions of a live and active church. Some one or some group must decide on the place and time for worship, who shall direct the singing, how the meeting shall be conducted, who will serve the Communion, and so on. In recent times many young people have protested against the "structured" meeting, saying that it is stereotyped, dull, lacking in life and interest; they prefer, they say, more spontaneity, more general participation, and more emotional warmth. In actual practice, however, experience has shown that the "unstructured" meeting soon loses its zest and appeal—even to the young—and the unplanned service begins to drag, with one person waiting for another to start a song or a prayer, or go give an exhortation; or, as sometimes happens, several will try to start songs at the same time. When nothing is planned in advance—not even the lesson or talk to be given—the more thoughtful members of the audience feel that time has been unwisely used, and go away disappointed. It is the view of this writer that in churches, as well as in college or high school classes, there must be planning, preparation, and a clearly defined aim if there is to be real meaning. Some worship which deemphasizes the teaching or sermon *can* be, and probably should be, more or less spontaneous; but even in such a meeting there must be a modicum of control. Someone, for example, must bring the meeting to a close.

Again the question comes: Is tradition a help or a hindrance in carrying out the will of God? As we have shown, many details regarding times and purposes of meetings, who shall teach, preach, care for the building, or carry on the programs of benevolence, for example, must be decided by those in authority. This may perhaps be what Paul had in mind in writing to Titus: "For this cause left I thee in Crete, that thou shouldest set in order the things that were wanting, and appoint elders in every city. . ." (I Titus 1:5). Judgment and expediency naturally enter into all decisions men must make, even in the regulating of worship or determining which of various Christian works are to be supported. These human decisions are always subject to change, suspension, or long continuance; and any kind of practice—if followed "religiously" for a considerable time—is likely to become a tradition.

It becomes clear, therefore, that as believers we must deal with two kinds of tradition, the divine and the human. One is based upon the truths given by God, Christ, and the apostles, i.e. the Scriptures; the other is temporal and subject to change, the ideas and decisions of ordinary men. Note the contrast in Paul's letter to the Thessalonian church: "for our exhortation is not of error, nor of uncleanness, nor in guile: but even as we have been approved of God to be intrusted with the gospel, so we speak; not as pleasing men, but God who proveth our hearts" (I Thess. 2:3-4).

A little further on Paul makes a very important distinction between "the word of God" and "the word of men": ". . . We also thank God without ceasing, that, when ye received from us the word of the message, even the word of God, ye accepted it not as the word of men, but as it is in truth, the word of God, which also worketh in you that believe" (I Thess. 2:13). Though Scripture was once an oral message (until recorded and tested, hence the word *canon*) it is now *fixed* and *unchangeable*. It is the "word of truth," the foundation of Christian faith, the final authority in matters of faith and worship. God's Word becomes the test of truth (though it was first given as tradition): "So then, brethren, stand fast, and *hold the traditions* which ye were taught, whether by word, or by epistle of ours" (II Thess. 2:15, emphasis added).

In each generation the judgments and decisions of men regarding the practical problems of church administration are but means to an end. They involve buildings, programs of service such as missions and benevolence, and the best ways for presenting God's message to man. What is good and useful at one time may be unnecessary or foolish in other times and places. In the days of the apostles, for example, foot washing was regarded as an expression of hospitality, and widows supported in some places by the church were expected to have a good reputation, to have shown hospitality to strangers, and to have "washed the saints' feet" (I Tim. 5:9-10). This act of washing feet sounds very strange in our culture, but it was a gracious act of thoughtfulness in the days of sandals and dusty byways.

During the nineteenth and the early twentieth century in America, gospel meetings were often held in "brush arbors," the crowds sat on rude, wooden benches, and the preacher needed a powerful voice to make himself heard in the open. The sermons were often long, and sometimes the crowds stayed for "dinner on the ground" and listened to more preaching in the afternoon. Customs change! Religious debates, once very popular in presenting the distinctions of various conflicting views on Scripture, are now largely a thing of the past.

The need for human interpretations (or judgments) is indicated by the fact that, although the New Testament says much about the importance of elders or bishops (Acts 15:6, 16:14; I Tim. 3:1-2 and elsewhere) nothing is said about *how* the men are to be selected or whether any ceremony should be used in installing elders. This being true, churches have used various ways of selecting men for their elderships and some have devised solemn and impressive services to set these men apart and to impress on them and on the congregations the obligations of the "office of a bishop."

It is always possible that any practice used for a considerable time will become a "tradition of the elders" and be regarded by some persons as binding.

An example of a fairly recent tradition in certain churches in the American Southwest was the formula used in the baptismal rite. Many preachers used, with slight variations, such a formula as "In obedience to our Lord's command, and upon the confession of your faith in Jesus Christ as Savior, I now baptize you in the name of the Father, the Son, and the Holy Spirit. Amen." But one man who used this simple statement caused great consternation in one of the congregations because he had not said "for remission of your sins." This expression had been used so often in the churches of the area (apparently to make quite clear to any visitors present the "real meaning" of baptism) that any omission of the phrase was a dangerous deviation from the truth. Some elders even took the position that a baptism without the "creedal statement" would be invalid, and that the candidate should be rebaptized.

Other customs which vary from the general norm, such as the use of solos or small singing ensembles in the worship service, the selection of elders for a definite term of years, the establishing of homes to care for orphaned or needy children, cause alarm in some congregations that have fixed and limited ideas about what can be done in the church service or in benevolence. Here the danger of the unwritten creed can, and often does, upset the peace of a congregation and may even lead to division. Many divisions have been caused by even less weighty matters.

Perhaps a graver threat to the unity and well-being of the churches is the tendency—in some of the more liberal churches—to substitute lectures on sociology, psychology, or so-called "divine science" for the "meat and bread" of Christianity. Such topics have their place in schools or colleges, but to offer these in place of the fundamental truths of Christianity is to betray one's trust as a minister and to defraud the children of God. Jeremiah the prophet described this kind of situation when he said, "For my people have committed two evils: they have forsaken me, the fountain of living waters, and have hewed them out cisterns, broken cisterns, that can hold no water" (Jer. 2:12-13).

Milton, the Puritan poet, described a similar situation in the church of England in his day:

> The hungry sheep look up, and are not fed
> But swoln with wind, and the rank mist they draw,
> Rot inwardly, and foul contagion spread,
> Besides what the grim wolf with privy paw
> Daily devours apace, and nothing said.   ("Lycidas," 11. 125-130)

Tradition in the Restoration Movement

The role of Alexander Campbell as preacher, debater, writer, and publisher is known to most students of modern church history. Early in life he became convinced of the evils of division among the followers of Christ and, in his search for truth, decided that one must go back to the Scriptures and especially to the New Testament records and Epistles to discover and to restore the simplicity of church doctrine and practice found in the early church. Many doctrines in his own day, he believed, were based on human creeds or tradition, and these, in his view, were the most prolific causes of division and strife. As a result he drew a sharp line between what he considered to be traditions of the apostles and those of modern men:

> I need not say much upon the chapter of *human traditions.* They are easily distinguished from the *Apostles'* traditions. Those of the Apostles are found in their writings, as those of men are found in their own books. Some human traditions may have a show of wisdom, but it is only an appearance. . . . I know of but one way in which all believers in Jesus Christ honorably to

themselves, honorably to the Lord, and advantageously to the sons of Adam, can form one communion. . . . Let human philosophy and human tradition, as any part of the Christian institution be thrown overboard into the sea, and then the ship of the church will make a prosperous, safe and happy voyage across the ocean of time . . . to gain a safe anchorage in the heaven.[23]

Mr. Campbell deplored the divisions which had multiplied so rapidly in the two centuries following the great Reformation, and in his view they were not only wrong and a scandal to Christianity, but also a major stumblingblock to the efforts of all Christians to convert the world. Man's self-will expressed in conflicting "private opinions" was, to him, the root cause of many of the divisions. Regarding this point he stated his position quite positively:

We will not hearken to those questions which gender strife, nor discuss them at all. If a person say such is his private opinion, let him have it as his private opinion, but lay no stress upon it: and if it be a wrong private opinion, it will die a natural death much sooner than if you attempt to kill it.[24]

Subsequent history proved his hopes to be too sanguine; many private opinions did not wither away and die. Nevertheless he sought to be liberal in welcoming into the church fellowship persons of various opinions so long as they did not try to force their views on others or make these personal opinions tests of fellowship. In his later years, Mr. Campbell noted "nine or ten distinct communions originated out of the Westminster creed . . . some as discordant and aloof from each other as were the Jews and Samaritans." He also spoke of the existence of twelve or more sects of the Baptists, and then observed, "No human creed in Protestant Christendom can be found, that has not made a division for every generation of its existence."[25]

Mr. Campbell's valiant efforts, as well as those of other "Restoration" leaders, only partially achieved their aims to unite the various segments of Christendom. New Parties and sects arose, or split off from the established churches; no basis could be found for Christian unity. His own movement, the Disciples of Christ, which had come through the Civil War without separation, finally broke apart into "liberal" and "conservative" wings, while maintaining for a time a show of fellowship. The "liberal" group, or Disciples, was found mainly in the northern and eastern cities of the United States while the "conservatives," or churches of Christ, were more numerous in the South and Midwest. Unfortunately, Campbell's pleas for undenominational Christianity and a return to "the old paths," though they met with success for a time, were frustrated and embarrassed by the division within the ranks of his followers. In most instances the splits within the movement came over matters not specifically mentioned in Scripture: the ways of organizing and financing missionary activities, the use of instruments of music in the worship, the calling of national or regional conferences, the right of church-related colleges to train missionaries and ministers, the addition of Sunday school or Bible classes to the church program, and many other like programs. Each of the two large groups in the Disciples fellowship splintered into several small and competitive fragments. Though none of these parties or factions had a written creed—Mr. Campbell and other leaders had stood adamantly against creeds—they had unwritten creeds, which are just as binding and galling as any written creed, and are more difficult to deal with.

As one surveys the history of Protestant Christianity, he is shocked by all the pleas for unity which ended in the constant multiplying of factions. As a member of the Church of Christ I feel that it may be proper to list what seem to me to be "traditions of the elders" which have added to the confusion of great numbers of good-spirited men and women and which stand in the way of unity, love, and progress. The statements regarding our "human traditions" are not meant to disparage but to make the church aware of attitudes and inconsistencies which weaken its plea and disturb the peace of the brotherhood. I shall forbear elaborating on these points, for persons related to the churches of Christ will, I think, see their validity and the need for a continuing restoration movement.

1. The assumption that debates on religious problems is the high road to truth. Rather, this method which may have been very effective on the frontier in the nineteenth century, has in modern times often led to evasion of the truth, ignoring the opponent's argument, and hardening those opinions already held by the disputants. Victory in the debate rather than a search for truth may become the principal concern. Debates have often engendered a bitter party spirit.

2. The danger of oversimplifying the meaning of conversion and neatly summing up the New Testament teaching as "faith, repentance, confession, and baptism," with baptism made the *sine qua non*. This kind of teaching has de-emphasized (or wholly omitted) the centrality of the cross, the atonement through Christ's blood, and the supreme importance of grace. In an effort to simplify the so-called plan of salvation, preachers have often shifted the emphasis from God's part to man's. This creates a false view of conversion and regeneration.

3. The danger of a legalistic approach to Christian doctrine which substitutes a rule or "law" for an apostolic admonition or plea. This tendency is seen in the preaching of a tithe, not

because a tithe was required in the Old Testament of all faithful Jews, but because Christians must "go beyond the law." No doubt many early Christians did give more than a tithe, especially in the Jerusalem church, but to make tithing a requirement would be to surrender part of the freedom—and opportunity for growth—which characterizes the new covenant.

Another example of hardening (or formalizing an exhortation into law) is seen in the emphasis given by some individuals to Hebrews 10:25 ("Not forsaking the assembling of ourselves together"). When this passage is used to *require* brethren to attend the service of the church, one may well ask what will be done with those who fail to attend some meetings. More important is the question of motivation: can pressure or compulsion ever be justified for getting men to serve the Lord?

4. Giving too much weight to the judgments or pronouncements of respected or "important" leaders, whether Luther, Wesley, Campbell, Lipscomb, or any other leader. These are but men, as fallible as the rest of us, and their opinions, though perhaps highly valued, should never be bound on Christ's disciples. There is always the danger of being drawn into the orbit of the "great" man and of forgetting that we are followers of Christ.

5. The tendency to act only on what has been done before, i.e., to follow precedent or tradition. For example, in some of the Churches of Christ the use of trios, quartets, and special groups is sanctioned widely at Sunday afternoon "singings" but not at a regular church service. Heaven forbid! Yet one of our favorite passages (Eph. 5:19) urges *speaking one to another* in psalms, hymns, and spiritual songs, singing and making melody with your hearts to the Lord. . . ." But since most churches in this fellowship look askance on solos, duets, and any special group singing, we deny ourselves this very effective means of teaching and inspiring one another. Antiphonal singing, i.e., groups singing in alternation, apparently common in the early churches, is also generally frowned upon.

6. Lastly I mention the danger of harsh and pharisaical judgments, name-calling, or impugning of motives of those who do not agree with "our" position. Sometimes human pride, rather than zeal for the Lord's house, may be the motive for judging one's brother or neighbor (see, e.g., Luke 9:54-55; Rom. 2:1-4; 14:4—5, 10). Some men in "contending for the faith" (Jude 3) seem to forget love and patience and become merely contentious! Naturally, error in doctrine as well as unchristian behavior must be reproved, but believers are admonished to act in love and forbearance, and to speak the truth in love. The proud, censorious spirit is foreign to the teaching of Christ and can defeat the purpose of a Christian who seeks to convert a man from his error—or from his evil judgment of others. The task of correcting

those who teach error or live unchristian lives rests both on elders (I Tim. 3:2-5; Titus 1:7-11) and preachers (I Tim. 4:12; 6:11-14; II Tim. 4:1-5).

Conclusion

This study has endeavored to show that tradition has played an important part in both the Jewish and the Christian religions. Some traditions have been based upon commandments or revelations given by God to men (to Moses at Mount Sinai, to Paul after his conversion), but many traditions are simply customs or practices of men which have been sanctioned by usage and passed on to succeeding generations. Readers of the Bible need to recognize that tradition had a great deal to do with the value placed on various books which were preserved from ancient times and given a place in the canon. This legacy from the past, i.e., the debt we owe to tradition, has often been overlooked. Rightly used, tradition is a very efficient servant.

At the same time we recognize that traditions may be man-made and are therefore as fallible or foolish as men. What may have been a useful and significant custom at one time can become useless and absurd under changed conditions. When human tradition has lost its meaning and is carried on only because of its venerable age, it should be humanely retired. When it was at best only the formalized judgment of a man or group of men, it does not deserve an endless life. And if, as sometimes happens, it obscures or overshadows the truth, it should be given up as quickly as counterfeit money.

The eternal quest of the Christian is for a fuller understanding of truth; the divine truth, for him, is the truth of God's revelation, a revelation made in times past to priests, prophets, and to other chosen vessels, but ultimately and most fully made in the person and teaching of Jesus Christ, who is "the way, the truth, and the life."

For Additional Reading

Henry Bettenson, ed., *Documents of the Christian Church,* New York, 1947, Chap. 3.

W. E. Garrison and Alfred T. De Groot, *Disciples of Christ: A History,* St. Louis, 1948.

Richard P. Hanson, *Tradition in the Early Church,* Philadelphia, 1963.

Henry S. Lucas, *The Renaissance and the Reformation,* New York, 1934.

A. C. McGiffert, *A History of Christian Thought,* 2 Vols., New York, 1949.

James Moffatt, *The Thrill of Tradition,* New York, 1947.

Elgin S. Moyer, *Great Leaders of the Christian Church,* Chicago, 1951.

Lars P. Qualben, *A History of the Christian Church,* New York, 1940.

Preserved Smith, *The Age of the Reformation,* 2 vols. 1920.

1. *The Outline of History* (New York, 1920), Vol. I, 204-5.
2. *Random House Dictionary of the English Language,* coll. ed., 1968.
3. "Tradition," *The Jewish Encyclopedia* (1905, 1925), XII, 218.
4. "Tradition," *The Universal Jewish Encyclopedia* (1943), X, 290.
5. Ibid.
6. Ibid.
7. Ibid.
8. Ibid., p. 291.
9. "Tradition," *The International Standard Encyclopedia* (1957), V, 3004.
10. "Tradition," *The New Catholic Encyclopedia* (1967), XIV, 225.
11. "Tradition," *The New Schaff-Herzog Encyclopedia of Religious Knowledge* (1964), XI, 488.
12. Ibid.
13. *The Thrill of Tradition* (New York, 1944), p. 85.
14. Ibid., pp. 94-95.
15. Ibid., p. 96.
16. *New Catholic Encyclopedia,* XIV, 225.
17. W. E. Garrison and Alfred J. De Groot, *Disciples of Christ, A History* (St. Louis: Bethany, 1948), p. 37.
18. Ibid.
19. Ibid. 2-3.
20. As quoted in Moffatt, p. 108.
21. Ibid., p. 124.
22. *The Jewish Encyclopedia,* X, 596.
23. *Christianity Restored* (a reprint of *The Millennial Harbinger,* VI, Rosemead, Calif., 1959), pp. 127-128.
24. Ibid., p. 123.
25. Ibid., p. 105.